59 0 969

D0418403

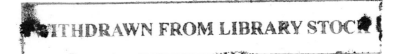

Writers in Conversation
With
CHRISTOPHER BIGSBY

VOLUME FOUR

ARTHUR MILLER CENTRE FOR AMERICAN STUDIES
&

UNTHANK BOOKS

First published in 2011 for The Arthur Miller Centre
By Unthank Books
www.unthankbooks.com

Printed and bound in Great Britain by Lightning Source, Milton Keynes

A CIP record for this book is available from the British Library

ISBN 978-0-9564223-5-4

Cover design by Dan Nyman

Contents

Introduction

- Christopher Bigsby -

The interviews collected here were all conducted as part of the Arthur Miller Centre for American Studies International Literary Festival held every autumn at the University of East Anglia (UEA). The festival began in 1991 and in the succeeding years has brought major writers from around the world to the campus, although the audience is drawn from a wide area. In one season a couple even commuted from Germany.

UEA has a reputation not only for studying contemporary writers but also for producing them, or at least for nurturing them. Its creative writing programme is known around the world. Though the Arthur Miller Centre focuses on American Studies, as its title implies it has a wide remit. Any Centre with Arthur Miller's name on the masthead is likely to be catholic in its interests. The Festival itself reaches out not only to novelists, poets and playwrights but to memoirists, biographers, historians, politicians and scientists. The common factor is writing. The Festival was not established with a view to publication and the format was not originally based on interviews, these forming only part of the evening. Over time, however, the interview has become more central.

As discussions of the crisis facing writers have become commonplace – regrets about the disappearance of bookshops, problems in publishing houses, the power of the web – so, apparently paradoxically, we have seen a growth of literary festivals, book clubs and signings. Reading may be a private enterprise but people obviously like to come together to discuss literature, to listen to writers read from their work and to ask them questions. Publishers, of course, see this as a marketing opportunity and writers are frequently leant on to go on the road promoting in a way that would have been unthinkable a generation ago. The surprise, perhaps, is not simply that on the whole they have embraced the necessity, if not always the pleasure, of doing so but that they so often respond with generosity and honesty, exploring the roots of their craft and acknowledging aspects of their lives usually closed to the reader.

Writers are not actors, except in so far as they stage the world they create in their own heads. Some do speak aloud the words they write as they write. Performance, though, was never part of the contract. A few writers are not the best readers of their own work, yet most take pleasure in reading in public, in making apparent rhythms buried in their texts suddenly evident as the words sound out. They also take pleasure in meeting their readers and responding to questions which sometimes offer novel perspectives on their work. Solitude may be the necessary condition to write but it is a rare writer who does not welcome leaving the study to engage with those who know them only through the books they read in equal solitude.

Once or twice in what follows audience questions have been incorporated in my conversations rather than break the text. The conversations have also been edited because as anyone who has ever transcribed a recording knows a literal transcription can be difficult to follow. We are liable to abandon sentences half way through, make redundant asides and punctuate our language with 'sort ofs' and 'kind ofs.' When I worked for the BBC I watched what were then called studio managers 'de-um' tapes, sometimes gaining minutes by doing so. For the most part, though, what you read is what was said and those who write with such apparently fluency speak with the same respect for language observable in their texts. Some of the interviews are brief, because the evening was taken up with rather longer readings than usual. All, however, I trust add something to our understanding of who these writers are and how they created works which are as varied as they are compelling.

For would-be writers there are exemplary tales. Some of the authors on the pages that follow had immediate success. Others suffered multiple rejections until, suddenly, a first book was placed and a career launched. All those interviewed spoke freely of their lives and of their approach to their craft. What is the attraction of first as opposed to third person narration? Is there an ethics to the appropriation of others' experience and, indeed, lives? What is the attraction of history to the novelist? What is the distinction between biography and fiction? Why are some drawn to the stage at one moment and the novel at another? Do some countries offer the writer a greater freedom for the imagination than others?

For the most part those included in this book spoke to an audience of 500 or more (sometimes those turned away watched on large television screens in an adjoining lecture theatre). It is the essence of interviews, however, that they have an intimacy belied by their public circumstance and to me that has always been part of their fascination. And when the event is over I am as anxious as anyone else to have my books signed. Why? For the same reason that I would have treasured Charles Dickens's signature or Jane Austen's or Thomas Hardy's. I know that on some level the sense of connection forged by that signature is factitious but I feel it nonetheless. Once, in a Salzburg bookstore, I found a copy of the life of Nathaniel Hawthorne written by his daughter. It was signed by a Catholic nun. I subsequently discovered that that nun was his daughter. I gave the book to Arthur Miller on the grounds that Hawthorne's forebear was Judge Hathorne who had presided over the trials in Salem in 1692 which he dramatised in *The Crucible*. It was no doubt a sentimentality but that signature itself contained a story even as it introduced one. Sometimes books do not belong to the person who possesses them.

If you were not at the festival at which these writers appeared you missed the party but I still think you can hear the voices of those who make their appearance on the pages that follow. You cannot now get your book signed, but there is a signature of sorts in their words and words, of course, are their stock in trade and the source of their unique identities.

- Christopher Bigsby -
Director of the Arthur Miller Centre for American Studies and Professor of American Studies, University of East Anglia.

In Conversation With David Leavitt

- 18th October 2004 -

David Leavitt was born in Pittsburgh, Pennsylvania, in 1961, and is a graduate of Yale University. He has taught at Princeton University and is currently a professor of creative writing at the University of Florida. His novels include *The Lost Language of Cranes* (1986), *While England Sleeps* (1993), *Martin Bauman; or, A Sure Thing* (2000), *The Body of Jonah Boyd* (2004) and *The Indian Clerk* (2007). His book *The Man Who Knew Too Much: Alan Turing and the Invention of the Computer* appeared in 2005. He is also the author of three volumes of short stories.

Bigsby: When you went to Yale were you already thinking you wanted to be a writer?

Leavitt: Yes. I started off wanting to be a poet. That lasted for about a minute because I was a terrible poet. All the poems I wrote kept turning into stories and it gradually dawned on me that my impulses were probably too narrative to make me a poet. I tried to write a sestina once. That is such a complicated form and every stanza just kept getting longer and longer and longer and I realised I just didn't have the kind of discipline that was needed to be a poet. I was writing fiction pretty seriously from early on and in my second year at Yale I took a course with Gordon Lish, who was a legendary writing teacher. That was what really cemented the desire in me.

Bigsby: Were the teachers of literature at Yale receptive to the idea of creative writing?

Leavitt: Not terribly. In fact the great evidence of that was that if you were an English major as an undergraduate you could only credit two creative writing courses towards your major. You could credit three but then you would graduate with what they called a modified English major, and the term modified, I think, indicated the attitude of the faculty. I

3

remember that John Hollander, who was a poet and English professor at Yale, said to me once, very disdainfully, that writing is not like macramé. It cannot be taught on an introductory level. So there was actually a lot of disdain about the idea of teaching writing. There was a tolerance of it but it was considered at best to play a very limited role in an education and that students who wanted to be writers should study literature, which to a great extent I agree with, even though I teach creative writing.

As I said, I took some workshops when I was an undergraduate and the one with Gordon Lish was immensely influential and important not only because he was such a great teacher, but because he started me reading a lot of writers whose work I wasn't familiar with. I found it immensely exciting because this was a moment, in the early eighties, when there was this real renaissance in the American short story. We were reading Raymond Carver and Grace Paley and Mary Robinson, who is now my colleague in Florida. Later on I was reading writers like William Trevor, Alice Munro, writers who were doing the most amazing things with short stories. It was thrilling to me to discover that there was so much that could be done with that form and that was what I began writing.

Really the earliest inspiration for me was reading. I would read these people and think, I want to do that too. I want to create short stories that are as good as these even though these writers were very different. It was the fact that they were doing such a huge variety of different things with the short story form that really got me excited.

My university started teaching creative writing in 1949, but there was the creative writing programme at the University of Iowa from, I think, the thirties. Flannery O'Connor was at Iowa in the nineteen forties. The question of why is an interesting one. I think principally there was a feeling among the people who started these programmes that as writers we had a duty to pass on the craft in the same way that say a pianist will take on pupils. It was an attempt to create a workshop environment, as opposed to a more strictly academic environment, in which students could bring their work and it could be looked at very much from a point of view of craft. You wouldn't be talking about the work in the way you would in a traditional academic literature class. You would be talking about punctuation and white space and point of view and whether you are going to write in the past tense or present tense, a very kind of nuts-and-bolts, craft-oriented approach. It was really out of that impulse, I think, that the writing programmes began and then flourished because there was a great hunger for that kind of approach.

The question that then began was whether you could study writing without also studying literature and my feeling was that the two were inseparable, though there are those who would argue that they aren't. My background, though, is as a student of literature and I always make my students read an enormous amount, often more than they want to, whereas I know other people who don't emphasise reading to the same degree. They really focus on just the student's work and nothing else.

Bigsby: One of the accusations is that there is a creative writing novel, that there is a kind of standard identifiable novel that people believe they know came out of a creative writing school. Do you see that?

Leavitt: I think that is absolutely true, unfortunately. I will say it doesn't come out of my programme.

Bigsby: It doesn't come out of ours, either, so where does it come from?.

Leavitt: Iowa. People talk about the Iowa story and the Iowa novel. Editors of magazines talk about that. I think the problem is that creative writing is taught in the form of a workshop. You have a workshop with seven or eight young writers and a professor who is presumably a more experienced writer. Each week you take one or two stories by the students which are read in advance. The student whose work is being discussed has to stay completely silent and everybody else picks the story apart. The danger of that is that a certain kind of workshop style ends up emerging out of the programme because each week you are doing this to another story and another story and another story. Certain kinds of criticism, certain objections, certain suggestions are made over and over again and the danger is a certain homogenisation where the student writer loses his or her voice. That is a real danger. The only way to fight it is to have to have a professor who doesn't let it happen. You also have to make sure you are not encouraging the group toward any particular kind of writing. I always consider my job as a teacher to help my students be the best versions of themselves that they can be, not to try to mould them in my image. But it is a real danger, and it does happen.

I don't think the problem is even necessarily who the teacher is. I think the problem is that the group itself ends up generating a group style, just as a result of working so closely, because there is so much intimacy involved in having eight or nine people through the course of a semester sharing each other's work in such an intense way. That is what you have to fight against. It has never happened in my classes. I haven't

5

noticed it happen. My students usually have a fairly strong sense of their voices to begin with, but I think it is a real danger.

I must say there are times when I read stories and I think this is such a workshop story. You balance the risks against the advantages and I think the advantages by far outweigh the risks because writing is such an isolated business and to be able to share work in an early stage with good readers helps you so much in the long run because it means you are able to correct a lot of the mistakes you are making before you send the work out to be read by editors who aren't going to be nearly as generous with their time as the other members of the workshop will.

Bigsby: It was while you were a student that you published a short story in *The New Yorker*, which I presume made you admired and hated in equal amounts by your fellow students. There must have been a certain amount of jealousy?

Leavitt: Yes, I would say so.

Bigsby: Am I right in thinking that was the first time *The New Yorker* had published a story with a gay character?

Leavitt: That has always been the story. In fact there was one other story before. Allan Gurganus's *Minor Heroism* had predated mine, but that was a story that didn't deal quite as openly or as frankly with the subject matter.

Bigsby: One aspect of your story is that the young man at the heart of it has to confront his parents and come out. Was that something you did before you wrote the story or did you publish the story and then have to do that?

Leavitt: No, I wrote the story and then I had to explain to my parents that I was coming out in *The New Yorker* in more than one way. I suppose I was trying to soften the blow by saying, 'Well Mom, Dad, I'm gay, but I am also about to publish this story in *The New Yorker* so that makes it a little bit better.' Actually I did a version of that scene in my novel *Martin Bauman* because it was irresistible.

Bigsby: Bookstores have a way of categorising writers. If you go into a bookstore you have to think do I go to the black section, the women's section, the fiction section, the literature section? Where do your books appear? Is it in the gay section, the literature section, the fiction section?

Leavitt: It depends on the store. I have a perpetual quarrel with Borders because Borders always puts my book under gay and lesbian fiction, which annoys me. It is arbitrary. I went to the local Borders where I live and looked up a bunch of writers to see who was where and Edmund White, I and Alan Hollinghurst were all under gay fiction, but Michael Cunningham was not, which I didn't totally understand. James Baldwin was neither under literature nor under gay fiction. He was under African American fiction. So when I saw that I thought this is ridiculous, this categorisation, and had a big argument with a friend who said, 'It is very useful for young gay men and women who don't know where else to find books that speak to their experience.' I said, 'Yes, that's true, but at the same time the price you pay for that is that you end up creating this idea that the only things that are good to read are things that in some literal sense reflect your own life.' That is the absolute opposite of what reading is all about. Reading to me has always been about discovering the commonality between all kinds of different experiences.

Bigsby: So you began with that story in *The New Yorker*. You then had a short story collection, but nemesis was waiting for you down the road in the form of the curious experience you had with *While England Sleeps*?

Leavitt: It was a total shock. I had written this novel based on an episode in the life of Stephen Spender. I told everyone this. It was no secret. I didn't call the character Stephen Spender, but it was so obvious to me that it was based on an episode from his life that I didn't think there was any question about it. He got very upset and sued me. It was a very complicated, strange episode that maybe some day I will be able to make more sense out of. What it was really about was this very tricky question of whether you can lay claim to own your own life. The thing I have noticed is that writers are much more sensitive about this question than anyone else. Writers, who habitually appropriate the lives of everyone they know, if they find themselves made into characters in other people's books are always going to explode much more quickly than would a non writer. A good example is Susan Sontag's response after Edmund White put an admittedly pretty mean portrayal of her into one of his books.

Spender's claim was that I didn't have the right to use this story, that it somehow belonged to him, but I think under the surface what was really going on was that Spender and his wife were trying very, very hard to control how his homosexuality was discussed. They didn't want to suppress it. They knew there was no way they could hide the fact that he had been homosexual for most of his life but they wanted to control it. I think my novel threatened that plan in a very profound way, and that was why he leapt to the attack.

Bigsby: In fact it was withdrawn. Was it pulped?.

Leavitt: Yes, Penguin caved, that is the only way I can put it, before it ever went to trial. It was pulped. I subsequently made some changes to it and it was republished.

Bigsby: How substantial were the changes?

Leavitt: There were plot changes. They were designed to distance it from the actual story of Spender's trip to Spain during the war to rescue Tony Hyndman, which was what the novel was based on. I had to change anything that too closely resembled what actually happened and that probably made the novel better, to be perfectly honest, though I resisted it mightily.

Bigsby: There is a story in *Arkansas*, your collection of three novellas, which makes a reference to the writing of that book, unsurprisingly because the character is named David Leavitt. You spoke about the appropriating of other people's lives. Here you seem to appropriate your own. What led you to have a character called David Leavitt whose life mirrored your own?

Leavitt: In some ways the story was written as a response to something that Stephen Spender said in an interview. He said that I had turned his life into pornography and he doubted I would be as relaxed about it if someone turned my life into pornography. So I thought, well, would I? Maybe I will do it myself. It is not really a pornographic story but it is about a writer named David Leavitt who has been sued by a famous English poet and is very depressed. He is having a major writer's block and he starts to write term papers for UCLA undergraduate boys in exchange for sex. He writes their papers for them and they pay him with sex. This was such an outrageous and funny idea to me, especially had it been me, that it was a very liberating, fun story to write. But I was in a sense trying to turn the tables on the whole idea that essentially writers disguise their lives as fiction. There is a point in which I give the game away. I write the line, 'Writers are always disguising their lives as fiction, what they never do is disguise fiction as their lives,' which is what I was trying to do in that story.

Bigsby: Although this story itself got into trouble?

Leavitt: This was an extraordinary thing. It was supposed to be published in *Esquire*. *Esquire* bought it and was going to publish it with a great fanfare because it was pretty long, about seventy-five pages, which was long for *Esquire*. They had already edited it and the graphics had been done when I got a fax from Ed Kosner, the then editor of *Esquire*, who had also been the editor of *New York Magazine*, saying, 'We regret to inform you that we have decided not to publish your story. You may of course keep the money you have been paid,' etc, etc. And it turned out what had happened was that the publisher had flipped out upon reading the story because she was afraid that Chrysler was going to withdraw its advertising. In fact Chrysler had never seen the story. I thought it was all because there was a sex scene in a Jeep. I don't know if this actually was the case, but it was one of those instances in which this effort on the part of the publisher to save herself trouble ended up causing the magazine infinitely more trouble because the fiction editor resigned in protest. Big scandal. All the newspapers picked up on the story and a huge article was written about it in the *Columbia Journalism Review* saying that this was the thin end of the wedge. The editor eventually resigned for this and other reasons and it completely blew up in *Esquire*'s face. Of course my publishers were delighted. They thought this was great and immediately slapped all these stickers on the book that said, 'Too hot to handle.' So it was a very, very curious chain of events that the story led to. Then at a certain point someone very cleverly interviewed Lady Spender about it and she said of me, 'I think he must be insane.'

Bigsby: In *Martin Bauman* there is a young man who has a story published in a famous magazine, clearly *The New Yorker*, who goes on to work for a publisher. So once again you appear in a work of fiction, though this time not under the name of David Leavitt. What is going on?

Leavitt: I don't know. When I wrote it the first thing that came to me was the name, Martin Bauman, and I wanted to call this character Martin Bauman because I wanted to do the opposite of what I had done when I had the David Leavitt character doing all sorts of things that I had never done. I wanted to write a novel that, at least as its jumping off point, used my own experience, but I didn't want to write a memoir. I wanted to be able to change things and I changed a lot. This book is less autobiographical than it appears. I was going back to doing the very old-fashioned thing of disguising my life as fiction and trying to do what I tell my students to do when they write autobiographical fiction. I always say write about yourself as if you are someone else, as if you are a different person. On whether or not I succeeded the jury is still out, at least my personal jury because I still don't have enough distance on that book to know whether it is a successful work of fiction based on my life, or whether it is kind of undigested mush of autobiography and fiction. I will decide in a few years what I think. In the meantime other people can decide what they think.

Bigsby: Jodie Foster makes an appearance in *Martin Bauman*. Was she at Yale with you?

Leavitt: Jodie Foster was my classmate.

Bigsby: I stood at the back of the room at Yale when Jodie Foster was on the stage. I just happened to be there giving a lecture.

Leavitt: You know the other actress in that play was Becca Lish, the daughter of Gordon Lish, my writing teacher, who is also the model for the character of Stanley Flint in the novel. I was at that performance too. It was Marsha Norman's *Getting Out*.

Bigsby: There is an organic connection between what we have been talking about and an aspect of *The Body of Jonah Boyd*. I suppose in the Stephen Spender case you were effectively being accused of plagiarism.

Leavitt: The phrase that kept coming up was that I had plagiarised his life. I thought that was a very odd phrase because to me plagiarism has a very literal meaning. Plagiarism is when you steal someone's prose, and it was never about that. It was about stealing his life. *The Body of Jonah Boyd* is about literal plagiarism, at least part of it is about a case of actual honest-to-God plagiarism.

Bigsby: And this is the first book told through a woman's voice?

Leavitt: It is also I think the first book I have ever written that basically has no gay or lesbian characters, which was a big shift for me.

Bigsby: Where did it start? Did it begin with her voice or with the notion of plagiarism?

Leavitt: It had basically two sources. The first was Edmund White, who is an old friend of mine. I was visiting him a couple of years ago when he was writing his novel *Fanny*. He was writing it in these leather-bound notebooks. He said he could only write in these notebooks. I said, 'Edmund, do you make copies of those?' He said, 'No, no.' And I said, 'Don't you worry about losing them? It is your only copy.' He shrugged off the question as if it wasn't really worth his time. But it stuck in my head and I thought, that is an awfully dangerous way of writing. I am incredibly paranoid and I make multiple backups of everything I write and leave them all over the place because I am so afraid of computer crashes. I print everything fifty times, whereas Edmund was very blasé. I got this idea in my head, the idea of a writer who was constantly tempting fate, who writes in these notebooks and is constantly misplacing them.

That was one origin. The other had to do with my childhood. I had grown up on a campus at Stanford University where my father taught. In those years there was this very strange arrangement that the university had with the faculty. There was a neighbourhood that was unofficially known as the faculty ghetto. It was actually on the campus and the university owned the land but the professors owned the houses. You would buy the house and the land would be leased to you for ninety-nine years for a dollar. If you lived longer than that the lease would be renewed and though the lease could be inherited by a wife or a husband, a widow or a widower, it couldn't be passed on to the children which meant that there was no possibility of inheritance. The house could but, of course, you couldn't have the house without the land. I remember when I was growing up this was a source of real anxiety for my mother because she had this idea that she wanted to leave the house to my sister but the only way my sister could get the house would be if she became a member of the faculty at Stanford.

This idea fascinated me because one of my two favourite novels in the world is *Howard's End* and that is of course about the inheritance of a house. In that novel the question of who will inherit Howard's End becomes a metaphor for the larger question that Forster was asking which was who will inherit England. I had always wanted to write a novel about a house and suddenly it occurred to me that this was my opportunity, that this strange situation could provide me with exactly the plot I needed.

So the two ideas came together and the result was *Jonah Boyd*. And of course the third was Danny, her voice and the idea of having the story narrated by an outsider who was at the same time very intimately involved in the family, but who was never allowed to forget her status as an outsider. I suppose in that regard Danny is a sort of proto-gay character.

Bigsby: I came across an interesting piece that you wrote about yourself when young in which you suggest that you had suffered from a form of Asperger's Syndrome. Was there a connection of any kind between that and writing?

Leavitt: That was a piece really about obsession and writing. I was specifically talking about Asperger's Syndrome, which is this syndrome related to autism. The example in an article which I read was of a child who was completely obsessed with washing machines. It was all he ever wanted to think about. He was constantly drawing pictures and making little models of washing machines. I was a little bit like that as a child and my particular obsession, because my family lived in London for a time, was the London underground. During the year we lived in London I was constantly making my mother take me to the end of the various underground lines. So we would go to places like Stanmore and Cockfosters because I wanted to say that I had ridden to the end of the line. Then, when we got back to the States, I would spend hours and hours drawing these imaginary underground maps, imaginary cities, and as I looked back on it I thought there was something Aspergic about that. But I also realised it was the beginning of whatever made me become a writer, this desire to create an alternative world. The underground thing became a metaphor for trying all the connections under the surface.

Bigsby: And I am inclined to say, almost inevitably, that comes into one of your books.

Leavitt: *While England Sleeps*, the original title of which was *The Train to Cockfosters*. Now mathematics is a new interest of mine.

Bigsby: Is that because you are working on Alan Turing?

Leavitt: I just the finished the book on Alan Turing which is a non-fiction book. Now I am contemplating a novel about a mathematician, but that is in the very earliest stages.

In Conversation With
Doris Lessing

- 24th October 2007 -

Doris Lessing was born in 1919 in what was then Persia (now Iran) and raised in Southern Rhodesia (now Zimbabwe). She moved to England in 1949 and her first book, *The Grass is Singing*, set in colonial Southern Africa, appeared the following year. She interrupted her Children of Violence series (*Martha Quest*, *A Proper Marriage*, *A Ripple from the Storm*, *Landlocked*, *The Four-Gated City*) to write the hugely influential *The Golden Notebook* (1962). *Briefing for a Descent into Hell* (1971) had already signalled a move away from realism that presaged a sequence of space fiction novels beginning with *Re: Colonised Planet 5, Shikasta* (1979). Perhaps the best of these was *The Marriages Between Zones Three, Four and Five* (1980), which has elements of fable about it, as did such later novels as *Mara and Dann: An Adventure* (1999) and *Ben, in the World* (2000). She has written for the theatre and opera. In 2007 she was awarded the Nobel Prize for Literature.

Bigsby: Michael Ondaatje has said that we are made by what comes before us and it seems to me that that is something you would agree with because you were born in 1919 and what came immediately before you was 1914-18. It is true, isn't it, that in some ways that fact has 'made' you and your generation, and, indeed, the next generation as well?

Lessing: I joke that I am a child of that war and it is true because that is what I was listening to throughout my childhood. My father was wounded in the First World War and talked about it the whole time. My mother, who was nursing throughout the war, also talked about it.

Bigsby: I seem to remember your father was presented with a white feather by a woman at a time when he had already lost a leg in the trenches.

Lessing: They had parties of women running around with white feathers presenting them to anybody who they thought should be in the trenches. My father had been in the trenches and lost a leg so this made him somewhat ironical, as you can well imagine, and it caused me to have a certain attitude to some aspects of the women's movement. My mother nursed hard throughout the entire war in the old Royal Free Hospital. That meant she was nursing the wounded and I don't think it did her any good. She had a bad time. This was what I was brought up in. I sometimes felt, when I was a child, that that war was closer to me than anything I could see around me. I was so underneath the trenches and star shells and tanks and bombs. I remember going out into the bush and thinking, 'Oh, for God sake just shut up, just shut up.' You see they couldn't shut up because some soldiers never stopped talking about it and other soldiers never talked about it. Interesting, that.

Bigsby: You were born in what was then Persia, now Iran. What do you remember of that, as opposed to remembering what people told you happened? Do you have vivid memories of it?

Lessing: I do. I have vivid memories that had to be accurate. I remember my brother being born, for example, and the height of the bed and the cot. There are certain verifiable memories. Then, in Tehran, there are certain ones that have to be true. After that I think memories came to be somewhat influenced by what my parents said happened to me.

Bigsby: Do you remember anything of the journey from Iran to England?

Lessing: The most vivid thing is just after the Russian revolution and the Civil War. My mother, intrepid as always, said she was going to take her little children back to Russia, which had never had a tourist industry since the war, and instead of coming back through the Red Sea, which was bad, we were on a train, first on the Caspian, where I got bitten by lice and could have got typhus but luckily didn't, and then on a train which had troops on it and was full of lice. I remember that journey very well. My mother got left behind at one of the stations buying something to eat. Of course, without knowing one word of Russian, she stopped the train following ours. She got onto it and said, 'Follow that train!' This is what my mother was like. She was a very formidable lady. I remember Moscow very well. I think it is very good for small children to be batted around the world because they remember it all. Memories are so vivid and children are so impressionable.

Bigsby: And then it was to Southern Rhodesia, as it then was. Your father had been in banking and now decided to be a farmer. He had some hundreds of acres of land and you were raised, as a child, in the bush. The pictures I get of your parents are that your father was a vaguely liberal person who tried to disarm difficult occasions. Your relationship with your mother, though, apart from valuing the fact that she told you stories, seems to have been an endless series of battles.

Lessing: Battles is the word, but you know she did order books for me and that involved writing letters to England, which was a horrible procedure. The parcels came back by boat and then up by train. These parcels were the great joy of my childhood and continued to be until I ordered books for myself. I will never forget the excitement of those parcels which she didn't open. She left me to open them. So, believe me, I am grateful to her for that, though we did fight about everything. You know parents don't necessarily get the children they want. I don't think I was what she would have chosen if she had had a choice.

Bigsby: In fact didn't she want a boy?

Lessing: Oh, yes, of course. I was going to be a boy. I was going to be called Horatio because my birthday is on the 21st of October, which is Nelson's day, and I would then have been called Horatia but I think somebody protested at that and said that would have been unfair. But then she had a boy, luckily for her, so she could adore that unfortunate child, which she did, much to his disadvantage, for years. She didn't like me very much because I was obstinate, difficult and, I can see, a pain in the neck. I do now see this.

Bigsby: Being awkward would later be a speciality of yours?

Lessing: I had to be awkward. I had to. It was a question of survival. I have talked to women who had mothers like mine. You have to fight or you would get swallowed up. This formidable woman, with unbelievable energy, which was what she had, was all focused on her unfortunate children. You had to fight.

Bigsby: There is a book of yours, not yet published, in fact not even at the publishers yet, which is about your parents. The interesting thing is that it is partly about the way they were and partly about the way they might have been.

Lessing: What I have done is to abolish World War I. That means no Russian revolution, no Soviet Union, no Soviet empire, no Hitler, no Holocaust and no World War II. Abolishing that war is quite a feat but I have done it. I have given them lives, ordinary, even humdrum, decent lives that they would have had if there had been no World War I. All his life my father passionately wanted to be an English farmer, but he never had the money to buy the land. My mother, who was this quite extraordinary woman, I have given scope for her talents, which were large. So in the book my father is a farmer and my mother does quite a lot of impressive things, which is what she should have done because she was totally wasted in Southern Rhodesia in what she could do, bringing up her two unfortunate children, with all her energy directed at us. She should have been running an empire. So I have given her an empire to run, which she would do brilliantly. That is the first half of this book. The second half is what actually happened.

So what this book has turned out to be is a very anti-war book. It is not what I meant when I started but that is what has happened. Some of it is very painful, because it was a painful story. My father was very ill. He got diabetes. He got this and he got that and my mother had to nurse him for years, and this is not a comfortable story. The first half of the story has given me great pleasure in giving them scope for their talents, because they were both very talented people in their different ways.

Bigsby: Back in the real world you were sent off to a Catholic boarding school, which sounds much like a lot of other Catholic boarding schools – not the happiest of experiences.

Lessing: We are talking about Southern Rhodesia, you know. The Catholic convent there was not a very good place. It was full of rather brutal nuns. It was not their fault. What I didn't realise until much later was that these were women who became nuns in the first place in Germany to escape the slump, the terrible economic conditions in Germany. These were women who probably wouldn't have been nuns. In the old days women often became nuns to relieve their family of having to feed them. So here we have these women, stuck in Southern Rhodesia with children like us who they didn't understand or particularly like. There were some good nuns, good teaching nuns, but it wasn't a good experience at all and I was homesick.

I don't think anything in my life could ever be as bad as the convent. I had dreadful homesickness and I wonder to this day why people in this country inflict that homesickness on their children. The upper classes still do apparently and probably say, 'Oh well, it didn't do me any harm.' Once on the television there was a matron in one of our posh boarding schools and she said that she had left because she could no longer stand hearing all the little boys sobbing their hearts out for their mothers night after night. No wonder some English men are peculiar if this is what we inflict on them, if this is what we make them do.

Bigsby: Then, in your teens, you did something that strikes me as fairly remarkable. You wrote a couple of novels.

Lessing: They were no good. Don't worry.

Bigsby: So you don't want to tell me what they were about?

Lessing: I was trying to write a man's novel about the bright young things of Salisbury of which I was only briefly a member. It was beyond my capacity. I couldn't do it. I didn't have anything. The other one was a real lesson. I wrote it in long-hand, very fast, and couldn't read it back. Inspired, I definitely was, but it was probably absolutely terrible and I am glad to say it was all torn up and I don't have to be embarrassed now.

Bigsby: Then you joined a group of people who regarded themselves as Communists, which seems remarkable given the colonial world of Southern Rhodesia.

Lessing: Not remarkable when you think that the war had come on and everything was topsy-turvy. Rhodesia was full of the RAF being trained. It was full of refugees from all over Europe. The men had gone up north to fight Rommel in the desert so nothing was ordinary or normal. So for us to start a Communist group, which I have to say no Communist Party in the world would have tolerated for five seconds, was quite normal. This kind of thing happened.

Bigsby: I have a suspicion that it may have had something to do with the battle with your mother. After all, you join the Communist Party, then marry someone, divorce him and marry someone else who is German and Jewish, who she didn't terribly like, and then divorce him. You seem to have done the things most clearly calculated to dismay your mother.

Lessing: I cannot think of anything I could have done worse to my mother than that history. It is terrible. She was a very conventional woman in every possible way, a believer in the British Empire, and people did believe in it and thought it was very good for everyone and God inspired. Then I decided to be a Communist, but what was much worse was that I didn't approve of race relations as they were. The words most often on her lips were, 'What will the neighbours say?' This was not very nice for her. In fact it was very bad. Then I married the German, the sort of stereotype German, big, fat, pipe-smoking, like Father Christmas, except that this one was a Prussian. Oh my God! And he was a real

Communist and stayed so all his life. So my parents and he had to put up with each other. Practically all of this I look back on and I need to laugh because it was all so appalling, but it wasn't funny then, you know. Believe me it wasn't.

Bigsby: Why exactly did you marry Gottfried Lessing, because you have said you didn't like one another very much?

Lessing: You don't understand at all. This was the Party, you see. We had to keep him out of the internment camp. He had already been in the internment camp and he said, 'Comrades, it is not as good as Baden-Baden health club.' So we had to keep him out of there. We didn't like each other very much but I have to say we behaved beautifully and we should have been given credit for this. No one is ever going to give us credit, except me, because we did behave very well. He didn't like me. That is the truth of the matter, and I can't say I was mad about him because he was such a cold fish. I will tell you what he was like. He was like the Communist in my book *The Sweetest Dream*. He was infinitely contradictory in everything, but he was always there, on the line or not on the line. So we behaved beautifully for about five or six years.

Bigsby: What got you writing your first book?

Lessing: I kept saying I was going to be a writer but I hadn't actually written more than short stories. I knew I was going to have to write a novel at some point and there was this moment when I walked into my boss, because I then worked in a lawyer's firm, and said, 'I am going to write a novel.' He laughed. I didn't blame him. What could be more ludicrous? So I then wrote *The Grass is Singing*, which is not as simple as it sounds because it was two thirds longer than it ended up. It was sent to England in the middle of the war and returned on the boat, threatened by U boats. And I looked at that massive manuscript and suddenly realised there was a perfectly good novel there. I just had to throw away two thirds of it, which is what I did. So that was *The Grass is Singing*.

Bigsby: In 1949 you made a big decision to leave Southern Rhodesia and go to England.

Lessing: I would have gone ten years earlier, but there was a war on. Nobody travelled unless you were a VIP or in the military. For years after the war you had to wait for the boats. The boats were crammed with returning soldiers, the RAF, people going back from India. It wasn't just a question of ringing up and going on the bus or the Queen Mary. You had to wait your turn. I would have gone in 1939 and I would have gone immediately after the war. All of us would have gone if we could have done.

Bigsby: The decision wasn't an easy one because you left two children behind and took one child with you.

Lessing: The thing about the children was that I was married to a civil servant living a life which I absolutely hated, the white life against the blacks. I hated all that. When I left I left for the wrong reasons. I really genuinely believed – though you might think it was mad and I think we were all mad – I genuinely believed we were floating into this beautiful utopia the Communists believed in and everything was going to be beautiful and quite soon. But I was right to leave because if I hadn't left I would have become an alcoholic or I would have had a very bad breakdown. This I knew almost immediately. So I give myself credit for doing the right thing for the wrong reason and I am very glad I did because I know what would have happened to me.

Bigsby: It was a strange London that you found because you had gone from Southern Rhodesia to an England where there was still rationing. There were bomb sites with weeds growing out of them. You must have been told a lot about England from your parents. Was it a shock?

Lessing: Not really. Somebody asked me in a television interview about changing cultures in my life. I have never changed cultures because I was brought up on English literature. This was my education. So my culture was English. I had unbelievably British parents. So I never changed cultures. When I came to England I knew what it was like because it was in the newspapers. It was also on things that we called newsreels, which people have forgotten about. So I knew what it was like. It was going to be tough. In those days we didn't expect things not to be tough. What happened to my generation was that we had to leave our parents as soon as possible and fend for ourselves, which we did. We didn't expect to be well off. We didn't expect to have a good time and we didn't have a good time, but then things were different. We weren't soft, as I think quite a lot of young people are. We were quite tough people, you know. So being uncomfortable and not having any money was not a big deal. It didn't matter.

Bigsby: But in literary terms there was a world available to you, in publishing terms, that there really hadn't been in Rhodesia because although the book you carried with you to London already had a publisher, it didn't have a British one.

Lessing: It had a Johannesburg publisher but he couldn't publish it because it was politically difficult. They bought it but said they weren't going to publish it. So when I got an agent in Curtis Brown she sent him a telegram saying that she was going to sue him for the most dishonest contract she had ever read in her life and sold me over the weekend to Michael Joseph. Then I got started.

Bigsby: So your literary career started with *The Grass Is Singing* in 1950, and not long afterwards, in 1952, you began *The Children of Violence* series. Then that sequence of novels was interrupted, in 1962, by *The Golden Notebook* which has never since been out of print.

Lessing: No, it has never been out of print. It gets published all over the place, all over the world. The essential thing about this book is that it has some kind of a charge because of the conditions I was writing in. Everything was extremely contradictory, battling, tight. This is when Communism was collapsing over there and most of the people I then knew were either Communist or had been Communists. You know that lovely ancient saying, everyone has been a Communist but no one is one, which is true excepting for South America. *The Golden Notebook* consists of several different notebooks and I would like to remind you that the second sentence in *The Golden Notebook* is, 'As far as I can see everything is cracking up.' This is what *The Golden Notebook* is about. It is not about women's lib.

It seems to me that if you are a woman experiencing life as a woman, as a writer, you are going to write about it one way or another. You don't really have to see this as fighting battles. I didn't like the nineteen sixties feminists for a large variety of reasons. I think that they did a lot of harm. I think the first bad mistake they made was to allow themselves to go political. From the very moment they were political it meant that they were going in for backbiting and schisms and it ended in a great frazzle of backbiting.

Women still do not get the same pay for the same work, which is something that has to be redressed. Women, it seems to me, or a large section of them, haven't changed at all. They still want to get married to Mr. Right, which is perfectly natural when you think of how we are biologically. They are obviously very much better than when I was young because the one great thing that has changed is equality of opportunity because women really can be anything now, anything. This is the great thing, and it is amazing, but young women today don't realise how remarkable it is because if you look back to my mother's generation, my generation, the terrible thing was that women who should have been working were not working.

Bigsby: It is a book in part about dreams as well as catastrophe and change, and dreams have always been important to you, haven't they, as a mechanism for writing? I know you once thought of writing a dream autobiography and that you said that sometimes you could almost instruct yourself to dream as a part of the process of writing.

Lessing: I can give an example of that. The book called *The Story of General Dann and Mara's Daughter, Griot and the Snow Dog*, which was a successor to *Mara and Dann*, was all in my mind. It was all planned out. It was all perfect, in the way we think, and then something quite unexpected happened. A griot, which is a name for a storyteller or praise singer for a king, just crept into this book, which I hadn't planned. I hadn't expected it so that meant that the whole book was out of shape, out of wack. It didn't fit to what was I going to do. So what I said to myself was, 'Help, help. I need to dream.' This doesn't always work quite so well but instantly I dreamt the whole dream where General Dann is standing by this marshy place and in it are three brown dogs and one of these dogs is a snow dog that becomes a very important character in the book. And because of this the whole book came back into shape. Suddenly it had a shape and everything was alright. So that is one example. Another was the beginning of *Mara and Dann*. When I was young I absolutely adored my baby brother and the whole of that beginning, where Mara is looking after the baby brother, I was dreaming every night. I dreamt what I was going to write the next day. I would wake up in the morning and it was all in my head ready to go. But that only lasted for about a third of the way through because Dann then disappeared from Mara's life so I had to stop dreaming.

Other writers have said this. I think perhaps we are rather shy in admitting it because it is regarded as creepy or something, but writers often use this. You can use your mind to tell you things that you don't already know. Your dreams can tell you things that you half know but need to be told properly. So the dream will tell you something. I don't think that whatever that world is, is as distant as we think it is if you put a little bit of effort into it, like thinking about it before you go to sleep. What do you need to know? What are you worried about? What plans are you making? Dreams can be very helpful.

Bigsby: Was your brief experiment with drugs simply to find out what it was like, or was it connected with the process of writing?

Lessing: I only took it once, because I am a coward. I took it once and I would never take it again because at that particular time I had a friend who took mescaline, with someone to watch her, and she had the most dreadful year. She said that for the whole year people's heads would roll off their shoulders. This God from Mexico, the cactus God, appeared to her the whole time and she had a dreadful year. Nothing, to me, is worth that. So I did do it once and I did learn a bit, which I am glad about. But only once.

Bigsby: You did something else once, rather strange, you starved yourself.

Lessing: Oh, that, yes. That was very interesting. Now we are back at the time when everyone was into this kind of thought. People who have been through initiation ceremonies often don't eat or sleep, so I thought I would have a shot at this and see what would happen. I do not advise this. It is not a good idea, although I am glad I did it. It was simply rather dangerous. I had a space of about five weeks and I went without food and didn't sleep for about three days. If I hadn't known what I was doing I would have gone to a doctor and they would have locked me up because I was having some very, very extraordinary symptoms, but I did know what I was doing and I kept my head. What I encountered was the figure you often encounter in people who have gone mad, what I call a self-hater. There was this figure, this incredibly powerful accuser, that is cultural since any small child anywhere will have this 'You are good, you are bad, you are naughty.' So I encountered this culturally-created figure and it was a very powerful figure. I am not prepared to laugh about it even now. It took me about six weeks to get rid of it. I could have gone bonkers and yet I kept my head, but I don't advise anybody to do it.

It was a very interesting thing to do because I understand a great deal now when I read accounts by people who are "mad". This figure, this accuser, this self-hater, the person who instructs you to kill people or kill yourself, is a culturally-induced thing and is very powerful. Then you have to ask if it is very powerful in us personally, is it very powerful in society? I think it is. Just think how easily we are intimidated, how easily we are made to feel guilty. You see that of course when people have been in torture camps or intimidated, how easy it is to get people to feel guilty. It is because of this figure that is in everybody.

Bigsby: *The Golden Notebook*, which interrupted *The Children of Violence* series, really jolted you away from your commitment to realism and the realist novel. You wrote a series of novels which you called inner space novels. But then, starting in 1979, came space fiction novels, beginning with *Shikasta*. In 1969 we saw the first picture of the earth as seen from space, whole and entire, blue and brown and white. There was, briefly, the sense of a whole humanity, but you knew that if the camera went in closer and closer what you were going to discover was division. I wonder if in some ways that image wasn't behind some of the space fiction series in that you became very interested in the connections between things, for example between the major religions. Christianity, Islam, Judaism all work from a common book. What led you into space?

Lessing: I don't regard *Shikasta* as the first because I had already written *Memoirs of a Survivor* and *Briefing for a Descent into Hell*, which were not realist. What happened was, somebody said that the three great religions, Judaism, Christianity and Islam, are in fact the same religion at different times. It is perfectly obvious when you start looking. He said no one ever did a simple thing like read the Old Testament, the Jewish books, the Apocrypha, the New Testament and the Koran. The cast of characters is the same in all these books and it is perfectly obvious that it is the same religion in a different state. So I got really turned on by this and I wrote *Shikasta*, though I have to say that while I think there are some very good things in *Shikasta*, I do not think it is the best of that series because I do think the series does contain some of the best writing I have done.

Bigsby: *The Marriages Between Zones Three, Four and Five* is a book I have always liked. I have an odd feeling, though, that it is almost as though you hadn't written it but simply written it down, that it was a pre-existing story, an archetypal story.

Lessing: It is like a myth or a legend, it is true. I had been wanting to write it for about ten years and I couldn't get the right tone of voice for it. I couldn't write it. But for some reason *Shikasta* was a great opener, very creative, and as soon as I had finished it I knew exactly what I should do. I needed the voice of the traditional storyteller. The solution to an impossible problem is usually very simple. The storyteller solved that book which I think was one of my best. Some people are so furious at that series and I feel quite embarrassed even mentioning it, but I do think it has some of my best work in it.

Bigsby: You have been given a whole set of labels. You were the African writer, a realist writer, a writer of space fiction. Then, suddenly, you wrote some books under somebody else's name, Jane Somers. Why did you do that?

Lessing: Mischief. I wrote the first one, *The Diary of a Good Neighbour*, and it went to my then publishers who didn't like it, but my first publisher, Michael Joseph, did like it and said, 'This is like the early Doris Lessing.' So I said, 'Please don't say this.' So she kept quiet, which was quite an achievement. The good thing was that two European publishers bought it not knowing it was by me and nobody recognised me. I thought this was impossible. What was interesting was that someone wrote a great piece welcoming the book but *The New York Times* wouldn't publish it. If *The New York Times* had published it, it would have done quite well, but as it was it was just a new writer that people patronised. Then I wrote the second book, which I rather regret. I should have left it.

Bigsby: We have been talking as though you only wrote novels. In fact you have written plays and operas.

Lessing: Yes, I wrote a couple of operas with Philip Glass, which was a very enjoyable experience.

Bigsby: Since the theatre is something that has attracted you – it is the background to *Love Again*, for example – would you like to have written more for it?

Lessing: Yes, I would, but when you look at people who are successful as playwrights, like Harold Pinter, they are usually those who have worked in the theatre even if they have been scene changers. They have absorbed theatre. My plays were too wordy. Now I look at them I can see it. I didn't have the right experience.

Bigsby: Do you prefer the process of being on your own and writing or being out there in the world communicating with people?

Lessing: I prefer being alone and writing, but as writers we are always at festivals. It is a fairly new thing. I don't know if you realise how new it is for writers to go around talking. When I first started being published, way back in nineteen-fifty, the publisher apologised to me because he wanted me to have a profile. They knew very much more then about writing than they seem to know or care about now. Now you can have it in your contract to go running around the world selling your books and I have to say it is very bad for young writers, or at least for some of them. They have all this attention focused on them. Sometimes they have a lot of money and sometimes they don't write again or they don't write as well as they did. It is not good for writers. Anyway, all us old lot talk away and chat, chat, chat, but it is not really what my job is. I think I am better writing than talking.

Bigsby: You are now eighty-eight. How old are you inside?

Lessing: I would say to any young people who see this decrepit old lady with her hair falling down and generally a bore, what they don't realise is that every old person is probably seventeen or twenty-five inside, and this is why there is a great deal of misunderstanding about old people. Just remember, they may look old but when they look in the mirror this is not what they see. You are looking at yourself when you were much younger and had more energy, so it would be very nice if I could do something to promote greater understanding of the very old. You know we are young sparks inside, believe me.

In Conversation With
Penelope Lively

- 17th November 2010 -

Penelope Lively was born in Cairo in 1933 and lived in Egypt before going to boarding school in England. She subsequently graduated in English from St. Anne's College, Oxford. She established her reputation first as a writer of children's books, the first, *Astercote*, appearing in 1970. *The Ghost of Thomas Kempe* (1973) won the Carnegie Medal while *A Stitch in Time* (1976) won a Whitbread Award. Her first novel for adults, *The Road to Lichfield* appeared in 1977. Ten years later she won the Booker Prize for *Moon Tiger*. Subsequent novels included *Cleopatra's Sister* (1993), *The Photograph* (2003) and *Family Album* (2009).

Bigsby: You were born in Cairo?

Lively: Yes, in what was called the Anglo American Nursing Home, but my whole childhood was spent in one of a group of three houses that were right out in what was then called "The Cultivation," which was about five miles out of the middle of Cairo and is now digested into the sprawl of Cairo itself, the urban sprawl. When I went back there with my husband and two friends we found the house in which I had grown up. It was in the middle of a teeming Cairo slum, but back in my days there had been fields of sugar cane.

Bigsby: Why did you go back?

Lively: I had always intended to go back. I was richly into adult life by then. I think the reason we hadn't been back before was partly because it was expensive and my husband was an academic and academics are not very well paid. We couldn't have afforded it and also, if you are sensible, you only visit Egypt in the winter and he really hadn't been able to take time off in the winter. But I wanted to go back. I knew I wanted in some way eventually to be able to write something that derived from my childhood in Egypt and from that first trip came *Moon Tiger* and later a childhood memoir, *Oleander, Jacaranda*, which came together in a haphazard way when I realised that I had had this very odd childhood growing up during the war in the Middle East. When my first grandchild was born I thought, one day these children might be interested in this and I started writing down all the fragments I had in my head as childhood memories and realised that it began to add up to a book, but the novel came first.

Bigsby: What is striking to me about your upbringing is that you seem to have been raised largely by a nursery nurse.

Lively: I didn't go to school. Allegedly, there was no school to which to send me. I now discover this wasn't quite true. I think it was really that my mother couldn't be bothered to drive me into Cairo every day and so the person who had been looking after me, effectively, my nanny, turned herself into a governess. She herself had left school at fifteen and was very canny. What she did was discover a do-it-yourself education kit whereby you could have the books and the timetables etc. sent out from England. It was designed for expatriate parents, mostly in India, and I have since discovered that quite a lot of other people had this education. Frankly, it was wonderful. It depended entirely on narrative. Before the child could write you read to the child and when it could write then it had to what was called "write back," but it mustn't use exactly the words which had been said. It must paraphrase. You told back, wrote back, did an inordinate amount of reading.

Some of the books never reached us because they went to the bottom of the Mediterranean – this was in the middle of the war – so then we just fell back on whatever was on my parent's shelves. They were a very middle-brow family so there was the canon of English poetry. We read the Bible, hugely. We gobbled up Dickens in a wonderfully naïve way. We entered into it totally. We were going to get Smyke and bring him home and feed him up and put him in the spare room. He would be all right with us. We were the original naïve and innocent readers. Science rather fell by the wayside I have to say. The science book was called *Eyes and No Eyes* and it was written by Arabella Buckley in the 1880s, so it was just a touch out of date. It had beautiful illustrations of the flora and fauna of Devon's stream life and I used to go outside and fish in the Nile, in the 1950s, and try to identify the kind of monstrous catfish against the illustrations of Arabella Buckley.

Bigsby: And you read Greek myths where you even found your own name.

Lively: Greek mythology was completely central. We had Andrew Lang's *Tales of Troy and Greece*, and this was the absolute centre for me because of being in there anyway, Penelope. So obviously this was relevant in some way – the solipsism of the nine-year-old. But I felt there was a way in which the mythology was a bit outdated because, after all, the Libyan campaign was raging on the fringes so I got Hector into an armoured tank and reinvented the myths. I was also in there with the wrong part because Penelope is said to be wise and kindly whereas Helen is far more beautiful. Nobody wants to be wise and kindly.

Bigsby: Is it right that you wanted to change your name?

Lively: Yes, I didn't care for Penelope. For an odd reason I wanted to be called Miranda. I really don't know why. I think this came from that Hilaire Belloc poem *Tarantella* with its line, 'Do You Remember an Inn, Miranda?' It sounded a wonderful kind of romantic name and I would have preferred that. I never have liked Penelope.

Bigsby: You were an only child, but invented a sister.

Lively: I had internal narratives. I was a very solitary child, not going to school, with no siblings. I have always assumed that everybody does this or did this, just lived in a state of internal narrative, but I now think possibly they don't. So I did live in this world of narrative, yes, and invented companions and messed about with Greek mythology and so forth and I think this probably was the refuge of a very solitary child. It wasn't, I have to say, a good basis for eventually being un-solitary. When I was twelve I came to England, effectively for the first time, and was sent immediately to boarding school. It was a kind of Calvary. Of course I was not used to the society of other children and I think I was completely hopeless. I couldn't cope at all, so I wouldn't really recommend this as a way to bring up children, but for the twelve years that it lasted Egypt was paradise. It was wonderful.

Bigsby: Did any of these interior narratives distil out into writing?

Lively: Creative writing had not been thought of then, and it hadn't occurred to Lucy, who was so-called educating me, to say, 'Write a story,' so, no, it didn't. I retold the stories I had been offered but there were no attempts at narrative. It was all going on in my head but I never thought of putting it down. The only writing that there is from then is an exercise book that still survives that is called *The Flora and Fauna of the Lower Nile*

Valley. It is written in the ponderous style of a nineteenth century clergyman. It is all about the jackal and the lesser sandpiper and stuff like that, but there is no story to it at all.

Bigsby: There came a moment when your mother walked out on the family. I assumed that would be traumatic for you but it seems that it wasn't. Was trauma delayed or did it never exist because your relationship was never close anyway?

Lively: Our relationship hadn't been close, no. She hadn't looked after me. She had been doing what middle class expatriate women of her day did. They didn't look after their own children. So I hadn't had a lot to do with her. She looked after me on Wednesday afternoons and that was about it. So we weren't close and I was far more traumatised by being sent to boarding school and losing Lucy.

Bigsby: You mention that you were living in Cairo during the Second World War, with Rommel's Afrika Korps doing battle with the Eighth Army not very far from where you were, seventy miles or so, and on one occasion you did leave for Palestine. Years later, you retrieved something of that in *Moon Tiger*. Did you know where that book was going when you started it?

Lively: I am very keen on beginnings. The beginning of a novel is tremendously important. You have got to jump straight in. I think for me it comes particularly from having written children's books. I always felt that if you don't grab the child on the first page you have already lost them and the same applies to the short story. I used to be a keen writer of short stories and I have written a lot. Alas, they have left me over the last ten years or so but the same applies to the short story. If you haven't seized your reader in the first two or three lines then something is already wrong and I do think that applies to novels as well. When I wrote the first page of *Moon Tiger* I do know that the first sentence came into my head before I really knew where the book was going. I knew I had this character and I knew what was going to be the first sentence of the book.

Bigsby: Your central character in that novel can, in effect, look back across the 20th century.

Lively: Exactly, and I wrote that twenty-four years ago. I am now the age that I think I imagined Claudia to be, dying in hospital. I was that much younger then so I look at it completely differently now. Someone else wrote it because, as a writer over twenty five years, you have changed into somebody else. I am not the same person who wrote that book. I am now somebody else writing different books.

Bigsby: Do you ever re-read your own books?

Lively: Never. Absolutely never.

Bigsby: *Oleander, Jacaranda* is subtitled *A Child Perceived*. Why that subtitle?

Lively: Because the working process for this book, as I said, came from thinking about my own grandchildren. So what I did over a few months was I fished in my head and pulled out those shards that we have all got and just jotted them down. Obviously they were in non-sequential order. We don't have a linear memory. We just have all these bits and pieces and I was putting bits down and putting bits down and then thinking that what I was putting down was what I wanted, what the child's eyes saw, but what I now found was that that adult eye was reinterpreting what the child had seen.

I was growing up in interesting times. I was a child in the Middle East during the war. It was raging, as you say, seventy miles away and Rommel was just about to get to Alamein. British women and children were being evacuated from Cairo. The military had already gone and families were leaving so my mother decided perhaps it was about time to go. So my father, who worked in an Egyptian bank, and who had not been able to join up as he would have liked to have done because he had crippling bad sight which he has left to me, stayed. My mother and Lucy and I went to Palestine where we spent the summer.

My mother stayed in a hotel in Jerusalem but Lucy and I stayed at Government House because Lucy, before she had been looking after me, had been looking after the children of the High Commissioner, Sir Harold McMichael. I am the last, and presumably the only-surviving, English woman to have seen General De Gaulle in his dressing gown because he was also staying there. This was apparently a kind of clandestine visit and we had to share a bathroom with him. We were told that we must not impede the General when he needed the bathroom so we must peep out of our door to see if he had finished in the bathroom before we could use it. I saw him loping down the corridor carrying a sponge and wearing a paisley dressing gown. When I came to write *Oleander, Jacaranda* I obviously wanted to put this in so I went to the De Gaulle biographers to check that he had actually been in Jerusalem at this point and could find no reference to this. He had been in Syria but not, apparently, Palestine. I remembered, though, that we were told that we must not mention that the General was at Government House, that his visit was hush-hush in the terms of the day. So I assume that this was a hush-hush visit to have clandestine talks with the High Commissioner.

Bigsby: But you have also said that childhood is irretrievable. I take that to mean not just that you can't go back but that you can't get inside the mind of who you were once?

Lively: No, it is the alien in our midst. You can't recover the child's eye view so that when I was writing *Oleander, Jacaranda* I was trying to look at what it was that a child sees, so it ended up by being a book about the nature of childhood perception, about what it is that I felt that children see. It is this extraordinary kind of immediacy. I was trying to discover how a child learns to interpret the baffling codes and instructions with which it is surrounded, how it learns to feel its way around socially. For me, it was peculiarly baffling because Cairo at that point was a cosmopolitan cauldron. It was a multi-cultural polyglot society rather more than I imagine it is now, so it was even more confusing and baffling and fascinating.

I could find no answers to this in the people who write about developmental psychology, although after the book came out I did get a letter from Margaret Donaldson, who is one of the great developmental psychologists, who had come across it and read it and she said that the reason we can't write about that kind of thing is because it is not scientifically quantifiable. She said it is very interesting. It is why we depend upon people like you to write about it because you are less interested in the science. You are interested in the perception.

Bigsby: When you came to England you lived partly with your grandparents?

Lively: Yes. After my parents were divorced and I was sent to boarding school I spent a great deal of time with my grandmother in Somerset.

Bigsby: You seem to have hated your boarding school which had a rather strange attitude with respect to reading.

Lively: I was actually punished. The only sort of privacy we had at this appalling nineteen-forties boarding school was a tiny little locker in which you kept your few possessions, and one of my most treasured possessions was my *Oxford Book of English Verse*. I read poetry a lot and I wrote poetry, which was more or less stamped out of me by that school, and this book was confiscated from my locker. I was summoned by the Headmistress who had it on her desk in front of her. She pushed it across towards me and said, 'There is no need for you to read this kind of thing in your spare time. You are here to be taught all that.' One of the punishments in the school was to be sent to read for an hour in the library, though there was actually very little to read beyond a few encyclopaedias. That was about it. It was a determinedly philistine school and I escaped from it at sixteen with a sigh of relief. Eventually, I can't think how, I managed to get into a university and discovered that there were other grey-haired ladies who had been encouraging teenagers to read books.

Bigsby: Rather miraculously, then, you ended up at Oxford where you studied history rather than literature. You said that studying history didn't make you a novelist but it determined the kind of novelist you were going to be.

Lively: It did indeed, yes. I read history very badly. I wasn't an assiduous student. I didn't get a good degree but in an extraordinary way it conditioned my mind for the rest of my life. I had no idea this was going on during those three years but it had this extraordinary affect on me and that is why I said it didn't make me into a novelist but it determined the kind of novelist that I was eventually going to become. If I had read English I think I would have been writing different kinds of novels and I am extremely grateful that I did this. I wasn't nearly as clued up about university as everybody is now. I applied for a college, St Anne's, where Iris Murdoch was then the philosophy teacher. I was interviewed by one of the historians who said, 'We might not have a place in history. If we don't would you like to read PPE?' [politics, philosophy and economics]. I didn't even know what PPE was. I had no idea, but being a kind of pliable girl I said, 'Yes, that would be lovely, yes.' So she said, 'In that case I think you had better have an interview with our Miss Murdoch.' So I was sent into Iris Murdoch and the only thing I can remember about this interview was she did ask a rather good question. She said, 'What were you reading on the train coming down?' I was reading an Ernest Hemingway, so we had a discussion about Hemingway. Mercifully, there was a place for me in history because I would have been completely hopeless at PPE.

Bigsby: One of the things about history, of course, is that it is a narrative and I presume it is partly that aspect of history that appeals to you.

Lively: Well, yes, except that the history syllabus, certainly at that university, has changed immensely since my day and the sort of history that I then realised I wanted in some ways wasn't even being written then. It was very much more political history then. My interests, subsequently I realised, were in cultural history and social history and the book that set me by the ears when it came out in the nineteen-seventies was Keith Thomas's *Religion and the Decline of Magic* and I suddenly realised this was the sort of history I had been wanting but that hadn't been around, or we hadn't been taught, at Oxford. Actually, it was around. It was being written by people like Marc Bloch, but it wasn't being taught at Oxford then, but Keith Thomas's wonderful book prompted, for me, a completely frivolous children's book called *The Ghost of Thomas Kempe*, which featured the sort of people who cropped up in Keith Thomas's book. So I was extremely grateful for that.

Bigsby: The other thing about Oxford is that you met the person who would become your husband, but you were both very unlikely people to be at Oxford.

Lively: We were. We met in what I call the clear blue air of higher education. I was a girl from the southern gentry, Jack was from the northern working class and we met, frankly, because of the Butler Education Act. Had it not been for that there would have been no way people from such completely disparate backgrounds could have met. After I came down I got the first and only job I have ever had. I came back to Oxford and worked as research assistant to somebody who was a fellow of St. Antony's graduate college. After I had been there for a year Jack came over as junior research fellow. I heard his name being mentioned before he came. Friends of mine said, 'There is this chap called Jack Lively coming over from Cambridge. He is said to be incredibly bright.' And I thought, what a wonderful name, Jack Lively. It sounds like something out of Smollett or Fielding, little knowing that it would eventually be my name.

Bigsby: So you married and raised a family, two children, one of whom himself went on to be a writer [Adam Lively]. You did not yourself, though, start to write until you were thirty and then it was a children's novel. Why then, why a children's novel?

Lively: You may well ask. I had always loved children's books, ever since a child, and I was hugely interested in reading with and to my children. I got more and more interested in children's literature, read more things that I hadn't read when I was a child. I had grown up and cut my teeth on children's literature and I just thought I would have a go. It didn't, at that stage, occur to me to attempt adult fiction and so I wrote a children's book and sent it off into the blue. I was incredibly naïve about publishers and I was just very lucky it got published. And then I wrote several more before I thought, maybe I will try writing for adults.

Bigsby: And that was seven years later. You were forty-four when that book came out.

Lively: I was an extremely late starter.

Bigsby: You have made up for it, publishing some fifty books. We talked earlier about history and that has always been a key factor in your work but you have insisted that you are not a historical novelist. Can you explain what you mean by that? Do you have a particular model of what a historical novel is as opposed to novels that contain history and are spread over long periods of time.

Lively: I suppose I would define a historical novel as one set in the past and I think when I first started writing fiction I had extreme suspicion of the historical novel. My experience of it then was that I didn't like people like Mary Renault. I completely changed my mind because the historical novel has been stood on its head by people like John Fowles and J. G. Farrell. When these people started writing I realised what the historical novel could do, but I think I also knew that I couldn't do that. But for me it was very important in writing fiction to peg private life to public life. I think because of this intense interest in history and the story of history and what history does for us I felt the importance of the way in which, whether we like it or not, and whether we admit it or not, all of our private lives are directed by public events. So I felt that when I was writing a novel I wanted this sense of people's lives being directed by public events to be there. I didn't want private life to dominate. History must be there as a backcloth, public life must be there. So inevitably, because of my interest in history, historians crept into the novels. I have had various historian characters. I am extremely interested in archaeology as well so archaeologists have elbowed their way into the fiction here and there and of course this has enabled me then to do all sorts of supportive reading, which is of huge interest to me.

Bigsby: How important is place to you?

Lively: I need to site a novel and I need to site the characters. For instance, in *Family Album* I had to completely imagine an Edwardian house. I had to know exactly how many rooms it had and what was happening there and although I don't name the provincial town in which it is located I had to have an idea of what it was. So certainly places are hugely important. I can't have a Sartrean vacuum in which events are taking place. I have got to know what the backcloth is and for some novels I have had to do a lot of leg work and tramping around. There is a novel called *City of the Mind* which is a London novel set in the nineteen eighties and I had to do a lot of tramping around London and thinking about that before I could possibly write it.

Bigsby: In *Perfect Happiness* you wrote about grief. That was 1987. Where did that come from?

Lively: I don't know.

Bigsby: In 1998 your husband died. In that earlier novel you had imagined what grief felt like. How far did you find that that turned out to be an accurate account?

Lively: I think I am rather glad that I can't answer that because I have never re-read the book since then, since Jack's death. I have never looked at it again and I probably hadn't for many years before that. I felt humbled after it was published. I had a number of letters from women who had lost their husbands saying that it rang true and I remember thinking, when I read these letters, that actually it had been presumptuous of me to write it. Well, I have now had that experience but I can't answer the question because I don't want to go back and read it again. I don't want to know whether I got it right or not. I probably didn't. In fact I am sure I didn't because until you have had that experience there is a sense in which you really do not know. When you are a novelist you are guessing at an awful lot of things because obviously there are masses of experiences that you haven't had and if you only wrote out of the experiences that you have had frankly you would be a very reduced novelist. So you have to make these guesses and try to achieve this kind of empathy over an enormous range of experience and that is just one of them. If I wrote that book now I would probably do it differently.

Bigsby: In 2005 you published a book called *Making It Up*, which is a kind of anti-memoir. One of your concerns, expressed in a number of books, is the sheer contingency of life. The chance of either of you going to Oxford was very remote, but that led to your marriage. People like to believe there is a narrative to their life and we unconsciously write and rewrite and edit those lives as we grow older. In *Making It Up* you go to certain moments in your life, when something might have been completely different, and offer an alternative version. How did you select those particular moments?

Lively: The absolutely terrifying thing I found was that they all happened when I was so young. I think that is partly because I hadn't had the kind of life where I have had a career and employment. Anybody who has had a career has made large choices or had contingent things happen much later in life but, given the sort of life I have had, they all happened very young.

As I said, I am very interested in archaeology and I think it was in my second year at Oxford that a Roman temple was being excavated in London by a Professor Grimes and I read about this in *The Times*. I was enthralled by it and so I wrote to Professor Grimes and said, 'I am a second year student at Oxford and I am very interested in archaeology and could I come and help on your dig?' He wrote a letter back, which I don't have any more but I remember it vividly, a charming letter in which he said he was very glad that I was interested in archaeology but unfortunately he was completely up to his ears with volunteers and he couldn't use another one. However, he said, 'When you have finished your degree at Oxford you might like to think of doing a diploma in archaeology somewhere and if so please write and I will make some suggestions.' Well, life took another turn and I didn't do that but that, I felt, was one of those nodal points when I might have turned into an archaeologist. I might have gone off and done a diploma in archaeology and become an archaeologist instead of a novelist and life would have gone in another direction. One of the stories in *Making It Up* is an imagined character who is sort of me but who is not actually the central character in the story.

Bigsby: Jack features as well because he might have served in Korea because of National Service, but Cambridge saved him from that.

Lively: He was saved by the bell, as it were.

Bigsby: But in the book you sent him to Korea, which was a rather cruel thing to do, and you leave him teetering at the end probably to be a prisoner of war.

Lively: I sent him to the Battle of the Indian River, which could very well have happened because he was in the Northumberland Fusiliers and the Northumberland Fusiliers were sent to Korea and national servicemen went with them. They were sent into the Battle of the Indian River when they arrived in Korea and Jack could have been with them but he was saved because he had been offered a Cambridge place. I have done a bit of research on this and apparently not all, but some, national servicemen who had been offered university places were allowed to go earlier. They were let off, I think, six months early or something, and he was one of those. So instead of going to Korea and the Battle of Indian River he went to Cambridge.

Bigsby: I said you were cruel to him but you were even more cruel to yourself because you kill yourself off and create a fictive sister, such as you had had in Egypt, who presides over your funeral.

Lively: Well, the killing off one was again something that could have happened. After I left Oxford I didn't quite know what to do and one of the things I toyed with was to go back to Egypt. I thought I would really love to go back to Cairo and the only skill I felt I might have was to teach English, so I made vague enquiries about this but it never came about. But I imagined the self who did do this and at that point people who are my age may remember there were aircraft called Comets and Comets were rather given to dropping out of the sky. There were a lot of Comet crashes and in fact a contemporary of mine, a girl of my age who had gone back to her family who were still in Egypt, was killed in a Comet crash. So I invented for the story a self who did go back to Egypt and died in a Comet crash. Many, many years later her bones are found on a Sicilian mountain side and retrieved by a sister who I do not have. So the story is really about the sister but, yes, I killed myself off in that story.

In Conversation With David Lodge

- 8th October 2008 -

David Lodge, novelist, playwright, critic, was born in Brockley, London, in 1935. He was educated at London and Birmingham universities and has lived in Birmingham (which appears as Rummidge in his fiction) for many years. His first novel, *The Picturegoers*, appeared in 1960. Subsequent novels include *The British Museum is Falling Down* (1965), *Changing Places: A Tale of Two Campuses* (1975), *Small World: An Academic Romance* (1984), *Nice Work* (1988), *Paradise News* (1991), *Therapy* (1995), *Thinks…*(2001), *Author, Author* (2004), *Deaf Sentence* (2008) and *A Man of Parts* (2011). In 1998 he was awarded a CBE for services to literature.

Bigsby: Your new novel, *Deaf Sentence*, has an autobiographical element to it.

Lodge: I would never have written this novel if I hadn't suffered the kind of hearing loss that my character is suffering. Also, the thread to do with Desmond's aged father, and the problems of looking after him, are taken from my own life. So I think in some ways this is the most autobiographical novel I have written for quite a long time in terms of drawing directly from my own experience.

Bigsby: And your hearing loss began quite some time ago, as is the case of the character in the book?

Lodge: Yes, it began I think in my late forties, though I can't exactly pin it down to a particular year. I recognised, as Desmond does, problems with hearing students and it was one factor which made me take early retirement from teaching. I was finding it more and more difficult, or I found I was talking too much because I wasn't hearing very well. At that point I had already had my ears tested and I had a single hearing aid of the old-fashioned NHS kind, which was rather cumbersome. I was told from the very beginning that it was a gradual but incurable condition and I would just have to improve the quality of my hearing aids as the hearing deteriorated, which is what happened. From managing with one you go on to two.

Bigsby: You retired in 1987, so that is twenty-one years ago. I remember when you came here to talk about your Henry James book, *Author, Author,* you said, 'I don't know that I am going to be doing this any more, reading in public.' Something changed after that and you decided to write a book about it. Was that an improvement in technology or a change of attitude?

Lodge: I was always a bit embarrassed at the handicap of poor hearing when it came to question and answer sessions. I would usually explain the problem but I suppose I felt, with this novel, since this was what it was about, and it is transparently autobiographical in that respect, there was no reason to feel any inhibitions. So in some ways it has been much easier to read than some previous books. Maybe I felt *Author, Author* was not an entirely successful book for reasons which were external, because somebody else [Colm Tóibín] published a good book on the same subject. In fact it greatly overshadowed it. I suppose I felt, well, I didn't want to end my public career with that book and in a way I hoped to recoup and recover my audience with this one. So I wanted to promote it and was glad to get opportunities to present and read it.

Bigsby: It is almost a campus novel.

Lodge: It is another version of a campus novel, I suppose, a retirement campus novel. Early retirement has become a very popular profession and a lot of academics are tempted or persuaded to take it, so that was one of the experiences I wanted to include in the book. But it is not my experience at all. In that respect it is not autobiographical. Desmond is feeling very much sidelined by having taken early retirement. He regrets it. He has lost status and a certain amount of self-esteem. He thought he would like the opportunity to devote himself to research but, having left the institution, and the kind of collaborative and competitive atmosphere of the institution, he feels there is really no point in labouring over a scholarly article any more. So he is feeling very much redundant and I turn the screw on that situation by making his wife have a second spring. Rather unexpectedly, she is having a successful career as a business woman. She has also rejuvenated herself physically so he is feeling more and more left out, or left behind. I haven't felt that at all. I have been as busy in retirement as I was before and have no problem filling my days. I think I recognise that syndrome, though. People have been dependent on their job, particularly if it is a professional job which they enjoyed and found fulfilling, and when it is suddenly taken away from them I think they feel very much at a loss.

Bigsby: As you say, there is another autobiographical dimension to the book in that the character's father seems fairly clearly to be based on your own. He suffered from deafness but also from early-stage dementia. Could you have published this while he was alive?

Lodge: No, I don't think I could even have written it while he was alive. He died in 1999 and the last year of his life held great anxieties for me because he was living in the little house in London where I grew up but he was getting increasingly incapable of running it, and looking after himself safely. He had done pretty well up to then, but I am talking about when he was ninety-two, ninety-three. I wanted him to move to some kind of residential care home near us in Birmingham but he didn't want to. Like most old people he didn't want to leave his house and in some ways the instinct is right because when you get very old it is difficult to adjust to a new physical location. Being in your old home tells you what you have got to do, but unfortunately he could no longer do it properly. So it was an anxious time.

The idea that I might write a comic novel about getting deaf came to me while I was cleaning my teeth and I made a note the next morning in my notebook. Immediately after that I thought maybe I could combine this with the experience of looking after dad in his last years, the reason being that he was getting deaf but, like many old people, wouldn't wear a hearing aid so we were always shouting at each other. The problems that were already there were exacerbated by that. So that is how he came into the novel and, of course, bringing him into the novel brought death into the novel because he was getting towards the end of his life. It seems to be that deafness is a sign of mortality and if you get deaf earlier in life than normal it concentrates the mind on that. Then I thought of the title of the novel being a kind of pun on death sentence. Those are the two main interwoven themes of the book.

Bigsby: You were something of an avid reader when you were young?

Lodge: Yes, I suppose I was, but for a long time I was a rather undiscriminating reader of boys' comics and that sort of thing. My father was a great reader, too. He didn't have much formal education. He was a dance musician by profession and largely self-taught as a musician. He left school at about fourteen or fifteen. He was a very intelligent man and very gifted and I owe most of my artistic genes to him, I think. He did encourage me to read things that he liked, British humourists like Jerome K. Jerome and short story writers like W. W. Jacobs, Damon Runyon and Evelyn Waugh, rather sophisticated tastes. He used to play in the nightclub where Evelyn Waugh and all the 'Bright Young Things' used to go so he got interested and read Evelyn Waugh's novels and gave me a taste for them at quite a precocious age. I was reading Waugh at the age of about fourteen or fifteen. I was absolutely fascinated by them, though those books couldn't have been more different and distant from my own social world. Dad was also a great reader of Dickens. As a boy I actually found Dickens very heavy going, apart from *Pickwick Papers*, which I used to love and read and re-read. But it was inevitably an English master, a very charismatic English teacher at my school – not a particularly distinguished academic school, a Catholic grammar school – who released in me a feeling for adult literature.

Bigsby: Did you start writing then?

Lodge: I started writing really not long after he came. I started writing poetry and essays and short stories and he encouraged me to read modern literature. He gave me suggestions, so it really took off from there.

Bigsby: You must have been almost literally one of the first beneficiaries of the 1944 Education Act.

Lodge: Oh, yes, my generation, my class, my sixth form, was the first in my school to all apply to university. I think they had had one or two people who had gone to Oxford or Cambridge before, but very few. We got very little advice. I literally didn't know there were any universities in England apart from Oxford, Cambridge and London. I didn't presume, or perhaps I was too timid, to apply to Oxford and Cambridge so I applied to London University, my local university, and got into University College, which fortunately happened to be an extremely good university, with a very good English department.

Bigsby: And English then presumably meant Beowulf and Middle English and dead authors?

Lodge: Yes, that is true. I think my year was the first that was allowed to do modern literature, twentieth century literature. We didn't have any particular finite dates but you had to study two authors – Henry James and Yeats – and then you could prepare other authors for another part of the paper. I chose to work on James Joyce's *Ulysses* and that was undoubtedly one of the crucial intellectual experiences of my life. It gave me a passion for Joyce and that book in particular. It is amazing how many novelists, when asked what is the greatest novel of the twentieth century, will say *Ulysses* because it embodied all the techniques of fiction and all the possibilities of fiction. I was particularly taken with the idea of basing a modern story on some precursor text that was well known or mythical, and I used that for several of my own novels.

Bigsby: You did a masters degree with a dissertation on Catholic writers and that seemed to have an enormous influence on your own first novels.

Lodge: Well, I had a Catholic upbringing. I had a Catholic education. It wasn't a very typical Catholic home by any means. My father wasn't a Catholic, and I was an only child, but Catholic education has a way of getting into the bloodstream. At that time, in the late forties, early fifties, it was a quite trendy thing for writers to be Catholic. Graham Greene and Evelyn Waugh were the two best-known English novelists. The greatest living poet was T. S. Eliot, who was Anglo-Catholic and theologically indistinguishable from Catholics. Obviously having aspirations to be a writer I found that rather inspiring and I think belonging to their small minority, which Catholics are in England, meant that you didn't want to rebel against it like Irish writers almost invariably had to in order to throw off the authority of the church to find their feet as writers. I didn't feel that. I felt it gave one an unusual or interesting angle on the secular liberal society. That you had those values and that system of belief was a great source of topics, themes, symbols, and so on. I guess I have always combined a critical literary-historical interest with a creative one. I wanted to find out where Catholic writing came from in English literature, how long it had been going on. So I was working back from writers like Greene and Waugh and it turned out to be a monster thesis.

In those days the Masters degree at London was two years, and a research degree, and there was no word limit on it. I produced a seven-hundred page thesis, so did another man on another subject, after which they changed the rules. I was discovering more and more generally rather bad Catholic novels in the British Museum Library, many of which had never been read, never had the pages cut. I was hacking my way through them and annoying my fellow readers with the noise of cutting through them. I produced this monstrous thesis rather than condense it. The two last chapters were on Waugh and Greene.

Bigsby: And they are the ones who were going to be very influential in your early novels. Indeed before you were called a campus novelists you were described as a Catholic novelist?

Lodge: Yes, I have always had two caps, I suppose.

Bigsby: Before you published your first book, though, which you did precociously young – you finished it at twenty-three and published it at twenty-five – you had to do National Service.

Lodge: I was very, very young when I went to university, too young really, just through the chance of my age on entering school. I was only seventeen-and-a-half, so I didn't have to do National Service right away. I did it when I finished my first degree. I was drafted into the Royal Armoured Corps, which was the most inappropriate place for me. I hated tanks, hated cavalry officers, but nothing is wasted on the writer so I wrote a novel about it in due course. I learnt something of life from it, but it was a terribly repetitive experience. I am not sure I learnt anything I couldn't have learnt in three months.

Bigsby: You started off as something of a realist writer, without the kind of humour we came to associate you with. Then there was a change, with *The British Museum Is Falling Down*.

Lodge: That was a comic novel and it was really a result of meeting Malcolm Bradbury when we were colleagues at Birmingham University in the early sixties, both having written one novel, both also taking the academic profession quite seriously and writing criticism. Malcolm was essentially a comic writer and was a bit ahead of me in the game of the literary world. He was writing for *Punch* and he encouraged me to write comedy. We collaborated on satirical reviews that were put on in Birmingham and I found I enjoyed doing that. Sitting in the audience hearing people laugh at the first revue we wrote seemed to me a nice experience. In those days my wife and I were both rather orthodox Catholics and were struggling with the absurd teaching of the Catholic church on birth control. I suppose, as with deafness, I thought I could write a comic novel about this and it certainly would be intolerable to write a serious novel about it. And so that is what I did, combining it with my research in the British Museum on the Catholic novel. My hero has Walter Mitty-like experiences. The novel owes a lot to *Ulysses* because it all happens on one day and the last chapter is a rather cheeky pastiche of Molly Bloom's soliloquy.

Bigsby: Julie Christie was in one of your revues?

Lodge: She was, yes, she was in this revue Malcolm and I, and a student called Jim Duckett, wrote together. It was put on at the Birmingham Rep in 1963 and was memorable to me, particularly, because I was sitting in the audience when the news of President Kennedy's assassination came through a transistor on the stage which an actor was very foolishly using as a prop. He had a music programme on but they suddenly interrupted it to say that President Kennedy had been assassinated and I thought it was quite a bad taste joke that had been put into the show, but it wasn't. In the interval everybody was talking about it and of course it killed our show. Julie Christie joined the Rep to learn the ropes as an actress. She was on five pounds a week, or something ridiculous. She had just finished *Billy Liar* and it hadn't actually come out, so she wasn't quite a star yet but was pretty well known. She wasn't actually a very good stage actress and I remember this undergraduate student Jim Duckett actually coaching her, coaching Julie Christie. She was willing but it wasn't her medium really.

Bigsby: Then in the late 60s you went to America, to Berkeley. That, too, would feed into a novel.

Lodge: I was in Berkeley in 1969. I went from the student revolution in England in the autumn of 68, which in Birmingham was a fairly well mannered affair, though it had its occupations which put the elderly professors into a tizzy, to Berkeley where there was something like civil war going on. I was hardly able to teach, although that was what I was there to do. That gave me the idea for *Changing Places* whose subtitle is *A Tale of Two Campuses*. Like *A Tale of Two Cities*, it is about revolution in two very different forms, two different countries.

Bigsby: And that was going to lead to *Small World*. At what stage did you realise that there was going to be more than one?

Lodge: I never intended to do a sequel but having invented Rummidge, and these characters, when I thought of doing a novel about what I called the global campus – this new phenomenon of international conferences and people swanning around the world – I thought I would use some of

51

the same characters again. So I started that novel with a very dismal British conference in Rummidge and then opened it out to the world. Then I used Rummidge again in *Nice Work* because why invent a whole new city when I could use the one I had partially invented already?

Bigsby: That is a technique of yours, the creation of two worlds?

Lodge: Yes, there are binary patterns in most of my novels, absolutely.

Bigsby: Another one in which you drew on your own experience is *Therapy*, because you had yourself undergone therapy.

Lodge: Yes, I tried cognitive therapy for a while. I was going through a period of depression but I was very aware that this seemed to be an epidemic in the world. Everybody was writing about it and I was also struck by the number of therapies that had sprung up to deal with it. So I thought I would try and write a novel about it. Of all my novels *Therapy* is the most like *Deaf Sentence* because it deals with a man who is the narrator of the novel. Desmond occasionally switches into the third person. Tubby, in *Therapy*, imitates other people in his life at various points in the novel. They are really both about people suffering psychological and physical affliction at the same time and coming to terms with it or working through the negative attitude to their problems. So I think there is a resemblance between the two.

Bigsby: You don't only write novels. You have also written for television and the stage. I seem to remember that when you adapted *Martin Chuzzlewit* for television, despite the fact that you won an award for it, you had an argument over aspects of that production?

Lodge: Yes, I had a struggle with the director. In the end I think probably it was good that there was some disagreement but it was fairly fraught at the time. Basically I wrote a script in which I was encouraged to take a very free hand with Dickens and it was approved by the producer. Then they gave it to a director who went away and read the novel and my script and wanted a much more faithful rendering. We battled over this and out of the debate came a stronger script. I didn't by any means go all the way to meet him but I think it was quite useful. I just regret the very end of the thing where he really cheated me.

It is both the pleasure and the pain of TV or film that it is a collaborative medium. This means that you get feedback from other people. You get input from other people, and that is sometimes exciting and enhancing, but, on the other hand, you inevitably run into conflict with other people as well and you have to compromise or try and resolve the disagreement in order that everybody involved can see the thing come to a successful conclusion. If the debate is really about artistic matters I think that is fine but often, particularly in feature films, and I think now in television, it is really governed by other factors: financing, selling the book, selling the product abroad, that sort of thing. Compromises are made which shouldn't have been made. I think I was very lucky with the people I worked with when we made *Nice Work* and *Martin Chuzzelwit*. I don't think there is the same ethos in television drama now.

Bigsby: How do you approach the writing of a novel? Are you one of those writers who keeps a notebook?

Lodge: I have a notebook but obviously now it is on a computer. I have this process of preparing to write a novel which has become more and more elaborate as I have got older. I suppose that is partly because the novels themselves have involved more research than they used to and this body of notes itself has sub-divisions. There will be notes on books I am reading that are relevant to it and there will be a series of memoranda to myself about ideas for characters, scenes and so on. This stage can take a long time, but at a certain point I decide to start writing. I used to write the novels out by hand and then type them up, changing them and revising them in the process of typing. Then I got an electric typewriter which speeded up the process a bit. Then I got a computer and I would write a few pages by hand and then put it onto the computer and edit it and then go back and write a few more by hand. Eventually I became wedded to the computer. I couldn't read my own handwriting any more. I was making so many corrections and changes and screwing up the paper and throwing it away and it seemed easier then to do it on the screen. But then I print out everything all the time.

Any given page of this book would have been printed out maybe fifteen times, maybe more, with tiny changes, because I can only read the text in a self-critical way if it is on the page rather than the screen. Then I make emendations and that is incorporated in the next version on the computer. So the computer has been a terrific tool in that respect. There was always a moment when you were typing your novel and thought of a possible change but couldn't bear to type out the whole page again. You would say, 'Oh, blow it.' But with computers it is so effortless. The danger is that you go on fiddling with it too long I suppose. On the whole I am enormously grateful for the technology.

In Conversation With
Javier Marias

- 11th November 2009 -

Javier Marias, an award-winning translator, journalist, novelist, was born in Madrid in 1951. He wrote his first novel – *Los Dominios del Lobo* at the age of seventeen. Later novels (publication dates are of the English translations) include *All Souls* (1992), *A Heart So White* (1995) – winner of the International IMPAC Dublin Literary Award – *Dark Back of Time* (2001), and the three-volume *Your Face Tomorrow* (2004-9). He also writes a weekly column in *El Pais*

Bigsby: Your father graduated in 1936, a year which marked the beginning of the Spanish Civil War. He was a Republican. What did he do in that war?

Marias: He was born in 1914, and so was a very young man at the outbreak of the war. He was called into the army and was a soldier of the Republican army. He was very proud that he didn't have to fight because he was in Madrid where there was practically no fighting. There were bombardments for three years, very heavy ones, but not real fighting, so he said that he was absolutely sure he hadn't killed anyone. That is in my latest novel. I certainly borrowed part of his biography for the character of the narrator's father.

Bigsby: What is the etiquette of borrowing real people's lives for fiction?

Marias: I asked his permission to begin with. There are two characters in this novel, *Your Face Tomorrow 3: Poison, Shadow and Farewell,* that are openly based on real people. One is the narrator's father, and the other is a character called Sir Peter Wheeler, who is based on Sir Peter Russell who was an Oxford professor I met when I taught in Oxford in the nineteen eighties and with whom I had a very good friendship until his death a few years ago. I asked them for permission, certainly in the case

57

of Sir Peter Russell. I asked him if I could use, for a character in a novel I was going to write, part of his biography, I don't mean gossip but the things that are widely known. I said, 'I might even call him Peter Russell.' He was a bit startled about that so I added, 'Or would you like me to call him Peter Wheeler?' The reason I asked him that was because Peter Wheeler was his original name. He changed it by deed poll when he was seventeen or eighteen, in the same way as in the novel this character called Rylands changed his name by deed poll to Wheeler. So I asked him whether he would like me to call him Peter Wheeler and he said, 'Yes, I would like that, because that way I will know what happened to that Peter Wheeler I parted with such a long time ago.' So I did that. He also wrote exactly the same books Peter Russell wrote so obviously I asked for permission.

The most important part in the book concerning my father's biography was the fact that at the end of the war he was arrested by Franco's police and taken to jail. He found out shortly afterwards that he had been denounced by a man who had been his closest friend since high school. I read that part to him before publishing the first volume just in case he had some objection. He liked it but said that he was denounced by two people, one of them his friend and the other a professor, but that he had not mentioned their names even in his memoirs, which he wrote in the nineteen eighties. Then I said, 'This is fiction. This is a novel. The character's name is not my father's name, so it is not exactly you. I am using the real names of these two people not in an article for the press, for instance, but in a novel. Therefore those names are not real any more because they are in a novel.' He never wanted to mention these names, but now I am telling the story and I am telling it in a novel.

Bigsby: When you said that he was denounced, he was at real risk?

Marías: Oh, absolutely. At that moment, of course. He was arrested exactly one month and a half after the end of the war. You can imagine how they were shooting people by then, the winners of the war. At that moment there were practically no trials, or if there were they were a farce, and I heard, as in most dictatorships, that the usual proceeding was that if you were accused that was enough to find you guilty. If you were accused you had to prove your innocence instead of someone else proving your guilt.

He spent about three or four months in jail and then he was lucky. I heard him say that one of the main things was that there was a witness for the prosecution who started to talk very well about him and say, 'This is a very good man. He has been a soldier in the Republican army, with the army of the Spanish Republic, but he didn't do any of the things he was accused of.' He had been accused of being the voluntary companion of the bandit Dean of Canterbury, the Red Dean. My father had never met him. This Red Dean was in Spain doing some serious things for the Republicans. So this witness for the prosecution started to talk well and then the judge said, 'Listen, are you aware that you are a witness for the prosecution?' And this man answered, 'Oh, I thought I was here to tell the truth.' So my father was spared and could leave jail, but he couldn't write in the Spanish press until the nineteen fifties. He would have been a university professor normally but he couldn't enter the university and therefore was obliged to teach in the United States and in Puerto Rico.

Bigsby: And you went with him as a child?

Marías: Yes, twice. He never wanted to go into exile. He thought that a writer, even if he is not a literary writer, needs to be in touch with his own language. He also said that many intellectual people of the time were going into exile and that if all the people with some capacity for speech, for writing, leave at the same time it would be much worse for the country than it was already under Franco. So he went to the States and came back, but twice he took his children to America. I was almost born there. In fact I was born the very day he left for the United States for the first time. As he put it, he shook hands with me and left, not because he was horrified but because it was the day he had to go to Wellesley College. One month after that, my mother took my elder brothers and myself to Wellesley where I spent the first year of my life. Afterwards, when I was four or five, he went to Yale and I spent one year there.

Bigsby: You were born in 1951. Franco died in 1975. So you grew up under Franco. What was that like? What was the cultural life like in Spain?

Marías: It was grey and dark, mediocre, but of course as a child you don't realise very much. On the other hand, I think that because I was raised in a family that was a family of losers of the war, and of intellectual people, I didn't notice that so much as maybe other people of my generation did. To begin with, I was very lucky in the sense that most people of my age went to schools run by priests. It was practically obligatory. The only co-ed schools in Madrid at the time were the foreign ones, and the school I went to was co-ed in a clandestine way. Apparently boys and girls were supposed to be in different classrooms and almost separated, but we weren't. We were together in the same classroom but now and then an inspector came and when an inspector came the teachers said, 'The inspector is coming, the inspector is coming, boys to this classroom and girls to that classroom.' So we ran and pretended we were separate but most of the time we were together. That was extraordinary in the Spain of those days. You won't find many people of my age who had girls and boys in the same classroom. So I was a privileged child in that respect. But of course the general atmosphere was one of some fear obviously.

In those days, even though my parents didn't have much money, there was a maid in the house and I remember that during lunch, when I was a small boy, I asked them – and I knew they were against Franco – if Franco died would you be happy about it. The maid was there and they said, 'Ssh!' Then I realised that of course I shouldn't say this in front of a stranger or semi-stranger. That was one of the first times I realised that there was no freedom of speech in my own country. When you are a boy you find out about all these things very slowly, but the fear is something you learn very quickly.

Bigsby: Is it true that at the age of seventeen you ran away to France to write a book?

Marias: Yes, sure, I did. I ran away to Marseilles in a rather privileged way because two of my uncles happened to live in Paris by then. One was a film director, and is still alive. He is well known here. His name is Franco.

Bigsby: Everybody's name is Franco. Your mother's name is Franco.

Marias: My mother's name is Franco, nothing to do with the dictator fortunately, though it recalls something about censorship under Franco. My mother wrote a book, an anthology of texts on the subject of Spain, texts written by Spanish writers throughout history. She wrote an introduction. That was in 1941 or 42. She was very young then. The title of the book was going to be *Spain as a Preoccupation* and then a subtitle which would be *A Literary Anthology*, followed by her name Delores Franco. She was called Lolita – all Delores are Lolitas or Lolas – but Delores literally means pain or grief. For the censors, though, *Spain as a Preoccupation* and Delores Franco, wouldn't go. She didn't know what to do and she said, 'Well, I can do one of two things. One, my sister could sign the book – her sister's name is Gloria, so Gloria Franco and *Spain as a Preoccupation* could do – or I can invert the subtitle and the title,' which she finally did. So, absurdly enough, the first edition of that book was called *A Literary Anthology* and then *Spain as a Preoccupation* in very small letters.

Bigsby: You wrote your first novel at the age of seventeen and published it at nineteen, but it was a novel inspired by America rather than Spain?

Marias: Yes, absolutely. I am still waiting for some critic to tell me how it is possible that the books I have been writing for the last twenty years or so, and that book, could be written by the same person because it has nothing to do with what I have been writing now.

Bigsby: Although your love of American popular culture is still there?

Marias: Absolutely, yes, but that book was very much like a film. It was obviously a little childish but it was a parody and also a tribute to Hollywood films of the nineteen forties and fifties and then sixties. It had a lot of dialogue and sometimes you could read it almost as a script, a cinema script. I wrote it just because I felt like writing, and of course I didn't expect it to be published at all. I suppose it is the only book I have written with total irresponsibility. I was very lucky. The book was published and there were some reviews of it. Some of them said, 'Well, yes, this book by this young man is not bad. He has some narrative capacity but why does he talk about all these things? Why doesn't he talk about his surroundings, about the world he knows, about Spain, in fact.' So I thought, 'Yes, why?' Then I realised that I didn't necessarily want to write on Spain.

In those days Franco was still alive and many leftist writers were writing what has been called social realism. Most of those novels were very well intentioned and very well meaning but from a literary point of view they were not very good. They tried to fight Franco with a novel, which is something I am sorry to say that is pretty ridiculous. You can't fight dictatorships with novels, or even with cinema, I am afraid. For a boy born in the nineteen fifties, in this mediocre dark country under Franco, one of the important things for us was going to the cinema on Saturdays or Sundays. So in a way I am reflecting what had been important for a boy growing up in Franco's times.

Bigsby: You quickly followed that with another book, which was also a kind of pastiche?

Marias: Yes, a kind of pastiche. I published that when I was twenty-one, and then I stopped for a while.

Bigsby: Yes, while you were at university. You went to the Complutense in Madrid, which is the same university your father had gone to. There are still bullet holes in the wall there and I was told that in order to protect themselves against the bullets they got the books from the library, by preference books of philosophy because they were fatter and stopped bullets more easily.

Marias: I have read about it too. It seems it was true, absolutely.

Bigsby: After two quick novels rather than publish another you became a translator?

Marias: Yes. I am not ashamed of those early books. They are okay. A lot of writers are ashamed of their very first book. I think they are readable and fun in a way, but I realised that I was very young. I didn't have much to say. Then, for about six years, I didn't publish anything and started translating a few books from English. I must say that that was marvellous training for a writer. Whenever I am asked in interviews what do you think of creative writing schools I say, 'I don't think you can really teach how to write. I think you can teach how not to write.' I think it must be a negative teaching rather than a positive one, but if I was ever involved in one, God forbid, I would only admit students who knew or spoke at least one language besides their own, and I would have them translate because I think that is the best possible exercise for someone who wants to be a writer, for several reasons. Certainly one of them is that, as has often been said, a translator is of course a very privileged reader, but I say he is also a very privileged writer. If you translate, as I did, Joseph Conrad or Thomas Hardy or Sir Thomas Brown, or Yeats or Wallace Stevens – of course if you have to translate Javier Marias you are not so brilliant – you have the opportunity of rewriting in your own language a great text and if you do it acceptably, you have done a lot. People don't realise how much you have done if you can do that.

Bigsby: Isn't there a curious metaphysical element to this? You take a book in another language but not one word of that book will appear in the translation. Even the structure of sentences, even the rhythms, can be different, and yet you are reading the same book.

Marias: Yes, it has been said that translation is a modest mystery, or modest riddle, but it is one of the biggest mysteries in the world. How is it possible that a book that loses the language that made it possible, that loses each and every word as it was conceived and written by the author, that sometimes, as you say, loses the pace, loses the rhythm, loses the alliterations (sometimes you can keep some of those and sometimes you can't), can still be the same book? If you read *War and Peace* in English, or I read it in Spanish, it is not. A professor of Russian would say, 'Oh, you haven't read *War and Peace*. You have to read it in Russian.' But normal people consider that they have read Tolstoy and not someone else. If you come to think of it if Tolstoy was here, and you gave him a copy of *War and Peace* in English or in Spanish, he wouldn't know what people were reading. When I receive a translation of my books into Hindi I don't even know where my name is. So it is a huge mystery.

On the other hand, coming back to the training of a would-be writer, there is another element which I think is important. If you have a style of your own, one of the things you have to do when you are translating is to renounce it and adopt somebody else's style. You have to try to be Conrad or try to be Yeats, try to sound like them in your own language and certainly not to sound like your own writing at all. The translator has to be an actor but it might also be said that he has to be a music interpreter. The original text is like the score in music. Of course the same score can be played by different people and still be a sonata but it will sound different even if you recognise it is the same thing. The same thing would happen with the original text and the possible numberless translations of a text there might be.

Bigsby: Is it possible for a book to improve in translation? Is Baudelaire's Poe better than the American Poe?

Marias: I think they can easily be improved in translation. They can also be ruined. It depends on the translation, but I think my books sell much better in English than in Spanish.

Bigsby: Why don't you translate them yourself, because you speak English?

Marias: No, I would need to be absolutely bilingual, which I am not. On the other hand, supposing I could do that, which I can't, it would be terribly boring for me to go back to the same text. I already write and rewrite each and every page of my books. To rewrite it in another language would be terribly boring so, no, I would never do that.

Bigsby: But do you check the translations once they have been translated?

Marias: I did in the beginning, when I studied to be a translator. I did that in the languages I know which, besides English, are Italian and French. I did that but now I don't have the time because that is a hard, long task. What I try to do, precisely because I was a translator for a period in my life, is to be available for my translators. They send me lists of doubts and queries and I try to answer them as best as I can and I know by the quality of their doubts and queries if I can rely on them or not so much. Sometimes you see that they are very good because of the kinds of doubts and queries they have.

Bigsby: You went to Oxford, where you spent two years teaching, and out of that came *All Souls*, part of which is extremely funny. There is a wonderful set piece at a dinner. There are figures in it that you feel are probably real but are, in fact, fictional while the most fictional character turns out to be real, at least in a way, which is the King of Redonda, not least because you are currently the King of Redonda.

Marias: Redonda is a small island in the Caribbean. There was a very wealthy ship builder in the late nineteenth century who had had one daughter after another, I think eight or nine daughters, and only one son. He decided he was going to buy this island. He was a native from Montserrat, a bigger island in the same area. He bought this uninhabited island and decided that his son would be King of Redonda. When the boy was fifteen there was a ceremony with the bishop of Antigua, which is another island close by. This son became a rather distinguished writer in the early tens and twenties of the last century. There was a moment when the British government seized that island because there were some interesting phosphates or something there, but following a dispute the British colonial office finally said, 'Forget about the island itself. There is no point in our returning it to you. But you can use the title King of Redonda.' He died in 1947 and named John Gosworth, a poet, to succeed him.

This is a kingdom that is not inherited by blood but by literature and this man was king until his death in 1970. He was a very obscure poet. John Gosworth in fact was a pen name. There are two photographs of him in my book, one dead, one of his death mask. The problem with him is that he was a drunkard and he ended up very badly. He was married three times but not even one of his wives was with him at his deathbed. The last years of his life he spent sleeping on park benches and things like that. He was a very close friend of some important writers like Henry Miller and Dylan Thomas. All of them were dubbed Dukes of Redonda, together with others.

The problem was that he had debts, he had many, to the point that he started selling titles to bar tenders and landlords to whom he owed money. At a given moment he decided he would sell the title of King of Redonda. He put an ad in *The Times*. He was selling the title for one thousand guineas, I think. That must have been around 1960. Apparently many people were interested in buying the title, among them, by the way, the brother of the King of Sweden. Apparently, as he couldn't be King of Sweden he decided he would be King of something. I have the royal archives. There was another one who, about ten or twelve years ago, wrote to me. He had read my book and he said that he wanted to abdicate on my behalf because I had written of the legend of Redonda in this book and I was a real writer, and the Kings of Redonda should be real writers and not the sons of bartenders or landlords which are those pretenders who are around.

I thought well, what kind of a novelist am I if something so novelesque comes into my life and I don't accept it. So I asked him what my duties would be. He said, 'You have no duties because you would be the King. Just keep fresh the memory of the former kings and the legend of Redonda, which you have already done in your book.' So I said, 'Well, okay,' and I accepted. It seems that those pretenders are very angry. I have been told that they say things like it was so difficult to throw the Spaniards out of the Caribbean and now that small uninhabited island has returned to a Spaniard. What I can assure you is that I am not going to enter any dynastic dispute. If someone comes and says I am the real King of Redonda, I will say, 'Yes, probably so.'

Bigsby: But you have been giving titles out. Didn't you give one to W. G. Sebald?

Marías: Yes, I thought why not go on with the Dukes and so I named my own Dukes. They must be distinguished writers or film makers and Max Sebald accepted. He was very kind to be one of the first ones to accept. He became the Duke of Vertigo, after the title of one of his novels, and he was very pleased. We never met personally but we exchanged two or three letters before he died. He completely understood the joyful character of the whole thing and the whole legend, and I keep his letters of course.

Bigsby: It seems to me that you and Sebald have a lot in common. You both seem to mix fact and fiction. You had already begun the process of putting photographs in your text, as did Max. What led you first to drop a photograph into your books?

Marias: The very first time I did that was in *All Souls*. That book was published in Spanish twenty years ago, in 1989, and Sebald published his very first book in German in 1990. Some people have told me that I have been following Sebald but I say, no, not really, because I did it before he ever did it. I don't mean by this, of course, that he followed me. He probably didn't read that book at all, so it is a coincidence. But the very first time I included photographs I remember that my Spanish publisher was surprised by them. He said, 'How are we going to include two photographs in a novel?' and I said, 'I don't see why not.' It is not comparable, of course, but when someone writes about a painting you can see the painting at the same time. It is an absolute pleasure when reading about something that does exist, be it a painting, a photograph, a poster or cartoon, to be able to see that physically. So I decided, why not have the photograph I am describing so the reader can take a look at it. Whenever, in one of my novels, I mention an image, be it a painting or a photograph, I may include it.

I did that only once in the first volume of *Your Face Tomorrow*. That was because an uncle of the narrator was killed during the war when he was only seventeen or eighteen and the narrator says that in his mother's belongings he found a very small photograph of his dead body, or rather his dead head with the shots around the temples, and that is exactly what happened to me. My mother died many years ago, in 1977, and in a small tin box in which she had kept a few things I found this small photograph. That uncle was killed by the so-called Reds, by the way. They also killed people that way, just because of nothing. So I had this photograph and that photograph is described in the first volume and for a long while I was thinking, should I include the photograph, as is my custom, or shouldn't I, because it belongs to a real person and some of my other uncles are alive, some of his brothers or sisters are still alive. To a certain extent you shouldn't ever show a dead man's face. But at the same time I felt as if I was stealing an image I was talking about from the readers. In the end I didn't include it because my respect towards the real source of that photograph was bigger than my respect for the readers of a fictional work. So I didn't include that one, but I generally do.

Bigsby: You have a way of being able to slow time down in your prose. The reader waits for an incident to be concluded but you circle around it. I think you use a phrase somewhere about going out on a branch. You digress and the digression becomes a part of the story.

Marías: That is what I intend. I intend it to be part of the story. The apparent digressions are also part of the story. You find out that they were not so digressive but the story is advancing at the same time. One of the interesting things you can do in a novel is to make time inhabit its real duration. Time is very fast. One minute is only sixty seconds, but in reality it is not like that. We know that when, for instance, we spend a long night somewhere, or with someone, in the end what we will remember is only one gesture or a few words or a few seconds, and that is what really lasts in our memories. In a way those things that cannot last become time. You can do this in a novel. In a novel things may have the real duration but by real I don't mean sixty seconds each minute, but something slightly more profound. I think we have all experienced that what remains of a long night or a long period is sometimes just a moment, a look. In a novel you can make things more real in that sense.

In the second volume of *Your Face Tomorrow*, there is a scene in a disabled toilet at a disco where somebody, at a given moment, takes a sword and there is a long passage about swords because a sword is absurd nowadays in London. There is a moment when he is about to strike somebody's neck and then I suppose the conventional reader will be saying well, will he cut his throat or not? But there are pages and pages and pages of digressions on the use of a sword nowadays, why it can be so scary, probably more so than a pistol, more so than a gun because we are used to people having guns but not people having swords. Why are we are so afraid of that kind of weapon? Then something else is said about Richard Burton, not the actor of course but the explorer, who wrote about the sword and there is maybe a flashback or something. I suppose a very impatient reader would say, 'Come on, let me know.' My intention is that all those digressions should be interesting enough to keep you reading but this is also a homage to something that happens in *Don Quixote*. There is what is called an interpolated story in *Don Quixote* in which two people are about to strike each other, and then the narrative is interrupted and he never returns to this incident so that those swords have been up for four hundred years and will go on like that forever. So in a way there was also a tribute to that kind of suspension of time that you find also in Cervantes and Sterne.

Bigsby: You are very frugal in your use of commas. You have seventeen-line sentences.

Marías: I use commas sometimes where very orthodox people would say I should be using something else, but it is a matter of rhythm or pace. I think that is very important. I think pace is extremely important in prose. Sometimes I use commas where someone very conventional would use a semicolon. I do that very often but this is a way of forcing the reader to breathe a little longer.

Bigsby: You once said you couldn't imagine writing out of a woman's sensibility, because you write it out of your maleness. That sounds very Spanish. Is it?

Marías: I have been using narrators in the first person for the last twenty odd years in my novels. They are men, and it is in that sense only. The one telling the story is a man and therefore he acts like a man, or a male if you want, and he behaves like one and thinks like one. In what I am writing at present – and I don't know if I shall finish it – the narrator is a woman and I think is not a very different narrator from the others. The difference between men and women is not precisely in language or in the mind. I think a story can be told very similarly by a man or by a woman but maybe it is convenient for me to think that now.

In Conversation With
Blake Morrison

- 31st October 2007 -

Blake Morrison, poet, novelist, memoirist, critic, was born in Skipton, Yorkshire, in 1950. He was educated at Nottingham University and University College London. He worked for both the *Times Literary Supplement* and *The Observer* as well as the *Independent on Sunday*. His first book of poetry, *Dark Glasses*, appeared in 1984. It was followed, in 1987, by *The Ballad of the Yorkshire Ripper (and Other Poems)*. His memoir, *And When Did You Last See Your Father?* (1993) won the J. R. Ackerley Prize for Autobiography. It was subsequently filmed. His account of two young murderers, Robert Thompson and Jon Venables, *As If*, was published in 1993. His first novel was *The Justification of Johann Gutenberg* (2000). It was followed by *South of the River* (2007).

Bigsby: You have explained that the immediate cause for writing *When Did You Last See Your Father?* was the death of your father

Morrison: At some level you think your father, or your parents, will live forever and you can be very unprepared for their death, even in middle life. I was forty when this happened, but at some level I was still the child of four who thought my father was immortal. When he died it was a huge shock and trauma. It all happened relatively quickly given that it was cancer. It was a few weeks between the diagnosis and the death and what else would I have written about? There was nothing else in the world that seemed of consequence at that time because of the state I was in.

Bigsby: So was it a way of dealing with it?

Morrison: It was entirely a way of dealing with it. I had begun to deal with it while he was dying in keeping a diary. I would spend a lot of time in my parents' home in Yorkshire for the last few weeks of his life rather than at my own home in London. I ran out on my family, if you like, on my kids, to be there at the end. I kept a diary of these extraordinary scenes, as it seemed to me, of somebody who was mortal after all and that was the first therapeutic element in it. The second was after his death writing little reminiscences, like short stories almost, which I suppose was a way of bringing him back to life or pretending he hadn't died. By the summer, after his death in the December, I had quite a lot of material which I thought was private. I showed it to Bill Buford at *Granta*, or he asked to see it, and he thought there was something more there. So what began as something very private and therapeutic became a book for others.

Bigsby: When you are growing up your parents are a kind of background noise. It is almost as though they don't have a life. You have a life and they are just around in some way. So beyond the therapy does this offer you an opportunity to go back and explore the lives that you almost ignored?

Morrison: Yes, the lives you took for granted, that you were callowly unappreciative of. That was one of the effects, undoubtedly so. Everything associated with my father suddenly seemed precious. Next to where I sit and write now there is a little cabinet inside which is, for instance, his pacemaker.

Bigsby: You do understand that that is rather strange, that most people would choose a watch or a book or an article of clothing. A pacemaker is decidedly odd.

Morrison: It is an intimate thing. It was inside his body. That is just one example of an object that suddenly acquired huge value and importance to me and, yes, you reappraise. All those stories that my father used to tell about the war – I was of that generation which thought, 'Oh, that boring old war.' Suddenly you realise how pathetic and adolescent you were and what a huge experience that was for that generation.

Bigsby: One thing you do capture is a sense of embarrassment about your father, because he would do slightly odd things.

Morrison: Isn't that a universal thing for any child to feel? Perhaps when you are four your parents are paragons and gods and goddesses but at a certain point, with teenage years anyway, embarrassment sets in. I think it sets in earlier and earlier now with children.

Bigsby: But he would do really quite strange things. He would try and avoid paying to get in somewhere.

Morrison: Is that strange?

Bigsby: In front of your children, with your children, petty criminality?

Morrison: The book veers between lighter memories of my father, when fully alive, and then really quite dark passages about the process of dying, because that was the other thing that this book tried to do, to be honest around death. My father having been a doctor perhaps gave me the licence to do that. He had taken me, when I was eight years old, to see the body of my grandfather lying in a coffin as if to say, 'This is what death looks like.' So I had that permission. My first book of poems was called *Dark Glasses*. It was quite an impersonal book. It took my father's death to make me in any way a confessional writer I think partly because it was written in a strange way over that year. I put things in that perhaps I would normally censor out. On the other hand I have to say that I think a lot of people respond to the details and the intimacy because at best they feel, 'Yes, I felt that too but I didn't know anybody else did and now I don't feel so peculiar.'

Bigsby: Your father was a doctor but so was your mother, so you were born into a professional family. Did they hope that you would become a doctor?

Morrison: Yes. There was a point when my father (I think it was one day while we were washing the cars) addressed it directly saying he hoped that I would be doing science 'O' Levels and I had to break it to him that I didn't seem to be very good at the sciences, and that it was more likely to be arts stuff. But his dream was that I would take over the family practice and then I could live just down the road. The next best thing, when it seemed I was getting into journalism, was that I would do my year or two in London but then I would get a real job working for the *Yorkshire Post* or maybe *The Craven Herald* in Skipton. He really wanted me to live close by and it was one of the reasons why it was quite hard to get away.

Bigsby: And when you decided that you would like to be a poet. How did that go down?

Morrison: I think the reason I chose poetry was because I knew that he wouldn't be reading poems of mine. It was the one area where I could be sure of escaping him. There was a risk with stories that he might, prose being easier, make the effort, but poetry was outside his domain and territory, so it was the perfect arrangement, really. It was something that wasn't monitored and wasn't controlled by him, this world of poems. So

I just mucked around and wrote bad poems as a teenager and then a bit later tried to take it more seriously, but it was all part of escaping, I think.

Bigsby: How old were you when your first poem was published?

Morrison: That was in a school magazine. Out in the world, in a little magazine when I was about twenty-four, twenty-five.

Bigsby: But of course from his point of view, even if it wasn't the Skipton newspaper, you had a real job as well so you could be a poet on the side, I suppose.

Morrison: Yes, that was acceptable, and he didn't know at all about the world that I was part of in London. I worked on the *TLS* for a bit and then *The Observer*. He didn't understand that world but he could see that I was doing okay. It was professional, middle class. OK, I wasn't boss of many people, that was disappointing, but I was making a go of it. I wasn't having to borrow too much money from him and he was spared having to read the poems.

Bigsby: And then you built a reputation as a poet, but there was a key poem, it seems to me. You wrote a poem about the multiple murderer Peter Sutcliffe which, on the face of it, is the most unlikely subject, except I suppose, historically, ballads were often written about crimes.

Morrison: They were. I think anybody who lived through that period of the Yorkshire Ripper and those serial killings was affected by it. Of course many men in the north were stopped and interviewed by the police. For me, the particular point of contact was that he grew up not very far from where I did. He was only a few years older than me. He went to places I went to and there was this sense of, 'How could this person growing out of the same soil, approximately, as I did, do this thing?' There was so much that was familiar in that story that I was drawn to write about it. Poems had always been things you waited and hung around for at odd times of the day and night. That would be my way with poems, anyway. But with this one – I had had appendicitis and had three weeks enforced convalescence – I just sat down in the morning in a nine to five sort of way thinking this is telling a story, hence the ballad.

Bigsby: And originally you wrote it in standard English?

Morrison: Originally I wrote it in standard English and that didn't work at all.

Bigsby: Why didn't it work?

Morrison: I thought, what was the motive, what lay behind exploring this man, re-inhabiting these terrible crimes? It felt somehow gratuitous to me and it bothered me and I put it away for a bit. And then I came across a Yorkshire dialect dictionary which not only taught me new words that I hadn't known, but reminded me of ones that I had known from childhood and had forgotten. I also realised just how tied into the absolute theme of what I was exploring, which was misogyny, this language was. This was a woman-hating culture with a number of dialect words that were demeaning, insulting, abusive of women. I don't think this is specific to Yorkshire. I think maybe it is there in any British dialect dictionary, but it was astonishing. There was just a rich vocabulary for abusing women. That was what interested me about Peter Sutcliffe. I was interested in him not as a psychopath but as somebody who had grown out of a woman-hating culture and woman-hating family. He killed those prostitutes, I think, in that spirit rather than because he was mad.

Bigsby: So there is a sense in which language shapes actions and assumptions. Or is language simply an expression of pre-existing condition?

Morrison: I am not sure, but certainly what it did is bring the poem to life. It enabled me to have a narrator who was a Yorkshire man but who, unlike me, hadn't moved away, hadn't, perhaps, been educated, still spoke in that tongue. OK, some of the words he uses are probably obsolete nineteenth century dialect words, but there was a kind of energy. It was his voice, not my voice. It gave me permission to go ahead and write the poem. There are a couple of little quotes I have at the top of the poem. One of them is something that Peter Sutcliffe said by way of explaining himself to his brother. He said, 'I was just cleaning up the streets, our kid, just cleaning up the streets.'

Bigsby: There is a level at which, even though you don't know what these dialect words mean, as a reader you are carried by the poem. You don't keep looking down for the footnotes.

Morrison: I hope the sense carries you and just the rhythm, the drive of the ballad. Of course the challenge was that the ballad now sounds to many people like an essentially comic form that we associate with Charles Causley, or some of Auden's more satirical poems, and not with a story about bloodthirsty crimes, something serious and dark.

Bigsby: You were going to go on and write about another crime in a very different kind of book. *As If* is about the Bulger killing (in which two boys were accused of murdering another). I know *The New Yorker* commissioned you to do this. Do you think they did so because of the Peter Sutcliffe poem?

Morrison: It was entirely because *And When Did You Last See Your Father?* had come out in May of 1993 and it had got quite good reviews. It was doing quite well that autumn and I had my fifteen minutes or three minutes of fame so they thought we will get an English writer who doesn't mind sitting in on the trial, with no guarantee of being paid or the article ever being published. And I was up for that.

I had never been to a murder trial before and just as everybody in the country had been fascinated and appalled by Peter Sutcliffe, so they were by this crime. I had a son of about the same age as the killers and another son about the age of the victim. So I could see that difference in my own home, if you like. I was just very curious and went along, I think naively, thinking that if you sat in on a trial it would give you the answers as to why two ten-year-old boys could kill a two-year-old. Actually, the legal process is not about bringing understanding, it is about establishing guilt or innocence, and all the insights came outside the courtroom in some bizarre way. But I did sit through that whole three-and-a-half weeks and it was obviously quite a traumatic three-and-a-half weeks. I did write the piece for *The New Yorker*, which is quite a long article, a few months after the trial, but didn't feel I had done more than scratch the surface and hence four years later the book.

Bigsby: Why did you begin the book not with the trial but with the Children's Crusade?

Morrison: I began with the Children's Crusade for two reasons. One was that I was haunted, as I think a lot of people were, by an image from the footage in the shopping centre where James Bulger was abducted. His hand was in the hand of a bigger boy and when I read about the children's crusade there was that same image. It has always been about bigger children leading younger children, in the case of the Children's Crusade on this extraordinary journey of hope and aspiration, and in the

Bulger case absolutely the opposite because they were leading him to his death. There was a sort of ironic juxtaposition.

The media had had their moment, and hadn't shed very much light on the case. The important thing was to wrest it back and find a new language to explain the behaviour of those boys, to approach it in a different way. I read a lot of children's literature. I read a lot of different theories of children down the ages, children's behaviour. I was interested in the question of what the age of responsibility should be because the whole point was that we had set the age of criminal responsibility at ten, which is the lowest in Europe.

The horrifying reality of this was brought home to me the first morning of the trial when these two little boys, who I knew were ten but had somehow been pictured as thuggish fifteen or sixteen-year-olds, came in. The case rested on the question of at what point do we hold children or young people responsible for their actions, at what point do they understand what it means to inflict serious injury or death. If the defence could establish that these two boys were in effect less intellectually and emotionally mature than ten, i.e. they were nine or five, then they couldn't stand trial, the trial couldn't go ahead, or they had to be found not guilty. But the expert witnesses, whose part in this trial, which lasted three-and-a half weeks, was about half an hour – two teachers from the school, two psychologists – agreed that there was nothing particularly immature about them. They were ten and so the trial had to proceed. Among many frustrations was that those experts, people who knew those boys, knew a lot about their families, were not allowed legally to address anything other than: 'Would they have understood what they were doing that day when they killed a two year old?'

My feeling is that children of ten do not fully understand the consequences of their actions, and there were a couple of things that brought that home to me. You may remember the trial. The little boy was killed on a railway line and I retraced the route that they took when they abducted him from the shopping centre. What I had read sounded horrific because the whole point was that they had walked him for two-and-a-half miles. What I hadn't realised, because the papers hadn't said this, was that they were actually walking him back home, back to their neighbourhood, and what became clear was that once they had got this little boy on their hands they didn't know what to do with him. The very last bit of the journey, before they went onto the railway, was an alleyway and, to the right of the alleyway, about a hundred yards away, was the local police station. They told various witnesses that they were taking him to the police station. But I suppose they would have got in trouble if they had gone to the police station, or would have been worried they were going to get into trouble. To the left, two hundred yards away, was Robert Thompson's home where he knew his mother would be very angry with him because he had truanted that day and he was under huge pressure not to truant. Unusually, he had managed to go to school all four days that week until that Friday and so he was going to be in big trouble for truanting that day. So what was the third way? The third way was up onto the railway embankment, and at some bizarre level that was the way not to get into trouble, to go up rather than in either of those directions.

The other thing that brought it home to me was when one of the barristers said that if ten-year-olds are intellectually and emotionally mature enough to commit murder, shouldn't they, therefore, be emotionally and intellectually mature enough to be jurors since you are supposed to be judged by your peers. Perhaps those boys should have been tried by ten-year-olds. But how would you feel about being tried by a jury of ten-year-olds? That brings home to you what limited intellectual and emotional maturity a ten-year-old has. So my feeling was that it was a monstrous trial and I guess that was one of the things the book was trying to say as well as exploring the backgrounds of the boys.

Bigsby: There is one moment in the book which surprised me, as there is in *When Did You Last See Your Father*? Suddenly, you sexualise it, that is to say there is a moment when you talk about the possibility of sexually responding to your own children. In the book about your father there is a passage about masturbation. Why was that there?

Morrison: I think they are two different things. The passage about masturbation is about the fact that there is nothing you need more than the affirmation of life and sexual release at such a time. That is my experience and a lot of other people I have talked to have said the same. So that is why that was there. I would put the passage about my daughter rather differently. I would say what that was about was a parent delighting in the body of a child. It seems to me the most natural thing in the world to delight in the body of a small child but we have got very nervous around that and the passage is written in such a way that you actually think this is a man undressing a woman in order to go to bed and have sex and you realise half way through that this is not that. This is about a father getting his daughter ready for bed in the most innocent way, but taking pleasure in her body.

Bigsby: The police suggested that the boys might have had a sexual motivation but that seems something of a desperate throw in an attempt to answer the question, 'Why?' I don't think the boys could have answered that question. Nobody in that trial could work out why they did what they did. Sexual abuse offered a packaged explanation, except it didn't make any sense.

Morrison: That was another theory of what they were doing so in that chapter I just explored that in a larger way, or tried to.

Bigsby: You wrote a memoir of your father. You subsequently wrote a memoir of your mother. One of the things that prompted you to do so was the availability of letters, love letters, effectively. Did you find that difficult?

Morrison: Yes, I did. I had always been aware of these letters. My father had actually said, 'One day, my son, you might find it interesting to read these.' So there was this invitation to read them, though not perhaps turn them into a book. Who knows? I was aware of them but after my mother's death it took me six months or a year to read them because her death was still too fresh. But having started to read them I realised it was an extraordinary gift. What is the period of your parents life you know least about? It is the bit when they are in love, when they are courting; it is before you came along, before you had ever been thought of, and there it was in immense detail.

They were separated during the war. They had just met in 1943 and were writing to each other every day sometimes. There was extraordinary detail about the lives they were living and to me it was interesting. There was mother, having come from Ireland to be a doctor, given this opportunity in England because all the English male doctors were away in the forces, steaming ahead with her career and my father, slightly jealous of this, stuck in strange places with the RAF as an RAF doctor. He was in Iceland, the Azores, not exactly hot spots, wanting a bit more action but being talked out of it by my mother and his sister and so on. So obviously at some level I felt transgressive. I was reading something quite private. On the other hand I had been invited to read it and it seemed an enormous gift, this archive of letters. The thing is it gave me my mother who had always been a bit of a mystery to me. There were things in there that explained my mother to me.

Bigsby: You have written two memoirs. The memoir as a form has been very popular these last twenty years or so. Do you have your own private explanation as to why that form has proved so attractive?

Morrison: I explain it as some need for authenticity, some need for books that we believe in, that we know to be true. Perhaps that need was quite strong in the early nineties because before that we had had magical realism, we had had a great flourishing in the eighties of British fiction and of the fantastic or of books that didn't invite you to believe in them. Social realism had been overtaken by other forms of fiction and it was, 'Let's get back to books where we know this is a true story.' The story might be quite limited in its way but the absolute conviction that it is true carries the reader through. That is my crude explanation as to why it took off and I think you are right, it has been a predominant form.

In Conversation With Toni Morrison

- 30th October 2008 -

Toni Morrison, Nobel and Pulitzer Prize-winning novelist, was born in Lorain, Ohio, in 1931. A graduate of Howard and Cornell universities, she published her first novel, *The Bluest Eye*, in 1970. Subsequent books include *Song of Solomon* (1977 – which won the National Book Critics Circle Award – *Beloved* (1987), *Jazz* (1992), *Paradise* (1999), *Love* (2003) and *A Mercy* (2008). Until her retirement in 2006, she taught at Princeton University.

Bigsby: In all of your work you tend to be drawn to the past. Sometimes it is not a very distant past, but sometimes a considerable distance back. Why the past?

Morrison: If you are interested in recasting the history that is handed to you in order to move forward into the future, or just accommodate yourself to the present, the past is critical. It is not just critical in a novel, it is critical in each individual. Everybody has a past and you have to deal with it. You have to understand it. It has to be yours, not somebody else's. You have to figure out how to get rid of the stuff that is not useful, although you may examine it closely, measure it. It is memory. An individual's memory is very much like a nation or a race's or culture's past and if the memory is distorted or erased or stained in some way you need to know what the truth is. And that is what culture is. That is what national myths are, and it is what individuals accumulate in their life. It is an accumulated past, not only of the individual self, but the whole family.

Bigsby: But you live in a society which has an ambiguous relationship to the past, a largely immigrant society that leans into the future, that wants to brush away the footprints from behind it. It is about pursuing happiness. The past tends to be visited as myth rather than as substance.

Do you feel ambiguously related to the culture of which you are a part and that you have to go back in time to reclaim?

Morrison: I was always very curious about that contradiction in the national story – individualism, moving towards the future, the frontier, a deliberate and sustained erasure of the past. You are newborn when you come to the United States and that is a very fierce and sustained drive, in the literature as well as in the consciousness, so I always wondered what they were running from. What is this frontier thing that they are always talking about even when they were in another part of the continent? Then the moon was the new frontier. There always has to be something out there beyond. So I thought, well, maybe it is not just that we are new, maybe it is that we are frightened of what is behind us. Something is chasing this dream as we pretend that the continent was empty. I thought that maybe it is the stain, the curse, but it goes back even earlier than that. Who were these people, where did they come from, not the clerics and the scholars and the merchants, but the ordinary people who came in boats that took six months to arrive? When they got here they didn't know anybody and they didn't have anybody. They were just thrown here, but they came just as they do now to the shores of European countries, boats from North Africa. What is it they are running from? Well, different things, so I was interested in a kind of deliberate blindness. I thought of all the gaps in history. Slavery existed everywhere. There was no nation that did not rest on an enslaved population, whether it was Athens or Paris or Belgium or Moscow. So that was not an unusual thing.

Then I began to look at the nature of the indentured servants who were understood to be different from slaves, but weren't. Their contracts went on and on and on and they were in people's wills. You could extend an indentured servant's contract for any reason and they had no respite. They had one benefit different from African slaves which was that they were white skinned and could run away and blend more easily than blacks. So looking at that I wondered what was it that made slavery and racism a married couple. I tried to construct what it might feel like without the racism. Racism was constructed. It was built, made legal for obvious reasons, to protect the landed from the poor and if poor whites had something that poor blacks didn't, that was a big benefit to the people who exploited both.

Bigsby: In *A Mercy* you go back to a very interesting but little explored period of American history, a period of incredible flux as different

European powers were still in contention, a time when different religions were in play – the Protestantism of New England and the Catholicism of Maryland.

Morrison: It was very ad hoc. It seems to me, even now, really unlikely that all these different States would pull themselves together in 1776. They had entirely different histories. The Swedes and the Dutch and the Portuguese, the Spanish and the English, were looking for resources, lumber and gold, anything they could find, and they fought each other and fought the local populations because of course there were natives there. This is before Indians were called Indians. So it was fluid. It could have gone almost any way. There was a lot of religious blood letting. So it suddenly became clear to my why, when they drew up the Constitution, they decided that no president should have to pass a religious test in the United States and that religion should be completely separate from government. When you see that ignored, as it has been in the United States recently, you see how the whole notion of democracy is shredded. America is a very beautiful country, a very bountiful country, and very dangerous at the same time.

Bigsby: Those component elements exist in *A Mercy*. There is an Indian girl whose tribe has been wiped out by smallpox. There is a slave girl. There are white indentured servants. They begin to come together in a place where there is a white man who is initially benign. He has come to America, like so many others, to make something of himself, to reinvent himself, but he is owed a debt and when he goes to collect the debt he realises he is never going to get the money back. In its place he is offered a young girl, a slave, Florens. He accepts her because he thinks his wife could do with some help around the place. He is not part of the slave culture but it is the beginning of the tainting of the man because for the first time he owns someone.

Morrison: He rationalises it nicely. He remembers being an orphan himself. He knows that children need to be with an adult otherwise they are just flotsam and jetsam. There would be no one to feed them and they would turn to crime, etc. He thinks maybe, since his daughter is recently dead, this might placate her, but it does open the door to something that he is repelled by, the idea of slavery and the intimacy of it. He knows it would require force to maintain and he is opposed to that. Subsequently, he is not opposed to the fruits of slave labour if he doesn't have to be around them.

Bigsby: Exactly, because though he is initially a farmer, he is not such by nature. He is an entrepreneur, quickly learning about rum and sugar which, of course, leads to a fusion of American capitalism and slavery.

Morrison: And then it takes him out of that constellation, that group of people who had made themselves without joining some extremist religion, without giving up the relationship among them. He goes away and then everything falls apart. The slaves have no last names. The widow is alone with a little bit of property. She is vulnerable. You have to belong somewhere.

Bigsby: And there are a number of people in the novel who have lost a sense of the context in which their lives had made sense. They had come from another country to a strange place. The native girl's tribe has gone. The slave girl has lost her mother. All of these people are floating. There is a sense of abandonment and equally a struggle to find some kind of an identity, some kind of new family.

Morrison: They are orphans, in that sense. They have either been abandoned by their family or they have escaped their family. Even the man, Jacob, has gone away from a marriage or relationship. The promise is there for all kinds of people in America, but something is missing. They all either need each other or they want to escape but it is as though a comet has hit and the pieces are flying apart. My conviction is that for the most part each of them survive quite well outside the group. They are changed profoundly, or something in their characters intensifies, as with the native American woman who prides herself on her loyalty.

Bigsby: She is almost the still point in the novel.

Morrison: Yes. She stays that way and her loyalty, even if she is mistreated occasionally, does not depend on the goodness of the person to whom she is loyal. It is something in her that she values, that she finds noble, that kind of consistency in devotion. It is that which maintains her. The lonely girl who has been raised on a ship and invents an invisible friend eventually becomes somebody. I heard her voice first and couldn't start until I knew that. Her language was askance a little bit. She can read, she can write. She is very needy. It is her journey through the book that is important and how she changes. She speaks only in the present tense but she is the one who says, 'I'. Others in the book are there as part of the narrative. They are the people with whom she associates. Their story is told because at the same time it moves her story along. Each person tells a little bit more of Florens's story until we arrive at her ability to tell her own story.

Bigsby: There is a passage in *A Mercy* in which a young girl has been whipped by her mother until she bleeds because she believes that demons possess her. Is there a sense in which that is a gesture of love, of mercy? Is there a difference between love and mercy in your mind?

Morrison: Yes, I think love has its own exchange of what is beneficial to the self as well as for the loving. I thought of mercy as she does in the book as something religious.

Bigsby: As you enter this novel you no more know where you are than when you enter Faulkner's *The Sound and the Fury*.

Morrison: I have to establish a certain level of trust so that you believe me when I say, 'Don't be afraid. It is going to be scary, but don't be afraid. Whether I am speaking through the voice of the character or not, it is dangerous thing to start. This is not going to be a happy ride, but it is going to be an enlightening one so don't worry. I am holding your hand all the way and if you stumble, or you don't understand, you have this delightful opportunity to do what I do all the time which is read it again and again. I am totally dependent on the reader's generosity and intelligence.'

Bigsby: How hesitant are you when you set out to write?

Morrison: I was afraid once when I was trying to imagine something that was for me unimaginable. That was when I was writing *Beloved*. It was a little unnerving and I could not do it for a bit. Then I thought, well, come on, if they can live it I can write it. What am I doing? Other than that, there are certain emotions that are not useful, like anger. I have never been angry when I write. I have always been curious. The problems are so exciting. The possibility of solution via language is so exciting to me. It is when I have nothing in mind, no project, that I feel a certain melancholy.

Bigsby: You said when you published *Jazz* that you wanted your work to be private but for public consumption. How far do you think that is what you have achieved?

Morrison: In some books, particularly *Jazz*, I think that was a successful venture. I once was signing books in a bookstore for people who had either read my books or were buying them and a young woman came up to me with a copy of my book in her arms. She told me that she liked the book, that she really thought it was wonderful, and I reached out my hand to take it from her so I could sign it and she said, 'Oh no, no, no, no.' She said, 'I don't want anyone to sign my book.' I realised it didn't belong to me any more. It was her book. The closest thing I can think to that is music. When you hear music you are in an audience but it really is yours, the way you are thinking about it, the way you are absorbing it and the way you remember it when you go back to it later. It becomes a deeply personal experience, even though it is shared by hundreds and maybe thousands of people.

In Conversation With John Mortimer

- 6th November 2001 -

John Mortimer, novelist, playwright, screenwriter, was born in Hampstead, London, in 1923. He died in 2009. He was a barrister who appeared in a number of free speech trials and drew on his work for many of his books. His first novel, *Charade*, appeared in 1947. His most famous character, Rumpole of the Bailey, would appear in a series of novels and a long-running television series. As a screenwriter, he wrote the script for Franco Zeffirelli's *Tea With Mussolini* (1999). He was knighted in 1998.

Bigsby: As a lawyer, your father specialised in divorce and there are two sides to your career. You are a writer of fiction and a barrister but there was a time when there was a high degree of fiction associated with the process of divorce?

Mortimer: There was a high degree of fiction associated with the process of divorce. I mean if you went skipping even further on I followed in my father's footsteps and became a divorce barrister. Picture me at the age of about twenty-three, a young, slim, slender, handsome upwardly mobile divorce barrister. It was a very interesting period of the divorce law in England. Now if you want a divorce you can go to the Post Office and fill up the form and cheerio. The first case I did – and in those days you had to prove something really serious like adultery – was a husband who was finding it inordinately difficult to persuade anyone to commit adultery with his wife. He was reduced to the terrifying expedient of putting on a false beard and false moustache and a pair of dark glasses and creeping into his own mobile home and pretending to be his own correspondent. He was actually sent to prison for perverting the course of justice. I thought that was a bit hard, the idea that you can't sleep with your own wife wearing a false beard.

My father, the divorce barrister, was an amazing man and it was a huge privilege to be his son because he taught me all about the two most important things in life which are the Sherlock Holmes stories and the plays of Shakespeare and I grew up with my father quoting Shakespeare usually in very inapposite moments. Some people sing little tunes in their head and my father just said lines out of Shakespeare. The wonderful thing he did was to take Shakespeare quotations and use them in a totally inapposite way. He was a great education.

Bigsby: The fact that he quoted Shakespeare didn't mean that he was in favour of you being a writer did it?

Mortimer: He said I could be quite a successful writer but writer's wives have horrible lives because the writer is always at home wearing a dressing gown, brewing tea, stuck at the work desk. You should get a job that gets you out of the house for the sake of your poor wife and go and divorce a few people. Anyway I went to Harrow, which was a deep disappointment to me as a school, except I met Byron. I formed a one-boy Communist party at Harrow. It was a very interesting period in history, the beginning of the war and the Hitler/Stalin pact. Germany and Russia were temporarily on the same side and I got instructions in my one-boy Communist cell to slow down production on my factory floor. My factory floor was a classical theatre and I went down and said, 'Translate Virgil very, very slowly,' which didn't need very much encouragement. Then Hitler was unwise enough to attack Russia and so I got the message to speed up production on the factory floor and by then I didn't really know what they were talking about.

I always really wanted to be a writer. I started life by wanting to be Fred Astaire but as I couldn't sing or dance it had to be put on the back burner, but from the age of about fourteen or fifteen I wanted to be a writer. That was all I wanted to be. I was going to be a barrister because my father was a barrister and I thought about all the things that you could be if you were a writer, like a school teacher, and I really didn't want to be a school teacher and so I really regarded being a barrister as my sort of day job, as girls who are going to be film stars get waitressing jobs. So really being a barrister was my sort of waitressing. Really all the things that I did were writing.

Bigsby: Not too long after this you had a brush with the film industry?

Mortimer. I did. I was about sixteen or seventeen when the war started and I went to Oxford and then I went into this documentary film unit at Pinewood studios where they made propaganda films about the war with the army film unit and the air force film unit. I was a fourth assistant director. I thought that was a very grand title but I found out that all the fourth assistant director had to do was to make tea for the director and say, 'Quiet please,' at the beginning of every shot and because I was very nervous and bashful, as I am today, I used to say it very quietly and they all went on sawing wood and playing pontoon and took not a blind bit of notice, so I yelled, 'Quiet, you bastards' and they all went on strike. It was then decided that I would do less harm if I was a scriptwriter. Larry Lee was the scriptwriter and he wanted to leave because he was bored with that war we were having, and he said, 'If you go to Watford junction and write a film script about Watford junction and it is alright you can have my job.' So I went along to Watford Junction on a bicycle and wrote this terrible script and he said, 'Right you can have my job,' I think because he wanted to leave anyway. So then I became the scriptwriter. I had a uniform with scriptwriter written on it. When the war ended I wrote a novel and then I became a barrister, so I had already been a scriptwriter and written a novel before I became a barrister.

Bigsby. And as you say you started out involved in divorce cases which were not without their fictional components. But you yourself were involved in divorce. Did that also involve an element of fiction?

Mortimer. I then wanted to marry somebody who had four children, a strange thing to want to do, and she was married to someone else so we had to provide evidence for this divorce. So we went to lots of hotels and set fire to the bed sheets and made each other blind drunk. I couldn't remember our visit at all and finally they sent a detective round and we confessed to this detective that we were living together so she got a divorce. The detective was called Mr. Galvin and a week later I became a divorce barrister and the first case I did I had to call a detective and it was Mr. Galvin who I had last seen entering my bedroom and inspecting the condition of the bed clothes and taking my confession. He never mentioned that and for the next twenty years, about once every month, I used to call Mr. Galvin, the detective, and we used to have coffee together in the law courts and became very friendly. Finally Mr. Galvin was on a pedestrian crossing somewhere up in Hampstead and a police car nearly ran him over so he hit the police car on the roof and they arrested him. He was very angry and sued the police for false arrest, false imprisonment. All he needed for his case was a character witness so I went to the law courts and stood up and I said, 'I have known Mr. Galvin, man and boy, for the last thirty years and I know him to be a thoroughly trustworthy man.'

Bigsby: It is often said that when people get divorced they go out and marry someone just like the person they have left. In your case you went out and married someone with the same name. That has enormous advantages when you are shouting someone's name doesn't it?

Mortimer: Yes, but apart from that they weren't very similar. I married a novelist first of all, a very good novelist, rather too good for my own comfort, and then I married someone who wasn't a novelist. Two people writing novels together is quite difficult.

Bigsby: And you switched eventually from dealing with divorce cases to criminal law?

Mortimer: I did, yes. I became a thing called a Q.C., which Rumpole calls queer customers. There is a very interesting ceremony you have to go through to be a Q.C. You have to go down to the House of Lords to swear an oath to help the Queen whenever she is in trouble. She has been in plenty of trouble but she hasn't sent for me yet. In order to swear this oath you had to wear this extraordinary uniform, black patent leather shoes with diamond buckles, black silk stockings and knee britches with diamond buckles and a long silk gown with tail coat with lots of lace at your wrists and lace at your throat along with a long wig with spaniels ears so you can't hear what is going on. I was standing in Fleet Street waiting for the car to take me down to the House of Lords to swear this oath and an old judge came hobbling by and he said, 'How are you keeping up your silk stockings? So I said, 'Mainly by faith, hope and prayer.' And he said, 'I will give you a tip, and this will be of enormous value to you in your future career in the law. There is a wonderful shop in Baker Street which sells suspender belts to outsize hospital matrons.' I thought that was enormously valuable. He must come as a great comfort to the criminals of England when they are sent down for ten years, the judge undoubtedly wearing a suspender belt made for outsize hospital matrons.

Then I began to do more important cases, including murderers. I never defended anyone who had done a murder but I have defended people who suggested they might have done murders. I found to my surprise that murderers are very agreeable clients. People in divorce cases are terrible clients. They ring you up at two o'clock in the morning and say, 'You'll never guess what he has done now. He has just gone off with the toast rack' or, 'He has asked me for custody of the bloody dog.' Murderers, on the whole, find it harder to get to the telephone. I used to find that my murderers had probably killed the one person in the world who was really bugging them and a sort of peace had come over them.

Bigsby: There was also a period in the sixties when you were appearing to defend books which were regarded as depraving and corrupting people.

Mortimer: That's right. I started off with a book called *Last Exit to Brooklyn*, which was about drug taking and homosexual prostitution in New York by a gentleman called Herbert Selby Jr. I did the appeal of that and my only contribution to the law of England was that I invented the aversion theory which said that if a description of sex in a book is so revolting it puts the British public off sex, at least until Thursday afternoon, it is of a highly moral nature. So *The Last Exit to Brooklyn* was acquitted. I met Herbert but I didn't tell him that I got his book off because I said it was so revolting it put everybody off sex. I did the cases which I used to call cases about free speech and liberty of the subject and my enemies called dirty book cases. A lady called Mrs. Whitehouse used to bring all those cases.

Bigsby: How was Rumpole born?

Mortimer: I was asked by the BBC to do *A Play for Today* and I thought I would try and invent a character that would keep me alive in my old age, like maybe a Sherlock Holmes, and so he figured in this one single play. I didn't know who was going to act him. I thought that Alastair Sim would be a wonderful Rumpole but I found that Alastair Sim was gay and couldn't take it on so Leo McKern played him, who has been wonderful ever since.

Bigsby: What was it like once Rumpole was really established in the public mind and you were still being a barrister? What was the attitude of judges, your fellow lawyers towards you in court?

Mortimer: I don't think it was substantially different. I used to get very irritated with juries who used to convict my clients and then come and ask me to sign copies of the book. I did put the things that judges say into the mouths of Judge Bullingham, which gave me a bit of satisfaction.

I remember doing the *Gay News* case. I was making an impassioned speech to the jury about free speech and everything else and suddenly the judge interrupted me and said, 'Members of the jury may be interested in knowing that during this very distressing sordid little case, England are 202 for four wickets,' and I thought that was the filthiest trick that any judge could play. I put that into Judge Bullingham's mouth and he said it to Rumpole. Then this judge came up to me and said, 'Is that anything to do with what I said?' I said, 'How could you mistake this brutal judge for anything like you my lord.' That was a comfort to me.

One of the nicest rude things that a judge ever said to me was when I started to speak to the jury on a very long fraud case and I said, 'You are to be congratulated on sitting through one of the most boring cases that has ever been heard at the Old Bailey,' and the judge started his summing up saying, 'Members of the jury it may come as a surprise to you to know that criminal law in England is not there for the sole purpose of amusing Mr. Mortimer.' Actually I think it probably is.

Bigsby: When you start a novel, and you have written some thirteen of them, do you know where they are going? Are you one of those writers for whom everything is in your mind before you write or is the writing a process of discovering what the book is?

Mortimer: I think you know what the theme is, which is not what the plot is. I think that you know who the characters are and I think you know where it is set and I think you should know vaguely what your destination is. The worst thing, though, is to write down a treatment which tells the characters what they are going to do because the most exciting thing is when they suddenly do something you didn't expect and also when you suddenly write something which seems totally unimportant but which gives you a thrill and which you can build on. So, yes, I think that the writing produces the writing. I think the only way to produce writing is by writing, not by making notes and charts. That is why film writing is so boring because everybody does treatments.

Bigsby: And you have worked on film. You wrote the screenplay for *Tea with Mussolini*. What was the experience of working on that film with Franco Zeffirelli?

Mortimer: Writing films is the best paid and the least enjoyable of all forms of writing because everybody changes everything and everybody thinks they know better than you do. As to Mr. Zeffirelli, first of all I used to have to go and stay in his house, which was very cold and dank and had a lot of dogs that stood on the table and ate spaghetti. I returned to England and worked with him in a hotel in England and at the end of every day he would say, 'Oh, darlings, you are a genius and have saved my life. It is the most beautiful script,' and then he went back the next morning and said, 'I don't think this is right at all.' So one night I said, 'For God's sake, don't read the script tonight Franco, go out and have sex,' and he said, 'I did that last night and the boy was not paying attention.'

Bigsby: You were also responsible for one of the most successful television adaptations – *Brideshead Revisited*. Did you have a sense what a phenomenon that was going to turn into?

Mortimer: Not really at all, no, because it was in the early days of that sort of big television, but I really loved doing it and I love Evelyn Waugh, worship Evelyn Waugh as a writer, although he is very different from me. I am a dedicated atheist. He was a high Catholic and an old Conservative and I am a liberal, but I found the religious part of *Brideshead* very moving. There is a letter of Evelyn Waugh's in which he said he didn't think more than seven Americans would ever like *Brideshead Revisited* and now they repeat it on television all the time and in San Francisco they have Lord Sebastian look-alike contests in which they all carry their teddy bears down to the marina, which is highly embarrassing.

Bigsby: The third volume of your autobiography is subtitled *A Year of Growing Old Disgracefully*, and growing old has evidently had its problems.

Mortimer: Yes, I have got practically everything wrong with me. I have asthma. I can't walk properly. I can only see out of one eye so I can't pour wine. When I was seventy I got this letter from the licensing department in Swansea regarding a driving license and they said have you got any physical defects and my wife said, 'Tell the truth,' so I said, 'Well I can't see out of one eye at all so I can't judge distances and the other eye isn't great and I have never been a very good driver' and by return of post I got a three year driving license with a letter which said, 'Happy motoring'. But I have stopped doing it now out of sympathy for the public.

In Conversation With
Michael Ondaatje

- 1ˢᵗ October 2007 -

Michael Ondaatje was born in Sri Lanka, in 1943. He moved to England in 1954 and then on to Canada in 1962. He was educated at the University of Toronto and Queen's University, Kingston, Ontario. He began his writing career as a poet. His 1970 book *The Collected Works of Billy the Kid: Left-Handed Poems* won the Governor General's Award. His first novel, *Coming Through Slaughter* appeared in 1976 and was followed by *In the Skin of a Lion (1987)*, *The English Patient* (1992) – winner of the Booker Prize and the Governor General's Award – *Anil's Ghost* (2000) – winner of the Irish Times International Fiction Prize – and *Divisadero* (2007).

Bigsby: Can I begin by asking you to explain the origin of your name?

Ondaatje: The name is a fake. I think it was originally an Indian name. The Ondaatjes came from India and when the Dutch invaded Sri Lanka – a lot of people invaded Sri Lanka – the smart merchants changed their names to look like Dutch names, so the double 'a' was added and the 'tj' was added. It was probably spelled much more naturally, phonetically, than it is now. So there is this odd Dutch connection that I don't claim very much but it is around.

Bigsby: But in fact what are the component elements of your DNA?

Ondaatje: It probably comes from India and then they came to Sri Lanka and married whoever they could, some Dutch, some Tamil. So it was really a mixed salad of sources.

Bigsby: You were born into a family that were at least at first reasonably well off but your father – I am looking for the right word – was a little strange in some ways, wasn't he?

Ondaatje: No, he was fine. He did drink. He was quite a shy person, but he did drink and when he drank he did become manic so that is true to a certain extent, but he was actually quite a sweet guy.

Bigsby: I didn't say he wasn't sweet but he began, for example, by apparently going to Cambridge University, but not really.

Ondaatje; Yes, he pretended to go to Cambridge. He lived in Cambridge. His parents thought that he had been accepted but he hadn't and when they discovered it they were furious. They came by ship to England to see him and he could offer them nothing to drink except champagne at eleven in the morning and this upset them even more, so the drama went on most of his life.

Bigsby: You were telling me he wasn't strange but I seem to remember that more than once he commandeered a train.

Ondaatje: He did capture a train a couple of times. But he wasn't strange when he was not drinking.

Bigsby: Right. And that world, before you were born, the world of Sri Lanka in the nineteen twenties and thirties, had a bit of a happy valley feel about it, didn't it?

Ondaatje: Yes, it was the jazz age in Sri Lanka. I went back there eventually as an adult and wanted to write about my family. It was really a case of trying to get these stories in order. I had various fragments of stories. My grandmother had had her breast eaten by a dog. She kept losing her breast.

Bigsby: I think you need to explain that.

Ondaatje: She kept losing her false breast. The dog would eat it. I couldn't believe all these stories. People would make the story even more dramatic because it sounded a bit boring the second time, so this was like research where I had to believe everything I was told.

Bigsby: You say somewhere that you think we are all influenced by what went before. What is it about that world before you were born that nonetheless you feel bears on you in some way?

Ondaatje: When I was at university the subjects I loved were history and English. I always thought that to write a historical novel, or to write about another time, is really to write about the reflection of yourself and your own specific interest today, your own emotional interest today, which you see in the eighteenth century or the nineteenth century or whenever. Not knowing my family, and leaving Sri Lanka at the age of eleven, meant that when I went back I had cut that part of my life out completely until I was about thirty-five. So it was this desire to understand how these people emerged, what brought them together, to try and find a context for all these stories that I had heard bits and pieces of before. In fact writing that book was almost like constructing a map of various uncles and aunts and other people.

Bigsby: I was waiting for you to use the word map because that word occurs in every one of your novels and several of your poems. It is as though you were setting out to map different things in different books, in a country, in terms of a psychology, and you have covered some territory. I will come back to that in a minute if I may. You left at the age of eleven and went to England. How long were you in England?

Ondaatje: From eleven to about eighteen.

Bigsby: Was it a shock to you going to England from Sri Lanka?

Ondaatje: A complete shock. It was a physical shock more than anything else. The mental shock came later. I went to this school in Dulwich, which actually had a very good reputation for writers and if you put the writers together who were there you would create a rather bizarre mixture – Raymond Chandler and P. G. Wodehouse, for instance. You can't get these two in the same room together mentally. Physically, I was wearing socks for the first time, and ties for the first time, and having to salute strangers in special ways. There were social codes to get used to. Essentially, I lived in England in a kind of state of shock for a while and then gradually settled. Then I left and went to Canada.

Bigsby: Why England, and then why Canada?

Ondaatje: Because I think there was a tradition in Sri Lanka that if you could afford it your parents sent you to school in England and then you were supposed to go to university and get a blue in rowing or something and then come back to Sri Lanka and join the family law firm. That was the expected line of career. I think our generation was the first one that came to England, went to school and didn't go back. Some did obviously but some carried on in England or went elsewhere. They went to

Australia or Canada. My brother had moved to Canada at that point and so I went to Canada.

Bigsby: When did writing begin for you?

Ondaatje: Writing didn't begin for me until I came to Canada. Reading began when I came to England. I loved reading books all through my teens but I never thought of being a writer until I came to Canada. My peers were writing and involved with small presses in Toronto and I had a great teacher. We all talk about how important teachers are to us but I had a wonderful English teacher who directed plays and read Browning very dramatically and swept out of the room after finishing one of those monologues. We took over the university magazine, captured it and put all our poems in it. That was the usual format.

Bigsby: And it was as a poet that you saw yourself as a writer?

Ondaatje: My first three books were poetry.

Bigsby: Although the third one was a bit different?

Ondaatje: Yes, I was happy for that book. It was going to be a book of lyrics about Billy the Kid and then gradually I wanted to write prose. I just wanted the landscape to be bigger. I wanted to be able to get on a horse and have a gun fight and that was difficult with a lyric poem, but the subject demanded it so I started writing prose for the first time. As a result the book ended up as some kind of mongrel of poetry and prose and fictional interviews with Billy the Kid and lots of almost half songs. It was structurally a very different kind of book to write for me. It was more like a collage, putting together things with various structures and colours and textures.

Bigsby: And was it that which began to nudge you in the direction of the novel? Why, suddenly having successfully launched yourself as a poet, did you, nine years after that, write your first novel?

Ondaatje: After *The Collected Works of Billy the Kid*, I wrote *Coming Through Slaughter*, which I claim was my first novel, but *Billy* gets dumped in the fiction category sometimes and this gets dumped somewhere else.

Bigsby: Because *Coming Through Slaughter* is a mixed form, too. It is a book about a jazz musician, but has a kind of jazz quality to it as well. It is not exactly a straightforward novel.

Ondaatje: No, I haven't written one of those yet. I like using every kind of method of discovery, impressionism, going around a figure and trying to piece him together. I wasn't trying to write a novel. I was not trying to write a mongrel poetry book, but it was all prose so that was why I claimed it as a novel.

Bigsby: When you came to your next novel, which was *In the Skin of a Lion*, you set it in Canada. In fact it is the only one of your books set in Canada.

Ondaatje: A lot of my poems are set in Canada but, yes, that was the first and so far the last book to be set there.

Bigsby: I remember Margaret Atwood and Jane Urquhart both saying that there were certain advantages in being a Canadian writer in that it wasn't worked over territory. It hadn't been mapped thoroughly. Did you have the sense that you had freedom there?

Ondaatje: Oh yes, I think that was very evident. It wasn't so much that it hadn't been written about but there was a sense that you could try it. That was the feeling I got when I was there in Canada. At that time, when I started to write, it was important to set your novel somewhere else. Canadians weren't supposedly interested in Canadian settings so if you wrote a spy novel you set it in Uruguay or New York and it really was quite a while before people suddenly realised they could write about their own place. Writers like Hugh MacLennan wrote about Canada and Quebec.

Bigsby: There are two constructions going on in *In the Skin of a Lion*. There is the construction of a bridge and the construction of a tunnel, and it is very tempting to see them both as metaphors. It becomes lyrical. We have just talked about the mixed forms in *The Collected Works of Billy the Kid*, a book of poetry, and your first novel *Coming Through Slaughter*. Is the membrane between poetry and prose permeable as far as you are concerned? Do they naturally mix or are they clearly distinct?

Ondaatje: I think we have been living through an age when the novel was very prosaic, crawling with realism everywhere. I really do believe that the novel is something that is so diverse, so various. Somerset Maugham talks about the wide liberty of the novel and it does have a wide liberty and it should have that. So it is not that I think that poetry and prose are naturally twinned, but I think the poetic structure, or the structure from a poem, could be within a novel and not be a problem.

Bigsby: There is, for want of a better word, a meander in your books.

Ondaatje: I do love the meander. I am not quite sure I think about this daily or anything like that but subliminally I am sure it is in every work. I do like the fact that there are numerous tributaries that come to the river of a plot.

Bigsby: We turn to literature like a dream as a way to shape things, give them a sense of coherence, but in *Divisadero* you quote from Nietzsche who suggests that literature is a way of escaping truth.

Ondaatje: Or protecting us from the truth. In *Divisadero* Anna, who is the governing character in the book, is someone who has gone through some trauma in her teens and cannot get over it. She is still preoccupied with it and blocked in some way, so she does quote Nietzsche and talks about how we turn to art, we hide ourselves in the third person, so that in the passages where she moves from the first person to the third person she does so to protect herself from being involved.

I think the thing about writing is that it does shape things for you. I find the world around me absolute chaos and the only time it is not chaos is when you are trying to make order of things and you want that order to be as complicated as possible. You don't want it too neat but there is a kind of shaping, forget order, shaping of something, the shaping of a scene which is what Anna is talking about in this book. It is a kind of protection and it is also a kind of awareness which can be the result of that lyricism and that reality.

Bigsby: There is a character which crops up in *The Skin of a Lion* who reappears in *The English Patient* and of whom there is an echo in *Divisadero*. These are completely different novels, set in different places, different times, so why this thread running through them?

Ondaatje: When I finished *In The Skin of a Lion* I had no idea of going back to certain characters but I noticed a kind of sadness at the end of the book at leaving these characters. Then, when I was writing *The English Patient*, I was about thirty pages into it and I thought well, the nurse could be Hannah or could not be Hannah, so I went back and forth on that for a while. Then Caravaggio turned up. I had not planned to bring Caravaggio into the novel but obviously there was something about those two that I hadn't finished with in some way. I was worried about whether it is a good idea to repeat a character, because if you do then you are not as intently focused on the discovery of that character because you have already done it in a previous novel. But they had both been through some huge change between the two novels so they felt like new characters.

Bigsby: *The English Patient* became highly successful, first winning the Booker Prize and then being made into a film. A lot of writers are associated with a particular book, and sometimes that makes them protective of another book which they feel has fallen into its shadow. Is that true of you at all or do you just celebrate the fact that this did so well?

Ondaatje: I was very happy that it did well. Obviously I am not going to turn my back on *The English Patient*. I don't see the books as like steps up a ladder, getting better and better. I do hope that they get better and better, or get more complex, or get more subtle, but I really don't see them as a route to some kind of final post. Go back to maps, it really is much more like a mapping. This book takes place here and this is the mental state of these characters and this is a preoccupation of these characters so it is more map-like as opposed to ladder-like, progression, perhaps.

Bigsby: Something you said just now bears on the way you write. Iris Murdoch famously used to say that she had the entire book in her head and then just wrote it out. My impression is that the act of writing reveals to you what it is you want to say or how you want to say it. Is that true?

Ondaatje: That is true. I think the problem with admitting that, or saying that, is that I am not saying that one should go and fully discover it as you go along. What happens with me is that there is a long period of time near the end when I go back. Half the time of writing the book is going back and rewriting, recreating and reorganising the structure of the book and discovering the characters even more. Usually the first draft is a discovery of what the story is going to be. I have to begin with some kind of situation or location or time period, so in the book there are these three young people in northern California in the late twentieth century. *The English Patient* takes place at a stage in the war but that is all I really had at the beginning of the book, then I stay with those characters and discover who they are and the situation grows into a plot. Sometimes it goes in the wrong direction and you have got all kinds of cul-de-sacs and you have to chop them off like too many arms. A great deal of time is spent rewriting the book so that it does have an order and a structure and a preparation for what will occur later on that may not have been there at the beginning.

The problem with writing the way I do, is that it is exhausting and terrifying, because I am not quite sure that things are going to work out until very much later on. I would much rather know exactly what I was going to do beforehand and feel more secure but I tend to get bored that way. I think the uncertainty sharpens the focus. When I was doing research on the building of the bridge in *The Skin of the Lion* it was simultaneous to writing it so it wasn't as though I had it all in my head and knew what was going to happen. I was going alongside it so there was a tension and that uncertainty matched the uncertainty over whether the bridge would be completed.

Bigsby: And both procedures offer pleasure or is the latter more like hard work?

Ondaatje: Both pleasure, completely. I love the part of discovering something. At the same time I love the craft and I have become fascinated by it, not just in books but in films. In a book, though, you can go back and burn the first fifty pages or rewrite them, but in a film you can't go back to Japan and film those first twenty minutes. It would cost a lot of money. That is a gift for a writer, to have that ability to rewrite, restructure and relight a scene in. It is a total pleasure.

Bigsby: Where did that stunning image that is in the book and again in the film of *The English Patient* come from where he is going up on a rope with a flare to see the paintings. Is this pure invention or is this derived from something?

Ondaatje: Pure invention.

Bigsby: You followed *The English Patient* with *Anil's Ghost* which took you back to Sri Lanka. What pulled you back to Sri Lanka, especially at that moment?

Ondaatje: I had been wanting to write about Sri Lanka for quite a long time and especially what had happened to the country and I really did not know how to write about it because every time I went there were so many voices, so many opinions, so many points of view. It wasn't until I thought I could do it with having two characters, Anil and Sarath, who are the two figures who try to investigate the case of a disappeared person, that I could make the book not the usual narrative voice but a debate, a constant debate between these two people. That allowed me to get the various points of view that I thought I had to represent in some way. It was really a book about what it is like to be there. It wasn't about choosing which political side is right, but what it is like to be there and to live in that state of fear or terror.

Bigsby: And although there is an actual map, there is another form because the central figure is a forensic scientist, who performs a different kind of mapping as the story turns around the discovery of a body and the attempt to prove who this was and when they were killed. Was forensic science then as it is now omnipresent when you started writing?

Ondaatje: No, this has been a curse for me. When I began the book I would turn the TV on and there would be some forensic show on and I thought I will turn the TV off. It is like gambling in the new book. Since then gambling has been on TV regularly, every week. Every actor is now gambling so it was a great annoyance to me when I was writing it.

Bigsby: It seems to me that many of your characters are displaced. They don't seem rooted. They are immigrants or they are caught in the war or, in this case, they are going back to Sri Lanka from somewhere else, but then leaving again. And there is a solitude at the heart of a lot of them. Do you sense this?

Ondaatje: That's true. I tend to get drawn to characters that I can't quite make out because they don't talk too much or they are in some mystery. I just think that when I am writing I am drawn to people who are very taciturn.

Bigsby: Can you explain your new novel's gnomic title?

Ondaatje: *Divisadero* is actually a name of a street in San Francisco. It is a Spanish word and literally means to divide, the division, the division line between the old city and the new part of San Francisco. The book begins in northern California, about seventy miles north of San Francisco. And there is another meaning to it. Anna and Claire and Coop, these three young people, grew up on a farm and then there was a traumatic moment in the family story and the family splinters and they all go off in different directions, so they are all divided. The fact is, though, that I couldn't think of anything else to call the book.

In Conversation With
Stephen Poliakoff

- 28th November 2007 -

Stephen Poliakoff, playwright, screenwriter, director, was born in London, in 1952, and educated at Westminster School and then at Cambridge, though he left before completing his degree. His first play – *Granny* (1969) – was written and directed by him while he was still at school. He was playwright in residence at the National Theatre by the age of twenty-four. He has always worked in the theatre and television. His stage plays include *Hitting Town* and *City Sugar* (1975), *American Days* (1980), *Breaking the Silence* (1984) and *Remember This* (1999). His television plays include *Caught on a Train* (1980), *Shooting the Past* (1999), *The Lost Prince* (2003), *Gideon's Daughter* (2006) and *Joe's Palace* (2007).

Bigsby: With a name like Poliakoff it is clear that you come from elsewhere, from Russia, and there is one of your plays set in Russia which features your grandfather. Is that an accurate portrait?

Poliakoff. I wrote a play in 1984 called *Breaking the Silence* which was about my Russian grandfather. My father was born in 1910 in Moscow and he and my grandmother and grandfather came from Russia in 1924, shortly after Stalin took over. They had various adventures. My grandfather was an inventor. He was one of the first people in the world to record sound on film. The reason we didn't get the talkies in 1900 was that the world couldn't invent amplification. It took another twenty-five years for them to do that and the result was *The Jazz Singer.* I wrote a play about my grandfather trying to invent amplification in the aftermath of the Russian Revolution, during the civil war that had ensued, and there was a certain truth in that.

My grandfather was given his own train. He was an inspector of telephones on the northern railway in the chaos after the Revolution. So I mingled fact and fiction in the play and when it was presented it was very clearly presented as a fiction, but nevertheless I did have quite a romantic Russian background from my father. I grew up with his stories, which he told frequently. They were very good stories, but quite long. Maybe that is where I get my pacing from. But you knew it was worth sticking with because they were very detailed. He described the wallpaper on the wall and what they had for lunch, but eventually they got to the action.

Bigsby: Presumably he saw the Revolution?

Poliakoff: They had an apartment just off Red Square. They could see Red Square clearly, and the Kremlin. He did literally watch the October Revolution from his bedroom window. It was a week of fighting and guns popping. It was a longer drawn out affair than in the films that celebrated it. A lot of the cavalry officers decamped from the Kremlin into their apartment block. They had one of them sheltering in their apartment. He had never tied his own tie before and had to be helped by my grandfather's chambermaid. So my father remembered all these images and the noise and the people up all night guarding their womenfolk. The people who lived in the apartment walked up and down in case the hordes rushed in. They were cinematic stories.

My Russian grandmother lived with us in our house and she lived to a huge age. She died in the mid-1970s, when she was very nearly one hundred. She had met Tolstoy, or rather followed Tolstoy down the road like a groupie because he was so famous. It was like following David Beckham. She had been to the first night of *The Cherry Orchard* but she was very, very monosyllabic. You knew her stories were true but you couldn't get much more out of her. She was living history at the top of the house and I would take my friends, when we were doing English literature and world literature, and bring her in and say, 'Look, she met Tolstoy.' She would say, 'Yes, I did,' and that was the end of the meeting.

Bigsby: Your father came over at the age of fourteen, which meant that he arrived with no English, I presume. Did he always speak with a Russian accent?

Poliakoff: Yes, he did. He was a very White Russian, a slight figure, very courtly. He kissed every woman's hand he met. It was a deep embarrassment to me as a child watching this happen and thinking it would be misinterpreted by the mothers of my friends. My parents had children quite late. They were both born before the First World War so they led back to a different time to most of my friends' parents. He was a fragment of White Russia and in the sixties and seventies, when I was in my twenties, it became obvious that he was this rather wonderful anachronism. He had a very, very powerful dramatic Russian tempo, which was really frightening sometimes. I had a difficult relationship with him in my adolescence but grew very close to him in my twenties. There are all sorts of things I probably should have found out, which I didn't. I think we probably feel that about our parents. I have a daughter in her twenties and a lot of the young actors I work with are very, very, close to their parents and bring parents to premieres, which I would never in a million years have done. I was of a generation that was trying to break away, very much reacting against the culture of our parents. I think kids are now much nicer to their parents as a rule.

Bigsby: You said of Jews that they always keep their bag packed because, having left one country, they are never quite sure they may not have to leave another. Did your father feel rooted in England?

Poliakoff: My father was a typical Anglophile. He loved English architecture, especially Georgian architecture. He loved good taste, what he regarded as good taste. He was a terrific snob, not literally, in a conventional way, but he loved fine wine, he loved Rolls Royces, though none of these things could he really afford. He had lived above his means. We weren't rich. His firm made the beeper – my father and grandfather invented the beeper or pager – for hospitals and the only time we were allowed to watch ITV in my youth was to watch *Emergency Ward Ten*, the hospital drama, because they had the beeper. Then, immediately afterwards the set would be switched back to BBC I or, even worse, be switched off entirely.

He was very much an Anglophile. That went right back and those that know about Jewish history will know that the Jews were chucked out of Moscow at the turn of the century, unless you were of the educated classes, unless you were lawyers or doctors, so my grandfather tried to look like a Russian prince or a gentleman of the world. He loved everything English and my father got that and when they came to England, with no money except a diamond, they behaved as if they were men of the world, very rich people, and sort of bluffed their way. So my father always retained that. I don't think he was worried about being in any way regarded as somebody who didn't belong.

Bigsby: Did you have relatives in continental Europe?

Poliakoff: We did. Some of my family went to France, and they were the only ones that perished in the Holocaust, but I have got quite a lot of relations left in Russia. My father was the only son of the family who came to England. I suppose he is the dominant influence on my life, compared to my mother who is a much gentler person.

Bigsby: Was she an actress?

Poliakoff: She tried to be an actress but gave it up when she married in the thirties. She was incredibly interested in the theatre and because I was the only show business one she took an absolutely obsessive, almost stereotypical Jewish mum interest in my career. At seventeen she told me that my career was going nowhere, even though I had had a play accepted, but then it was cancelled and that is when she told me that my career was going nowhere. I remember thinking that was a bit harsh.

Bigsby: You were shipped off to a public school. Was that at all like the naval academy in *The Lost Prince*?

Poliakoff: I went to a boarding school which even for the early sixties was an incredibly old-fashioned and deeply racist establishment. I'd better be careful naming it, even after forty-five years. In the sixties there was a part of Kent where there were lots of boarding schools, and we played each boarding school at all the games. There was one just down the road and we suddenly stopped playing football. I asked why – I was near the top of the school, then, and could ask teachers such questions – and they said, 'Oh, because they have got a coloured goalkeeper.' This was in 1965. It is a long time ago but it was in the middle of the swinging sixties, so it was a different world. But I thought nothing wrong in it. I was the only Jewish boy there. I realised that it was a side of England that I hadn't seen before and I wasn't to see again because I then went to a very liberal public school, Westminster, which was completely opposite. But that was a very strong reminder of a certain period in Britain. It left a deep scar because it was quite a horrible place.

Bigsby: At fifteen, you wrote a play that got reviewed?

Poliakoff: Yes, well this is again to do with that culture. It was a different world in the sixties. Plays at public schools were reviewed in the national press. Winchester would do a Greek play and would have a big review in *The Daily Telegraph* and *The Times*. I was the unwitting beneficiary of that because I wrote a play that was put on by an English master and was reviewed in *The Times*. I got an agent out of that and that was a real bit of luck, but it is amazing to think about now.

Bigsby: Then you went to Cambridge where you read history. Your parents, one of whom was an immigrant, must have been very proud. Then you blew it all, because you left?

Poliakoff: Yes. Funnily enough they kept quite quiet about their disappointment, I think because it wasn't a huge surprise. I had been told to have two gap years because I was quite young when I took my A levels, not through academic brilliance but just because of when my birthday was. I was only sixteen when I took A levels. I was trying to write plays, do plays with youth groups. My parents knew I was very interested in that. So when I announced I was leaving Cambridge to write plays I think they thought, well, that's his vocation. That is what he has got to do. I had already had one performed professionally at the Royal Court, albeit for a try-out Sunday night performance, while I had been in Cambridge so it wasn't completely whistling in the dark. I had had professional encouragement. I thought, if I can sell a play by the time I would have left Cambridge anyway, then somehow I would have repaid their investment. I just made it.

Bigsby: Can I just take you back to the very early plays. By 1975 we had grown used to state-of-England plays by such writers as David Hare, Howard Brenton and David Edgar. Your plays don't strike me as ideological, but they did offer a comment on the state of England, an England that you dramatised as being incredibly bleak in many ways?

Poliakoff: Yes. I suppose I established myself writing a group of urban plays about young characters reacting very strongly against the urban setting. It had obviously been happening but people hadn't really noticed amidst the euphoria of the sixties, by which I mean young people hadn't noticed, and suddenly all these town centres had been ripped up and built for the car – Birmingham, Newcastle. They were going to knock down parts of the old town in Edinburgh as late as 1975 and were stopped by a weird group of people ahead of their time, environmentalists and hippies. It is extraordinary how recently that was the mentality. It has only changed in the last twenty-five years. So I wrote about that, about the darkness of sixties euphoria and about the powerlessness of young people.

It was the beginning of celebrity culture, the beginning of the world of the phone-ins, of what we see now on reality TV. Commercial radio was a new thing with young people entering competitions and being offered prizes to meet rock stars. I wrote about that a lot. They were political in a wider sense because they were about the dispossessed, but they were reflecting the landscape of the seventies which was quite uncompromising – the architecture, the atmosphere, IRA bombs going off. It was a dark time, as I am sure a lot of people remember. Interestingly, it was an incredibly rich time for new work and an incredibly rich time for American cinema. The culture was really rich, incredibly rich. It is almost impossible to find an uninteresting work from the mid-seventies from America. It was one of the great periods of American cinema, in the history of cinema, and it was an incredibly rich period for new writing both in television and theatre in this country. So I was part of that world. I had a lot of role models to inspire me.

Bigsby: In 1977 you wrote a *Play for Today* at a time when every week there would be new plays on television, very often by new writers. It is almost unimaginable now.

Poliakoff: Yes, there was a tradition that went from the mid-sixties to the mid-nineties, about thirty years, where there were original works played not just on the BBC but also on ITV. The tradition was still alive at the BBC until about ten years ago, then it just died almost overnight. That was a terrible tragedy, I think, for British culture because there was an enormous amount of interesting work but it was also a unique forum for people to offer a wide audience. What we got was a writer's original vision, not ruled by the box office and not ruled by having to be in genres, which is very important. You had all sorts of writers' dreams and visions. You never knew what was going to come at you across the carpet. I remember watching a play, when I was about thirteen or fourteen, made by Granada on ITV, about two girls carrying a giant cheese between two northern towns. It stayed with me for forty years. You could see very social realist things or you could see Dennis Potter's strong metaphors or political dream plays by David Mercer. There was an extraordinary range, and it was terrible that we lost that.

It is not completely lost, and it may be about to revive again, but it was a tradition that I was brought up in and found incredibly inspiring. I think all our culture is worse because of its loss. New writing was terribly dependent on the theatre. A lot of writers wrote for both, but it was much more difficult for playwrights to earn their living because the theatre paid so badly unless you were Tom Stoppard. But they were able to work in television and now that is not open to them. It is a terrible loss to the theatre as well because writers therefore can't sustain a career, but I think people are waking up to that now.

Bigsby: Many of the *Plays for Today* were shot in the studio. In fact people had to fight for ten minute's worth of film. When you made *Caught on a Train* you made a decision that it was going to be shot on location and that you were going to get hold of a real train, or part of a train, to do it in. And that has been true of you ever since. You don't like shooting in studios?

Poliakoff: I don't like shooting in studios. I have virtually never shot in a studio. I like using real locations. I didn't direct *Caught on a Train* but I was quite instrumental in the production even though I was very young at the time. I think that where I have been lucky is that I have been able to write for television in exactly the same way as I write for the theatre, and to write what interests me. Then I film it as I want, cast who I want in it, cut it how I want. Obviously, people are watching me. I am not completely left to my own devices, but nevertheless I then present it to the world. I have had a lot of ratings success. The encouraging thing is that all my work, not just recently, has been watched by very good sized audiences and so long as I hold my audience I am allowed that freedom. I like the incredible democratic nature of television in that you can reach so many different people from all sorts of backgrounds and they will stay with it, if you believe how they measure these things, which is another question.

So that was the tradition that was open to loads of writers and now is open to only a few. But I am fighting very hard to try and make it so that other writers benefit from that, are able to make things on film that aren't in genres, aren't ruled by American box office. That is an extraordinary tradition which I am trying to uphold. What it does mean is that you can make things unlike other things. In the cinema you have got to make something that is like something else because then it can be marketed. There are very few films that aren't in a genre, especially in this country, though less so in Europe. If you look at the history of English cinema nearly all our movies are in a genre of some nature, certainly since Film Four was abolished. The only chance to do this is in television and the audience, when they do get those surprises, do show up for it.

Bigsby: *Caught on a Train*, featured Peggy Ashcroft as an old Viennese woman who is taken off her train by men with guns. Seeing that now brings back that sense of threat that people were feeling even as we were in what is now the European Union.

Poliakoff: I am a great believer in Europe. That story was written very much at a time of the first real fears. There was a wave of consciousness about terrorism in the seventies and eighties. There was a great fear of people behaving suspiciously. Planes were being hijacked and there was an irrational fear about Europe being a dark place.

Bigsby: In a lot of your work things seen in the background, by a kind of peripheral vision, seem important. In *Caught on a Train* the characters go through a station and we are aware of people dossing down on the ground. In some way what we glimpse in the background is telling another story.

Poliakoff: I write a lot of first-person stories because they don't tend to be multiple stories. They may have different levels but they are basically seen through one person's eyes or, at the most, two person's eyes. In *Joe's Palace* everything is seen through the boy's eyes while in *Capturing Mary* it is Maggie and her younger self. I like telling first person stories and then you notice what the character notices, or he walks past something. We notice things as he walks past. That is my style, I suppose, because it is then possible for me to say to the audience come with me in this character. The beginning may be a little bit different to something you have seen but stay with it and you will get a story. You will get a situation and it is just like what is happening to the character. I do feel that audiences will be with it and therefore will be led into a world which maybe they haven't seen before.

That has governed the way I have approached writing for television. It is not possible to do that in the theatre but television is a perfect medium because it is intimate. It comes to people in their homes. They don't have to struggle to the cinema and sit through all those bloody ads just to be entertained. They say, 'I am in my home. Alright, here I am, surprise me, interest me.' They don't want that every night but they want that sometimes. It is a fantastic challenge and a fantastic privilege to be able to address millions of people like that or coax them into your world.

Bigsby: It seems to me that *Shooting the Past* is a crucial work for a number of reasons. One has to do with the pacing of things, allowing things to happen slowly, the sort of pleasure you got from watching the television version of John le Carré's *Tinker, Tailor, Soldier Spy*. The other is that, for virtually the first time, the Holocaust is invoked, though there is a reference to eugenics in *Century*. That element was going to come more and more into your work.

Poliakoff: I think it took me a while to look at my Jewish background. I have always been quite happy being a Jew. I have never had any difficulty with that, but I think my parents were slightly old-fashioned, with an emphasis on good manners, so that I reacted by being this hairy, urban playwright. Oddly enough, my early work was criticised for being a bit too fast. I moved around. I had short scenes, which is now very common in the theatre and was less common then. I wrote quite televisual scenes but they were theatre plays and it was only when I came back to television in the late nineties that I was thrown a challenge by the then controller of BBC 2 who suggested I write something unlike anything else that has ever been on television. So I thought, right, television then was very, very into multiple stories. The whole idea was that nobody could concentrate any more. That was one of the accepted wisdoms. It was said with huge authority that children could not concentrate for more than seven minutes or maybe five and a half minutes. Wind on eight years, only eight years, and every kid's movie is three hours long – *Lord of the Rings* – and they will go and see it two, three or four times, and they sit there absolutely still. So that was complete rubbish. I am always terribly sceptical when you are told things by anybody in authority. The pseudo-science of market research and management consultancies is nearly always wrong when they project into the future.

I decided to go back to really long scenes, as in *Tinker, Tailor*, which had very, very long scenes which can be incredibly compelling. So I thought, I can do that and use photos in a true story of a photographic collection that I knew was threatened. So I wrote *Shooting the Past* and all hell broke loose when I finished it. The BBC said, 'Oh, it is so slow,' even though that is what they had asked me to do. I was resolute in saying I had no idea if it was going to work but I knew it couldn't not work. You couldn't make it what it wasn't, and so it went out completely as I had cut it. When it was first broadcast on BBC2 even the continuity woman's voice shook with uncertainty. I remember shouting, 'What do you mean? Not even you are on my side.' I was shouting at the television. This voice said, 'Now a very strange group of characters.' Yet it got a very good audience and it held its audience over three weeks and it had a much bigger effect than I ever anticipated.

Bigsby: In *Shooting the Past* you seem to have a real sympathy for still photography. How important has that been to you, not just in that particular work but in other work as well?

121

Poliakoff: I am not a great expert on photography, but I really love still images and when I responded to that challenge of the controller of BBC2, way back ten years ago, it was because I had noticed, as a viewer, that when a film camera looks at the still image in a documentary it is very, very difficult not to be drawn towards that image. I am sure we have all watched documentaries and thought, 'God, that was a wonderful image. I wish it had stayed longer,' and I thought I could use that in a drama, the power the still image has when the film camera looks at it. Obviously a still image looks great if you are looking at it in real life, but it is that magical mix of the movie camera and the still image that I find attractive. I like the stillness of pictures in this busy world since I was trying to make the slowest piece of television. So it suited my purpose as well.

Bigsby: Was it with *Shooting the Past that* you got control over your work?

Poliakoff: Yes, because that was a major success and I had been, I suppose, brutally right, though I was as surprised as anyone that it had such a big reaction. I think the reason for that was the work. It was to do with the fact that it was a surprising world and I think people liked the surprising world. But it was also to do with the fact that a lot of that authored television had vanished and here was a work that reminded people of the pleasure of seeing something unlike other things. There is a strong appetite for that, not every week but once a month certainly.

Bigsby: *Perfect Strangers* focuses on a family reunion. It is an ironic title in some ways because they are family and hence not supposed to be strangers. There are secrets to be uncovered, a past to be explored which has the power to destabilise the present. One of those secrets has to do with the Holocaust. You followed that with two films, set in the eighties moving into the nineties. In between came *The Lost Prince* a full-blown costume play. At its heart is the figure of the lost prince, a damaged person who everyone wants to displace, remove from history, push into the background. It's a film that almost seems to set out to restore this person.

Poliakoff: Exactly. I wanted to reclaim the boy from oblivion because generally the public didn't know about him. He was born in 1905 in the middle of the royal splendour. The adult world was engulfed in an extraordinary catastrophe involving the symbolic heads of the nations. The Kaiser was his cousin and he was related on both sides to the Russian royal family, which George V didn't allow to come to England, but it was also a celebration of a child who was different, a child that had learning difficulties. He had both epilepsy and learning difficulties, quite what they were we don't know. Basically he was on the autistic spectrum and also an epileptic, so it was obviously a very touching story, but I thought it was also a great way of looking at a piece of history that we think we know but from an angle that is fresh. It was a celebration of all children that are slightly different and what they are capable of.

Bigsby: *Friends and Crocodiles* takes you from the eighties into the nineties. *Gideon's Daughter* is set in a very precise year, 1997, the death of Princess Diana, the election of the Labour Party and the beginning of spin. Does that pose you a particular problem in that this is a history which is alive in everybody's imagination?

Poliakoff: I wanted to write about what you might call work marriage. We are often incredibly obsessed with the people we work with and it can be like a form of love story. We start to work with them and really admire them and then they let us down in some way, or vice versa. Though work is such a huge part of our lives, it is very seldom part of drama except as a background. I really wanted to write about the great changes that have happened over the last twenty years and which we have all lived through and I thought that it hadn't been written about enough. So I made that pair of films and I tried to approach it the same way as I did *The Lost Prince*, dropping people into the middle of history as opposed to having a saga. So there are leaps in time. It was a very interesting exercise, writing about recent history, because it is difficult not to be self-conscious about mobile phones or things that we all take for granted now, but I like those sort of challenges to see if you can make them work.

Gideon's Daughter was about a PR guru who is asked by the government to help sell the millennium in 1997. His life starts to unravel partly because of his guilt, being slightly a philandering man. His wife is dead and he wasn't very nice to her. His teenage daughter is punishing him. There is also that extraordinary difficult time when children go off to university, or they go on a gap year to dangerous parts of the world and maybe don't get in touch. It is one of the worst times.

We first meet the daughter when he goes to her last assembly at her school and she sings a song about George Simenon, the writer who was one of the great philanderers of the twentieth century, who claimed to have slept with two thousand women. She sings straight at her philandering dad. So it is somewhat pointed.

Bigsby: What you didn't mention was that George Simenon's daughter committed suicide.

Poliakoff: She is punishing him and he tries to think what she was trying to tell him through that song. We slowly realise he is having a breakdown. He is the one who is nearer suicide than the daughter. But it has quite a life-affirming ending. She forgives him. I think one of the more interesting experiences of my life was when the BBC had a big showing of the film for what they called the great and the good and I was sitting there with my daughter next to me, at that time my nineteen-year-old-daughter, watching that film. That was an interesting moment.

Bigsby: It seems to me that virtually all of your plays move towards some moment of redemption, of reconciliation.

Poliakoff: Yes. I think that is true. My recent work, *Capturing Mary*, does have a slight redemption but it is more pitiless. It is about a life ruined and it is quite startling in that way. It is much, much darker than most of my work. It was deliberately written as a much darker work but it is certainly true of that film and of *Joe's Palace*. There are redemptive qualities, because I think that basically I am a humanist. Are we cruel animals, highly intelligent mammals? En masse, under a certain political situation, madness and darkness can flow, but individually I am a humanist. I do believe that people are essentially imaginative, much more intelligent than most political or marketing systems give them credit for, and nearly all my work for television celebrates that fact.

Because I am in a mass medium what I find exciting is to create work that may be quite challenging, may be quite difficult, in the sense of it not easily falling into one category or another, or saying that you can assimilate this immediately after it is finished. That is not true of my work. I find it really exciting to say to the audience, come with me because I believe a mass audience is very intelligent. So far they have come with me. You can't generalise about four million people in terms of watching it to the end because a million people leave, like that, in television. It is very brutal. They just go because it is very easy to leave. It really doesn't take much to press a button and say, alright, that's enough. I find that a very interesting and potent and powerful interchange with this unseen audience. I am saying, 'Come with me,' and I suppose my work is celebrating both my characters' intelligence and the audience's intelligence.

I don't think audiences need pat solutions. I don't think audiences need happy endings, but I do believe that if they come on a journey like that they don't want to be in a pitiless place. I think *Capturing Mary*, which is about a life ruined, is quite pitiless, and it suited that story, but I am not a pessimist, despite climate change, the end of the world. I am extremely sceptical about people saying they are in control. I am extremely sceptical of all accepted wisdom, but as to the belief that people are basically creative beings, that is where the optimism in my work comes from.

Bigsby: How much of the impact of your work is owing to those professionals who are working with you to produce this?

Poliakoff: Well obviously I am very dependent on the people I work with and I choose everybody. I choose the cameraman, I choose the designer. I look at their works and try to choose people that I know will be on the same wavelength. The casting is all me so I try to have brilliant actors and then I try to encourage them to be at the top of their talent. So when you have got a Maggie Smith or Michael Gambon that is a great start. And there is always some amazing talent coming up. Then you try to surround yourself with the best technicians. But I do plan the look of the thing very, very carefully because it is not the same cameraman on, say, *Joe's Palace* as it is on *Gideon's Daughter* so I work with different people sometimes but the look tends to be the same in the recent work because I am not a great believer in the social realist tradition, although there has been wonderful work in that tradition. I personally don't think the world looks like that. I think the world is very richly coloured. And the work owes a lot of its hypnotic power to the music as well. All those pieces are very important in plays and a lot of work goes into them from other people. It is a very collaborative thing and I try to work with really gifted people.

Bigsby: If you were beginning as a writer today would you find it as easy?

Poliakoff: When I was a young playwright if you couldn't get a play on at the Royal Court or Hampstead, you were in trouble, so I think it is probably about the same in an odd sort of way. There are great disadvantages and great advantages. There are many more outlets than when I was young, but on television at this moment it is tougher. I think it will get a bit better in the next two, three or four years. Television is going to remain a very powerful force in this country for the next ten years. Terrestrial audiences are still enormous. Nineteen million people. That is the same as twenty years ago. *Caught on a Train* went out on

BBC 2 when there were only three channels It got three million viewers. *Capturing Mary* went out twenty-seven years later against *I'm A Celebrity*. It got three million viewers. That is quite extraordinary, the symmetry. Three million is a lot on BBC 2 for a hundred minute drama. That was a very good audience. So I think the audience has still got an appetite for new drama. People will make new drama, so I think for the determined, talented new writer the future isn't bad. My career would have gone slightly differently probably. I might have been making low-budget British films rather than a *Play for Today* sort of thing, but some of those are made for nothing. It is reasonably hopeful. I think I would have had a slightly different career but I think I probably would still have got the work.

Bigsby: Are there disadvantages in being both the writer and the director?

Poliakoff: There is a huge financial disadvantage, because when you are a successful writer you earn far more money if you could keep writing rather than directing. My peers are much richer than me because they pour out scripts and it takes me two years to make four hours of television and direct. So, economically, it is a very dumb move. But since that is not one of the governing principles of my life, that doesn't particularly worry me. The reason I did that was because although I had my work done early on by some very good directors, and I got on with several of them really well, I was spending more and more time with them. They wanted me round all the time because my work is very particular. If it works, it works in a particular way. So I was spending so much time on the set it was really tiring being there all the time with somebody else directing. You don't have the adrenalin of making it yourself, and various producers and leading cameramen said, 'You should direct your own work.' I thought, well, if they are telling me to do it I must take that very seriously. So it was actually the people in charge who said, 'Why don't you try?' rather than the other way around.

Because I really liked working with actors I found I could do it and actors liked working with me because they have quite a lot of rehearsal time and quite a lot of inspiration. One thing I am really proud of is the consistency of acting in my work because it is not just getting the famous actors. *Joe's Palace* had a complete unknown. *The Lost Prince* had complete unknowns at the centre, and it takes a lot of time to find them. The main advantage is that it gets you away from the desk and you get new ideas being away from the desk. I would go mad after thirty-five years sitting at a desk because a lot of dramatists, as I am sure you are all aware, have quite short creative lives, though not all by choice. It is often said theatre dramatists only have a short time because it is a young person's game. I remember reading Max Stafford Clark, who ran the Royal Court for many years, saying playwrights are like athletes. They have a very short life and I thought that is all very well for you to say because you are not a writer. So the reason I am sitting here now, maybe, is because I started directing my work, not being consigned like an old athlete to hobble around in some pasture.

As regards who is controlling your work, there is quite a strong structure of producers and executive producers watching and advising, but also I think there is a slight snobbery about because nobody asks Mike Leigh if he has too much control. But he has the ultimate control because nobody ever sees a script. The financers never see a script. Nobody asks Ken Loach if he has too much control, even though his work is mostly improvised. So it is just because I am working in television where it is more unusual for people to have control. In cinema it is quite common, so I see myself as no different from that.

In Conversation With
Irina Ratushinskaya

- 30th October 1996 -

Irina Ratushinskaya was born in Odessa in 1954 and studied physics at Odessa University. When her poems were perceived as being anti-Soviet she was imprisoned for seven years but was released after four. In 1987 she left for the United States and was stripped of her Soviet citizenship. After living in London for a number of years she returned to Russia and her citizenship was restored. Her books include *Poems* (1984), *Beyond the Limit* (1987) her memoir, *Grey is the Colour of Hope* (1988), *The Odessans* (1992), and *Wind of the Journey* (2000).

Bigsby: You were born in Odessa in the Ukraine, a place that has its own history, its own culture, its own language.

Ratushinskaya: For me, Odessa is a very special city. What was interesting about this city is that in those days there were so many nations living in peace together and coping with each other, enjoying their differences, not denying their differences, that it gave us a sort of very special culture: Russians, Jews, Italians, French, whoever. I wouldn't say these people mixed up through marriages. I wouldn't say Odessa was any sort of melting pot. It was not. Somehow those cultures didn't melt together but when my generation grew up we were taught, and took it naturally, to make the most of our differences. Perhaps because of the Odessa climate people would never take life too seriously. They would never take themselves too seriously. There was fun, humour. That was the tradition and it still is and of course I was very interested in the history of the city. Odessa was founded a little more than two hundred years ago so one can follow its history and not be overloaded with historical notes.

Bigsby: You mention a mixture. There was also a mixture in your own family in that you have Polish roots. Was that something that you were taught about by your parents or was that an aspect they wanted to suppress?

Ratushinskaya: My parents belonged to what in Russia they call the scared generation, those who had to grow up under Stalin's rule. So my parents would never talk to me about my roots. I cannot blame them because I understand how dangerous it was, but my grandparents were more open and to me the mutual understanding and sympathies skipped a generation. That is why I would say that grandchildren and grandparents understand each other better than parents. Relationships in Russia are different from this country. People live together. Old people are not sent to old people's homes. No one would shake hands with a person who sent his mother or father to an old people's home. So the parents work and grandparents belong to the children.

Bigsby: Was there a moment when you became aware of growing up in a world which didn't have freedoms?

Ratushinskaya: One of the first moments was when I went to school and my father didn't allow me to exchange letters with Polish children. There was a project in our school that involved us becoming pen pals with some Polish school children. My father said that I wouldn't be allowed to do this because as soon as you start writing abroad you would be drawing attention to yourself. I couldn't blame him because his father was one of twelve sons and all of them were killed in the civil war, revolution and so on. Only one survived and I was an only child, so he wanted to protect me as much as possible, but it was difficult for me to accept this double way of thinking. At home I was taught not to lie but at school we had to lie. It was officially demanded. From the age of four we had to say that we loved Lenin. We didn't have the honour of knowing Lenin. We didn't have any feelings about such abstract things as Lenin's personality or the Communist Party. We were supposed to say that we knew that socialism was the best system that ever existed. It was nonsense. We were taught to comment on political events. I personally felt it was a betrayal. There is something very dishonest in getting little children involved in politics. When you are six or seven it is none of your business and you don't know who to believe, but we were taught to speak politically, to be involved in political demonstrations and so on. In history lessons I was supposed to repeat what horrible people nobles were, how the whole country suffered from them and so on. I simply couldn't repeat it because I respected my grandparents, I respected my parents, and I wouldn't say dirty things about my family. Why should I? So perhaps I took things too seriously for an Odessan and that is why I landed in a labour camp.

Bigsby: You were at school at the time of the Prague Spring. You must have been about fourteen. Can you remember that event and how the school dealt with it?

Ratushinskaya: My parents didn't let me go to school for a week. My mother was a devoted communist at this time. Now she is a devoted Catholic but then she believed that the Czechs were horrible people who had attacked our soldiers for no reason and that if we didn't go there then America would. I was fourteen, which is a difficult age. So I started arguing. My mother was horrified at what I said and afraid that I would repeat it at school, so I spent a week under a sort of house arrest. I still don't know – and I never asked – how they explained it to the school. It was the best of weeks for me since I was simply sitting at home, reading and reading, and enjoyed myself enormously.

Bigsby: After school, in 1971, you went on to university and had only been there a year when the KGB tried to recruit you.

Ratushinskaya: How they went about this recruitment really shocked me. I was about seventeen or eighteen. They invited me to some young communist organisation do without any explanation. The great idea was that various young girls were supposed to establish contacts with foreigners who visited Odessa, because Odessa is a port city, and make friends with them. They were supposed to have a nice time with them and carefully get information, who they knew in the Soviet Union and whether they had some relatives in the Soviet Union, get addresses of those people, their Soviet contacts and in fact estimate whether it would be a good idea for the KGB to recruit those people. I didn't know much at the time. I think in my generation we thought that it would be easier to sign a contract with the Devil than say 'Yes' because we knew there would be no escape ever. So I said, 'No' straight away and hoped they would let me go. Then they said, 'You cannot actually get out without our written permission,' and it was true because the whole building was surrounded by soldiers. Then they said that if I said, 'No' I would have to leave the university and my mother and father would lose their jobs. They said they knew where my little sister, who was twelve years younger than I, had to cross the road twice on her way to school. I was absolutely terrified.

When I was older I discovered it was all bluff. I was told that they were simply scaring young girls. They could do such things in Stalin's time, but not in the seventies. Then they produced a big lamp and shone the light in my eyes. One was standing behind my back and for two hours they were shouting at me in turns. I was scared to death. I couldn't actually talk. I was just saying, 'No, no, no, no,' and that was it. So they told me I could go home but forbade me to tell anyone at home about this meeting or they said that that person would have the same trouble as me. So when I left the building I thought of committing suicide. That was the clever way I thought of to protect my family but the sea brings some sense into people's heads, at least in Odessa. So when I was by the sea I had another great idea. I decided I would walk around Odessa, because in Odessa most people know everyone, and tell people so that if something happened to my parents or my sister it would be too much publicity. So I did that. I never heard from the KGB any other propositions and I wasn't even kicked out of the university. But at more or less the same time I had a friend who committed suicide. She hanged herself without any explanation and her friends didn't understand what had happened and still suspect that she was raped or something.

Bigsby: You went to university to study physics. Why physics?

Ratushinskaya: The worst possible place to learn about literature would be a literature institute because the ruling idea was that everything is political, everything is divided into two parts, communist or anti-communist. So Soviet writers were supposed to make propaganda. In Russia you had to involve Lenin's name in all your essays. You had to explain your devotion to the Communist Party, quote from Marx, Engels, and so on. The best writers to have come out of Russia during the past twenty or thirty years didn't have a literature education. I always knew that I was a poet but I always knew I would never be able to publish my poems in the Soviet Union, not because they were political, but because they were not political. So I had to support myself with something else and why not physics. I was good enough at physics and later, when the KGB started to prosecute me and fired me from my job, it was such a relief that I could work as a tutor and make reasonable money without being officially unemployed. There was nothing wrong with my learning physics.

Bigsby: You said you had always been a poet, but only in a sort of dabbling amateur way for a long time. Then there suddenly came a change when poetry really did become central to what you do. What brought that about?

Ratushinskaya: I don't know, because I didn't notice that moment. As a girl I started very early. Actually, before I could write I loved to compose poems in my head and I didn't understand why people bothered to write them down. Writing is such a hard thing to do for a little girl and it was my very private place. I didn't want people to make fun of me so my parents only learned that I was writing poetry from the KGB interrogator. When I was arrested I didn't want them to be involved. So I was writing happily, privately, without any urge to show anyone at all until I became a student. Then I started writing, mostly jokes for student shows, and had a reputation as a person who could write verse for any song in fifteen minutes. Then my friends started to ask for some of my poems. In those days if people liked some stuff they simply copied it, sometimes in writing, sometimes making photos of each page, sometimes using typewriters, and distributed it underground. When I was arrested the interrogator told me that my poems were confiscated in Moscow and even Siberia. I didn't know where they were circulated. I didn't mind, actually. I thought it the most natural process.

Bigsby: When you married, you became involved in the issue of human rights in the Soviet Union and almost inevitably found yourself in court and getting a savage sentence. Was it the sentence you expected?

Ratushinskaya: I had mixed feelings when I heard the sentence because, for our generation, it was a kind of privilege to become a political prisoner, especially for poetry. Of course it was not nice to be separated from my husband and parents and from my friends, and to know that I would be forty (I was thirty odd when I was arrested) when I completed the sentence. Also, there was the possibility that they would add another sentence while I was in the labour camp. So the best way was to keep a brave face, remember that I am from Odessa, and to follow the advice not to believe them, not to be afraid of them. So, like others of the young generation of political prisoners I knew how to deal with the KGB from the very beginning.

Bigsby: You asked once, what do we know of values until we are in prison? Did you discover a set of values in prison or did you simply apply the values you had instinctively learnt?

Ratushinskaya: The whole thing is a matter of proportion, because I think all people have more or less a full system of values and more or less the same ethical system but in what proportions. This makes all our differences I think. It is quite a special experience to be robbed of everything, including a toothbrush, isolated from the rest of mankind, without much hope of surviving. But then, when one doesn't have anything, when one is not responsible for anything any longer, and is absolutely one hundred per cent care free, as only prisoners can be care free, one can see the proportion of those values in a different light. My first discovery was that the whole world could not be taken from me. I still felt the connections. I was not allowed to exchange letters. I was not allowed to have meetings. Actually I only learned that Brezhnev had died in my courtroom, where the prosecutor mentioned it. There was no radio, no news at all, but I still felt these very live connections, emotional connections. It is difficult to explain but I didn't feel shut off at all.

The experience also gave me a feeling, which is with me till now, that all our problems are conflicts, like children playing in a sandpit. They take it seriously, fight over a spade or bucket, and it is very emotional. But that is only the beginning of adult life. After a few weeks of imprisonment I felt myself a more conscious Christian than I was before. I had heard from my priest, and I had read in theological literature, that the human personality is more important than the history of any state because the state is temporary and human personality is made for eternity. I knew that we were leading this life as if we were in a quite cruel boarding school but that one day we would be taken home, and it is natural for our development. So I didn't have any reason to take it too seriously. Perhaps it is a very personal approach but it is my approach.

Bigsby: But even an Odessan must have found it difficult to see the funny side of some of the things that happened to you. You were knocked unconscious a couple of times. You were frozen. You went on hunger strike. You suffered all kinds of illnesses. What was the lowest point of those years?

Ratushinskaya: The most difficult thing for me to bear was the constant fear for my husband's life because when the KGB deals with a dissident they start blackmailing you both. So they told my husband, Igor, 'Ah, you are not arrested, she is suffering, she is dying and you don't want to renounce your views in writing,' while to me they said, 'Ah, here we are responsible for your life. We will think twice before we will kill you but he is in Kiev and there are so many hooligans and who knows what might happen. No one would know.' They wanted me to renounce my views, betray my friends, abandon my religion. They wanted the same from all the inmates in the labour camp and wanted the same from my husband. I had to live more than three years without knowing whether he was alive or dead. For me, that was the most difficult point. Though there was physical suffering, of course. I was younger and didn't know a lot of things so when I had a toothache in the KGB prison I complained about it and a sort of dentist came. I was taken to the cell where eleven KGB officers were standing and watching as they simply drilled the nerve out of my tooth without injection. So I lost consciousness and when I came back to the cell I promised myself not to complain again while I was in the labour camp.

Growing up in the Soviet Union you knew it might happen at any moment. We grew up having at least some of our relatives in the labour camps or being murdered in the labour camps, so one could bear a lot. We learned not to panic, to control one's emotions, and it was very important not to hate the KGB officers. I have seen some prisoners who did, who allowed themselves to hate – and there were so many reasons every day to hate those people – and became insane. I have seen such cases. But in the labour camp, under pressure, I came to understand the practical everyday value of the commandments. I understand that we must not hate our enemy. At the same time that system corrupted the warders and KGB people enormously. We were actually sorry for them and they started to help us secretly. They started to help us send messages out of the prison. That is why the government had to change three sets of the KGB officers during the existence of our labour camp. You can corrupt people with kindness.

Political prisoners are like computers. They come in generations. The first generation of political prisoners were simply average people arrested by chance. Some were priests, monks, nuns, some of them were intellectuals, but millions were arrested because their neighbour wanted their flat and wrote a false report to the KGB. That was enough, in the thirties, to arrest someone as a political prisoner. Now, because we had absorbed all the experience of Solzhenitsyn's generation, we were the third generation. We knew what to expect. We were ready not to be broken down and, by the way, in Russia there is great shame at the idea of a poet or priest being broken down. All other people would be forgiven but not priests and not poets.

Bigsby: You went on writing poetry, in fact poetry became in some senses even more important to you. You described how the KGB officers could be a conduit, a way of getting word out, but how else did you get your poetry out of those prison camps which after all were supposed to be secure?

Ratushinskaya: Of course they were secure, as much as possible. I still cannot speak about all opportunities because while there are no political prisoners in Russia at the moment to be on the safe side I will keep our little prisoner secrets. Once someone who worked in customs at Heathrow told me that some of the ways we communicated were better than those used by drug smugglers but I wouldn't like to give those methods away. Our labour camp was for specialist, dangerous, criminal women but we were political prisoners so there was no punishment cell in our small zone. To break us down the KGB sent us to a punishment cell in the labour camp for criminal women where they kept a special isolated cell for us. I spent about one fourth of my labour camp time in the punishment cell. But on our way there and back we were accompanied by soldiers and I don't remember any case, when I asked a soldier to take this little thing and to post it or to pass it somewhere to some address, when he would refuse. In our times political prisoners were respected by the population and everyone – criminals, soldiers – was on our side. I wouldn't say I enjoyed going to the punishment cell. It was a horrible place and I never knew whether I would come back alive or not, but I knew that while I was there I would certainly be able to send another message.

Bigsby: In 1986, released from imprisonment, you decided to come to Britain. Why Britain?

Ratushinskaya: I would say it was the other way around. When I was in prison I had no idea that people were campaigning for me in this country and in other countries. All the letters which people sent to me were confiscated and never reached me, but what was useful was that while the KGB people never read those letters, they counted them, so that when they decided whether to keep me in the labour camp or not they had to take into account what publicity the case had had. When I was released I learnt how many people, in various countries, had campaigned for me and immediately there were telephone calls, interviews. I started thanking people for helping me and starting campaigning for my friends who were still in the labour camp immediately. Then I was invited by various countries and organisations asking me to visit them. They seemed to want to see me alive because they had been campaigning for me for years but all those invitations had simply disappeared in the post. They telephoned me from America. 'Did you receive our invitation?' 'No,' I said, and when British friends wanted to invite me that invitation disappeared as well. So then the British Embassy simply called me and my husband Igor in Moscow by telephone, and gave us the invitation. Without this invitation we couldn't appeal for permission to go abroad in the Soviet Union. We went to the Embassy but immediately after we left we were arrested and searched. The letter was taken away and then the police telephoned someone for two hours. Finally they decided to give us the invitation and my husband and I came to this country for three months to see our new friends, to say thank you and to remind people about other political prisoners.

It was the time when almost everyone was so fond of Gorbachev, and so charmed by him, that people were ready to forgive despite the fact that there were thousands of people still suffering, political prisoners still suffering in the labour camps. So we came. We could bathe once more. Finally I went to a proper dentist and so on but we could not go back. In 1987 the Politburo took away our citizenship. The decree was signed by Gorbachev personally. So we found ourselves stranded in England, with one suitcase and no English having to start our life afresh. I never complained. I find this country a very good place for exile. [in 1998 she reclaimed her citizenship]

Bigsby: I must now leap over ten years and bring you to the latest development which is a novel, *The Odessans*, which is a long way away from your poems, which are for the most part quite small. This book has epic dimensions. What led you to move in this new direction?

Ratushinskaya: Actually I started writing my first novel when I was twenty-three. This novel, the manuscript unfinished, was confiscated by the KGB. It was clear that Russia was not a good place then to write big things because it is difficult to hide them. It is much easier to memorise a poem than a short story, leave alone a novel. So, I started writing, but it was confiscated. Actually I didn't complain much – well of course I still do because they never returned it – but I think I was not mature enough when I was twenty-three and I didn't actually know how to finish it. I couldn't bind the ends together, but before I was arrested I had written a collection of short stories which circulated in Russia and they were published in France and in America. So I didn't write only poetry. By the way, the whole idea of writing a novel about Odessa is not mine. I had lunch with my publisher and he said, 'Irina, you collect so much about Odessa, why shouldn't you sit down and write about it?' I said, 'No, no, no. I am not prepared,' and in three days I said, 'I will.'

Bigsby: It is a novel that goes back to the immediately pre-revolutionary period, almost as though you are going back to when this whole system, under which you suffered, began, as though you want to find where the incubus started. It also has echoes of your Polish background almost as though you wanted to trace that element that was in your background but got suppressed. Were you deliberately going back to that moment because it was when the machine started to move?

Ratushinskaya: I am not sure. First of all the machine started to move long before that revolution actually happened. It started in the second part of the last century. I think I was fascinated by the generation of those who were old enough to remember and understand the revolution and young enough to go to the battles of the Second World War. Just to think of all this generation, what they had to pass through, for me they were very special people. Luckily for me most of them were Odessans and when Odessans are old they love to talk about their past, so I had as many life stories as I wanted. What was interesting for me was that very few people had had key roles in those revolutions, the civil war and such events. Most people had their own lives, wanted to survive, wanted to protect and develop their personalities somehow, and what I wanted to show in this book was how little even all those horrible events could alter human personality. If the person is not ready to be broken down he would never be broken down by any means. The KGB even tried drugs but they didn't work. It was a myth that they could give you drugs and you would unfold all the secrets, you wouldn't be able to stop talking. Alright they gave such drugs to one of my friends, a dissident. He was taken to the hospital and said he couldn't stop talking. He talked all the time but it was up to him whether to reply or not. What I wanted to show was this miracle of human survival.

Only one out of eight in Odessa survived through the period I describe. People used to beg, young girls were murdered, people were killed in all manner of ways but some people did survive and they remembered. They were very special people. They wouldn't be shocked by anything. They would never forgive betrayal. They were in a way very straightforward, never thinking about their belongings except books sometimes. They had a very philosophical approach to life and very strong ideas about good manners. I don't know why. People would have difficulty dealing with them. Normal people could hardly communicate with them because the demands on themselves were reflected in their demands to others. But this is the generation I am fond of.

Bigsby: And what does freedom mean to you now?

Ratushinskaya: Freedom, for me, always meant something which you would give up only for a very important thing. Freedom is the opportunity to lose one's freedom but according to one's own choice. If I am a Christian that means I give up much of my freedom and accept restrictions and obligations, some of them hard. Those who have children know where their freedom goes when the little darlings are born. Those who are married know where their freedom goes with family life. Freedom is just the open opportunity. I wouldn't idolise freedom simply because if you have such a thing and never use it, you don't need it.

In Conversation With
Salman Rushdie

- 24th October 2005 -

Salman Rushdie was born in what was then Bombay in 1947. He studied history at King's College, Cambridge. He published his first novel, *Grimus*, in 1975 but it was his second that established his reputation. *Midnight's Children* (1981) won the Booker Prize. It was his 1988 book *The Satanic Verses*, however, which changed his life as a fatwa was declared which necessitated his going into hiding for some years. Subsequent books include *Haroun and the Sea of Stories* (1990), *The Moor's Last Sigh* (1995), *The Ground Beneath Her Feet* (1999), *Shalimar the Clown* (2005) and *Luka and the Fire of Life* (2010). In 2007 he was knighted for services to literature.

Bigsby: I have always thought of you as a comic writer. Am I wrong to think that?

Rushdie: I have always thought so. It is one of the things that I think people forget to say about these books, because there is a very strong comic strain, sometimes black comedy. I think one of the things that people didn't say very much about *The Satanic Verses* is that quite a lot of it was comic in its manner. It made me feel that comedy is what gets up people's noses further than anything else. Maybe if the book hadn't been so funny I would have been all right. I think the battle was between people who had a sense of humour and people who didn't. It is not only comic. There is a point in this book where it becomes very tragic, but I think until that point it is quite funny.

Bigsby: The other thing that strikes me, especially when I hear you read your work, is its rhythmic quality. Do you read aloud when you are writing? You were once an actor. Does that inform your work?

Rushdie: It is very kind of you to say that I was once an actor. I was once a person who did some acting. I think the questions of rhythm and pace are very important. I don't know if I read it aloud that much but I imagine it being read. I sit there going through it in my head for the rhythm because sometimes whether a particular bit of the story is told quickly or slowly can affect the way it is experienced by the reader.

I have often been fond of fooling around with the pace at which a story is told, which is something I learned from a short story by the great German novelist Heinrich von Kleist, who wrote a short story called *The Earthquake in Chile*. The story is four or five pages long. It has the most extraordinary amount of plot, a quite ludicrous amount of plot, and as a result the story hurtles along as if it was a speeded-up film. Every single thing that happened in the story was absolutely horrible. There is an earthquake and there is mayhem and calamity, and then there is more mayhem and more calamity. It is told at such an amazing break-neck pace that it becomes funny and you find yourself giggling at this hideous, atrocious sequence of events. Yet somehow it also fails to lose that note of atrocity underneath. I thought this really interesting. All he is doing is telling the story too fast. If he told exactly the same story in a hundred pages instead of five it would not have that comic note in it. There would only be the atrocity. So at that point I began to think that this was something to play with, the pace of the story. Sometimes accelerate it, sometimes slow it down, sometimes tell it in what seems to be the naturalistically correct pace, other times fool with the tempo. So I have always been interested in that.

Bigsby: Your new book, *Shalimar the Clown*, also packs a great deal in, though not in four or five pages.

Rushdie: *Shalimar the Clown* starts off as a murder story which reveals itself to be a love story which turns into a story of the betrayal of love which turns into a story of revenge which turns into a story of hatred which turns into a murder story. At the end I think it is in some danger of turning back into a love story. At the heart of it is the story of a place. It is the story of Kashmir, a place of great physical beauty but also a place where the closest thing to a harmonious culture that one can imagine was created and then, in recent times, destroyed. What happened in Kashmir was that the people were caught between the rock of India and the hard place of Pakistan, two countries which have fought over it with relatively little concern for what the people of Kashmir wanted. What they have said rather consistently, for almost sixty years now, is would you both please fuck off, but that is the option that nobody considers.

The love story takes place against that background. It is a story about two young people who are both members of a village troupe of travelling players. There is an old tradition of folk theatre in Kashmir going back hundreds of years. The Kashmiri word for these players literally translates as clown, hence Shalimar the Clown, although in fact they are by no means only clowns. They are not just actors. They are also gymnasts and tightrope walkers and magicians and singers and dancers. It is clearly a dying, or nearly dead, form these days. Shalimar the Clown is a clown on the tightrope, on the high wire, and he falls in love with the village troupe dancing girl who is called Boonyi. That goes well for a while, even though he is from a Muslim family and she is from a Hindu. Unlike Romeo and Juliet, the families think it is fine, but she begins to have second thoughts about it. So the problem doesn't derive from the Montagues and Capulets but, so to speak, from Juliet who eventually makes the bad or rash move of running off with the American Ambassador. That unleashes the revenge tragedy which is the heart of the book.

Bigsby: As you first describe it, Kashmir is a kind of paradise, and that was the Kashmir you knew, or you heard of, when you were growing up. In a sense, then, you are returning not only to Kashmir but to your own youth?

Rushdie : Yes, it is true. My family originally came from Kashmir but had left before I was born. My grandparents moved south into India and settled, but it was made very clear to us, as we were growing up, that that was where we were from. If you ask Indians where they are from they will tell you about the region before they tell you about the country. They will say they are Bengalis before they say that they are Indian. They will say that they are Kashmiris before they say they are anything else. The region, and regionality, are very, very important. We were certainly brought up to think that that is who we were. We were Kashmiri people who were living, in my case, in Bombay and we would go to Kashmir as children every summer because Kashmir was India's playground. It is where Indians went on holiday in the hot season to see such magic realist things as snow and to experience such magic realist things as cold. So, for me, it was this enchanted childhood space. But when I went on going there as a grown up I slowly watched its ruin. Now it is in very bad shape.

Bigsby: There are, as you say, all kinds of pressures that are tearing Kashmir apart, most especially the tension between India and Pakistan both of which lay claim to it?

Rushdie: Yes. When the partition took place between India and Pakistan it was based around the Punjab, in the west, and Bengal, in the east.

States which had frontiers in common with those areas were allowed to choose which way they wanted to go. The problem of Kashmir was that it had a largely Muslim population with a Hindu ruler and there were only five million people, not a lot. It looks quite big on the map but almost all of it is mountains and impassable. The Hindu ruler completely panicked at the independence of India and would not make up his mind. He dithered in the most spectacular way. In the end the Pakistanis tried to force his hand by sending over the border irregular forces, not in uniform, tribal warriors probably containing large numbers of Pakistani army soldiers in plain clothes. This irregular army came across the border to invade Kashmir and the Maharajah reacted, as Maharajahs will, by running away. He left behind this difficult situation.

The Kashmiri political leaders of the time turned to the Indian army and asked it to come in to defend them against these marauding tribe. That took place in 1947, the first battle for Kashmir. As a result Pakistan got hold of essentially the northern one third of the province and India held on to the southern two thirds of the province, including the main valley of Kashmir. Thus was created this thing which was in those days called the Ceasefire Line and is now called the Line of Control. So you have this partition valley. Ever since then you have these huge armies staring at each other across this Ceasefire Line.

There have been two further wars fought over it. Now both India and Pakistan are nuclear powers. The last Kashmir dispute came very close to a nuclear exchange and yet the rest of the world doesn't give a damn. Then it was further complicated, in the last fifteen years, by the arrival, in the Pakistan section, of Jihadist terror groups tolerated by, and in some cases set up and trained by, the Pakistanis in Al-Qaeda training camps. The Pakistani General responsible for this was President Musharraf. So that complicates it. Now you have terrorists coming across the border for whom Kashmiris are not Muslim enough and who get beaten up a lot so that they can be more Muslim than they are in the habit of being. So there you are: terrorists from Pakistan and the oppression of the Indian army, which came to protect but has stayed to harass and occupy and terrify people. It is a mess.

Bigsby: Despite the centrality of Kashmir it seems a story of paradise lost, of lost innocence, on a much broader scale.

Rushdie: Yes. Kashmir is Kashmir but it also plays a metaphorical role in the story. I do think we live in an age beyond innocence. It is hard to have a wide-eyed view of the world as beautiful. Those things that we thought were beautiful in the world have in many senses been despoiled, and I am not just talking about places but also ideas. It is very difficult, therefore, not to write about this moment in the history of the world as a tragedy. It feels like a tragedy. But my inclination being what it is, I try and disguise the tragedy as a comedy and that works for most of the book, but then there is a moment when the tragedy bursts out of the comedy because it is as if the story is saying to you, 'Okay, it is not funny any more,' because you get to a point which is beyond comedy and I hope that what that does is to increase the shock of that moment. If you have been living in a world which might be full of horrible things but they are described to you as black comedy, then that is palatable in a certain way, but if at a certain point the smile is wiped off your face it becomes slightly stark. I hope that that increases the shock at what happened.

Bigsby: Yes, as it does for *Shalimar the Clown* who begins as an innocent, as a performer, and ends up as a murderer, or, indeed, your American ambassador who starts fighting against fascism and turns into something quite different.

Rushdie: I am always interested in characters who change a lot. I have always been attracted to write about characters who don't stay the same all their lives but who shift. I think it is partly because what we know about human personality these days, as opposed to what Jane Austen knew or what Dickens knew, is that human personality is not homogeneous. It is actually very mutable. Even without anything awful happening to us we are very different in very different circumstances. We can be very different when we are young to how we are when we are old. We can be different with our loved ones to the way we are with our fellow workers. We can be different with people of our own race than we are with people of another race. We are a shifting bunch of responses and selves, some of which contradict each other. So it has always interested me to explore that. How much can a personality shift?

In the case of Shalimar the Clown, who starts out as this rather sweet boy about whom people say that he wouldn't hurt a fly, that change is obviously very great and it became a challenge to show that that was possible, that in a single human life it is truthful to say that such a change can take place. I remembered, when I was writing the book, that years ago I had met the film maker Bernardo Bertolucci the day before he was flying to China to make what became *The Last Emperor*. I asked him what the movie was about and he said it is about this boy who is told he is

God. He is not told that he is like God or God's representative, he is told he is God and he is brought up believing himself to be God. But at the other end of his life he works as a gardener in the palace in which he was formerly God and he says that he is happy and content with the change. And what Bertolucci said was that he was interested in whether a human being could change that much. Was that brainwashing or was it a genuine shift in consciousness? And I remember thinking that that was a really interesting subject. In some ways that is not the film he made, because it got taken over by more epic dimensions, but I thought that that psychological subject was fascinating.

Bigsby: In the case of Shalimar it is not ideology that changes him, it is a sexual betrayal.

Rushdie: It is a sexual betrayal, but it is also to do with honour. Yes, I think the thing that triggers it is, as I said, the fact that his wife breaks his heart by running away with this man of great power and charisma. Everybody, except she, can tell that it is going to end in tears, and so it does, but before it does it doesn't just break his heart. It damages him in, if you like, his manhood. There is a scene in the novel which I think of as one of the key scenes. After she has gone off he meets his mother on a village pathway and bursts into this tirade about how she is lucky she is not a man because a man has to suffer this, and has to put up with that, has to respond to this or his honour is destroyed. A man must do this and cannot do that. It is as if he is trying to put back together his sense of himself, his un-emasculated sense of himself as a man, and I think it is something to do with that, not just with the fact that she runs off. It is something to do with that honour issue that makes him pick up the gun. But it is not ideology, you are right.

Bigsby: And there is a connection between the personal and the public. In fact they are not quite opposite. They bleed into one another.

Rushdie: Yes. Those of us who are old enough to remember the sixties have always known this, that there is no frontier line between the personal and the political. I think nowadays less than ever. Jane Austen could write about the private lives of her people without needing to refer to the public stage. Now I think that gap is so small, and the public world impinges on our private life so often and so directly and in so many ways, that for a novelist it is hard to leave it out. It is not because one wants to write political novels, but because it is a part of the explanation of what happens to people in their lives and it seems to me a wrong decision to ignore that. It doesn't even have to be violence or terrorism. If, let's say, you live in a country with a weak economy and some currency speculator attacks the currency and the currency collapses, you may very well, as a consequence of that, lose your job because your firm collapses and you are fired. The thing that has made that happen is an action by a person whose name you don't know performing that action in a room whose existence you are unaware off, and yet it changes your life. This has great implications for the idea of character being destiny, and probably at the root of the novel is the idea that character is destiny.

At the very foundation of the novel as a form is the idea that people determine the things that happen to them and the life they lead. And now it seems to me there are many ways, very dramatic ways, in which that is not true. To an extent it was always not true. There were always wars and accidents, and so on, but sometimes character can be shaped by destiny rather than the other way around. But that question – the question of the relationship between the individual and history, the question of the individual and the society in which he lives, which is after all an old novelistic question – seems to me has an extra edge right now because of the world we live in.

Bigsby: That came home to me very powerfully in the book. You used the word frontier before. This novel moves from France to Kashmir to Los Angeles. It moves in time, and as it does all those frontiers dissolve in some way. You can't stand outside this system and be disconnected from it and, as you say, that in turn raises the question of whether we are the victims of history or whether we are the motor force of history.

Rushdie: Saleem, in *Midnight's Children*, asks himself this question about whether we are masters or victims of our time and I guess I have been worrying away at it ever since. I now think that this question of interconnectedness is again a new thing. Human history hasn't in the past been quite as interconnected as for various reasons it now is. The subject of the shrinking planet is not one that I invented. It is partly because of economic globalisation, partly because of mass migration, partly because of new information technologies, partly because of things like globalised terrorism. We suddenly live in a world in which one bit of it smashes into another all the time. In our cities we see the stories of many other parts of the world jostling with each other. The realistic novel is the novel which tries to take into account this interconnectedness and to understand what it means to live in such a world. Alsace is in the novel partly because Max, the American ambassador, comes from there, but also because in a strange way it balances Kashmir. Alsace, in a way, is Europe's Kashmir, another place where people have fought over a frontier and where France and Germany have battled backwards and forwards, most recently and tragically in the Nazi period.

Bigsby: And why did you give Max the name he has?

Rushdie: My view is that very few people remembered the name of Max Ophüls, the film maker, until I used him as the name of the character. I think I have done him an enormous favour, but actually I am slightly irritated with myself that I did it because now I am having to explain it a lot. The truthful reason is that I wasn't planning to call him that but I wanted a Franco-German-Jewish name because of his background and I remember writing down in my notebook something like Max Ophüls. Then every time I tried to change the name the character would not accept it, didn't like it, and insisted on being Max Ophuls. So, in the end, I thought okay, people are called all kinds of things and there is going to have to be another Max Ophuls. Then I went through a whole process of self-justification and I had many, many, justifications. For example, Max Ophüls, the film director, wasn't called Max Ophüls. It wasn't his name. That was a name he took. He was really called Max Oppenheimer, and I thought if he had used that as a stage name I could pinch it back. Then I thought, this is a novel about the betrayal of love and one of the film-makers greatest films is *Lola Montez*, which is a film about the betrayal of love. So that is another reason. Then I thought this is a novel in which everybody is miserable about their name. All the characters hate their names for various reasons. It is a kind of running gag in the book. Everybody wants to change their name except Max who is perfectly happy with his though it is not his name. Then Max, in the Resistance, is a forger, forging identities to help people escape the Nazis. The fact that he himself has stolen a name from somebody else seemed not inappropriate, so it just went on and on like this.

Actually, the clincher for me was remembering that in my young days in advertising I had once met a man who was a PR man for a mattress company whose name was William Shakespeare, and he was very proud of it and fierce about it. He would answer the phone, through gritted teeth I suspect, and say, 'Hello, William Shakespeare here.' He didn't call himself Bill Shakespeare or Billy Shakespeare, he called himself William Shakespeare, and I thought if there can be two William Shakespeares, that's it. None of those are the reason. The reason is that the name got stuck and I couldn't change it.

Bigsby: How do you respond to those critics who have called *Shalimar the Clown* a return to form?

Rushdie: You can imagine how I feel about that. It is very odd to me this business of giving retrospective bad reviews to previous books, books that were perfectly well reviewed at the time. *The Ground Beneath Her Feet*, for instance, was a book which got, I would say, ninety per cent terrific reviews and now in many of the newspapers where it was highly praised people say that it was a terrible novel. Excuse me for not agreeing. In the case of *Fury*, people really seemed to not go for it, in the critical fraternity at least, but that is not my experience amongst ordinary readers as I travel around lecturing and reading. I very often get people coming up to me, particularly younger readers, saying that they think it is one of the absolute favourite books of mine that they have read. I also find that it is enormously well liked amongst other writers, even writers I don't particularly know, like Joyce Carol Oates. It seems to be very well liked in the academy. People studying my work seem to have a good regard for it. So it seems to me that of the various categories that there are of people who read books, ordinary readers, academics, other writers and book critics, it seems to be just one out of four that don't like it. That is aright.

I never thought that I lost form particularly. On the other hand it felt very unusual writing this book, to tell you the truth. When I wrote it I did things I had never done. I showed people the book while I was writing it, which I have never done before. The reason I had never done it before is that I have always been very insecure to show unfinished work because I have felt that work in progress is very, very, fragile, that if people just say slightly the wrong thing it can really knock you for six and it can be difficult to regain your sense of what you are doing. So I have always hugged it to myself until I felt that it was more or less done. This time I felt able to show the book, a hundred pages at a time, to four or five friends and publishers. I don't know why I did it. I just did it because this time I didn't mind doing it and I think it might have been because I felt okay about it. I felt that there was something that was quite solid there and I wasn't scared that I was going to be deflected from my work by people not liking it. In fact people did like it, so I do think there was something unusual in the writing of this book. I can't really pin it down better than that.

I don't myself give my books marks out of ten so I don't have a view about which of my books is better. I know that the writing process of this one felt unusually safe. It felt as if there were these four characters at the heart of the book that were strong and solid and that if I just paid attention to them properly the book would write itself. So I don't know what that means, whether that means it is a return to form or a better book or what, but I did feel unusually on safe ground writing it.

But there is no accounting for people's responses. It reminds me of one of the very first encounters with audiences I ever had, which was in New Delhi, at the university, just after *Midnight's Children* came out. There was a young woman reader, extremely beautiful I may say, who put up her hand, and so I immediately chose her. She said, 'You see, Mr. Rushdie, your novel, *Midnight's Children*, is very long. Does it have a point?' I said, 'Does it have to have just one point?' And she said, 'Well, fundamentally, yes.' I opened my mouth to answer and she said, 'I know what you are going to say. You are going to say the whole novel from the first page to the last page, that's your point.' I said, 'Actually, yes, something like that.' She said, 'Well it won't do.'

So what can I say? What was fundamentally my point? One of the points is the question of the relationship between history and memory. When I started writing the book I probably had a more Proustian idea of what I was doing, which I later abandoned, because I had this desire to go beyond memory in search of lost time, to try and bring the past back as if it had not gone away, which is the project of Proust. At a certain point, though, I came to think that that really wasn't what I was interested in and that actually the distorting power of memory and its relationship to the facts was much more interesting because the truth is that when we remember our lives we all remember them incorrectly. That difference between memory and event fades away, particularly in private life when other people are not there. The way we remember our parents, after they are dead, is just something that lives in our minds. We may be wrong about the way we remember them but that is what we have. And so I began to think a lot about that.

The novel is not an objective history. *Midnight's Children* is about somebody remembering his life and the events that happen in his life. In some cases there are some quite deliberate errors of memory which he clings to. I remember, for instance, when I was planning the book I was thinking about the period in the sixties when India went to war with China briefly, and I remember thinking how frightened everybody had been when the Chinese army defeated the Indian army on the high Himalayan slopes. I remembered people talking about the probability of China invading north India and capturing Delhi and how we would all be in the new Chinese empire. I remember people saying that they had better go and get Teach Yourself Chinese books because you would need them soon. I remembered all this stuff. Then, when I was talking to my parents about it, my mother said, 'I don't know what you are talking about because you weren't here.' I said, 'What do you mean I wasn't here?' And she said, 'No, you were at boarding school in England when this happened.' We looked at all the dates and she was quite right. It was school term and I was in Warwickshire, not in Bombay, and yet in spite of the fact that it was proved to me beyond any doubt that I had not been in India at the time my memory refused to give up the truth of what it had remembered.

I thought this was an interesting thing, that when we are faced with the choice between memory and fact we always prefer memory and I thought therefore that would become the policy of the book, that Saleem would tell his story as he remembered it and where his memory differed from the objective facts of the time, he would say, 'To hell with that' and prefer his memory. So it became a novel about the battle between memory and fact. In some places in the book that took on a political dimension because, of course, one of the things that has happened in India, as elsewhere, is that people of power tried to falsify the record and memory can then sometimes become a witness. To give just one example, in the struggle for Bangladesh the Pakistan army committed terrible atrocities. There was genocide, there was mass killing of intellectuals, for example, trades union offices set on fire with people inside etc. There was a whole list of atrocities. I am not merely making them up. They were a matter of record at the time. There is photographic evidence of this, reportage, eye witnesses, etc. and yet ever since then, 1971, the official Pakistan line has been to deny that any of this ever happened and that it is an Indian conspiracy to say that it did. Then you find yourself in a position where you confront this with what you remember as having happened. What you are doing is setting your memory up against a version of history, against official history. That is one of the things I was trying to do. It was one of my "points."

In Conversation With
Nawal El Saadawi

- 16th October 2007 -

Nawal El Saadawi was born in the village of Kafr Tahla in Egypt. She graduated as a doctor from Cairo University in 1955. When in 1972 she published *Woman and Sex* she was dismissed from her post at the Ministry of Health. In 1981 she was imprisoned and wrote *Memoirs from the Women's Prison* (1983). Her books include *The Hidden Face of Eve: Women in the Arab World* (in translation, 1980), *The Fall of the Imam* (1988), *Walking Through Fire: A Life of Nawal el Saadawi* (2002).

Bigsby: You were born in 1931 in a small village.

Saadawi: I was born in a village in the middle of the Nile Delta. It was a very fertile place, a lovely village.

Bigsby: Your parents were fairly poor.

Saadawi: My parents were not at all rich. I came from two classes, the very poor peasant class of my father and the upper bourgeois snobbish class of my mother. I was brought up between two classes and so was really class conscious because of that. My father's mother was a peasant. She worked in the fields with no shoes. Her hand was like the hand of a man because of working and digging, but she was a great personality to me. She shaped my character, my peasant grandmother. But my mother's mother had Turkish blood. She was very white, very fair, very domesticated, very submissive, like many upper class women, and I was very, very aware of that.

Bigsby: How central to your life was your father?

Saadawi: Both my mother and father were very important. My mother felt that the wife has a lower status than the husband. We live in one world, dominated by the same system, the capitalist system in which women are inferior to men in all families, in all religions, in all countries.

Bigsby: You say that but it was especially true in Egypt at that time, surely? I remember you once said that you felt an exile from the moment of your birth and by that I think you meant you had the misfortune to be born a girl in a society in which that was inherently an inferior thing to be?

Saadawi: Yes, like all women in all societies, because there is a tendency now to portray women in Egypt or in the Arab countries as oppressed. We are oppressed but in a different way. For instance, my name is Nawal el Saadawi. That is my father's name. In Egypt we never carry the husband's name. I married three husbands, in fact. I had to divorce two husbands because they didn't like my writing, so I had to leave them. If I carried the name of my husband, as here in Britain or the US, I would have three names. So this is a positive element in our culture, and this came from the ancient Egyptian civilisation, with its female goddess. So we inherited the power and dignity of women from ancient Egyptians and that is why we carry the name of the father. It is still patriarchal but it is better than carrying the name of the husband, much better.

Bigsby: I am interested in the fact that you are so resistant when I talk about the position of women in Egyptian society at that time, or perhaps I should have said Islamic society at that time, because this is a point that you yourself make in your own books. You have written that you discovered very early on that there was a difference between the way you were treated and the way your brother was treated, and under Islam there is a distinction between the role of women and the role of men?

Saadawi: As there is in Christianity and Judaism, because I spent ten years of my life comparing Judaism to Christianity, comparing the Old Testament and the New Testament to the Koran. They are similar in relation to the oppression of women. To be fair, women in Britain or in the United States are freer now, a little bit freer, especially in their personal and sexual lives. Virginity, though, is still respected in our region, in our countries, but not respected here. This has nothing to do with Islam but what happened was that our political, economic and social development was stunted, obstructed by colonialism, British colonialism. Egypt became a cotton farm for the British. Our resources were exploited. Now we have become an American colony. We are becoming more and more poor. Sixty per cent of the people in Egypt are below the poverty line because of American and European colonialism.

Virginity in Britain lost its value because of the industrial revolution. Women had to go out to work so that the capitalist system didn't care much about virginity. They wanted women to be a commodity, working in the factory, or a sexual commodity. They didn't care about virginity but in the feudal society, in the society that did not develop normally because of colonialism, religion did not develop. It is a political, economic, social matter, rather than religious.

Bigsby: When you were about five or six you were subjected to what was I suppose a physical assault, and this became a cause of yours later: clitoridectomy Can you recall what that was like?

Saadawi: I am against cutting any part of children. I am against male circumcision because in many societies, even in the United States, they sometimes circumcise boys. I am a medical doctor and we have to respect the human body, especially in childhood. The child is helpless so we cannot do that. But I am also against psychological clitoridectomy. Sigmund Freud cut the clitoris of women psychologically when he said that a mature sane woman should have only vaginal orgasm and not clitoral orgasm. So he cut the clitoris psychologically, which is sometimes more dangerous than cutting it physically.

Some people say that women in Islamic countries, or in Egypt, are veiled, but make-up is a veil. I call it the postmodern veil because it hides the real face of the woman. So, what is the difference between hiding my face with a piece of cloth or hiding my face with powder and colour? It makes no difference. That is why I say women are oppressed by the capitalist, patriarchal system. They are all veiled; they are all circumcised, either psychologically, educationally or physically. When we feel that men are much better than women, and when we marry and take the name of our husbands and our husbands do not take our name, this is discrimination, this is educational circumcision. So I like to broaden the discussion, because wherever I go Islam has now become the enemy.

After the collapse of the Soviet Union and communism, capitalism needed a new enemy, so Islam has become the new enemy. Now everybody says, 'Oh women are oppressed because of Islam.' This is not true at all, and we have to correct this. The struggle is political and economic. We are now living in a neo-colonial period, not the post-colonial, and Egypt is now suffering more than under British colonialism from a subtle globalisation, a subtle post-modern globalisation and neo-colonialism.

Bigsby: On the subject of colonialism, your father was a part of rebellion against the British, was he not?

Saadawi: Yes, and he suffered. My father was a rebel and I inherited this from him, and from my mother and my grandmother, my peasant grandmother. She was a rebel. Her husband died when she was young. He had oppressed her so after he died she flourished. I notice that many women flourish after the death of their husband. She now had the freedom to be active politically, so she left the village.

Bigsby: Your father was an enlightened man and believed that women should be educated, you in particular. How usual was it for a girl at that time to go on to medical school in Egypt?

Saadawi: Not at all. They tried to marry me off when I was ten years old. Most of the girls in both my father's family and my mother's family were married before they were fifteen. When a girl was seventeen or eighteen they called her an old maid, so it was normal that when I was ten, and was tall and developing very rapidly, they brought men to marry me. I developed various tricks to frighten them, so that a man would come only once and then disappear.

Bigsby: You eventually went to university and studied to be a doctor. By the nature of things, part of your training required you to look at cadavers, at naked dead men, and this despite the fact that when you married you never undressed in front of your husband. Sex, in other words, was a fraught world.

Saadawi: Yes, my mother too, or we would do it in the dark, when it was very dark. I can't say this is universal, but it is very prevalent. People were ashamed of sex. Sex is also a taboo in Christianity which is why the virgin Mary should be a virgin, should not be a wife or a mother, because of the negative connotations of sexuality. People are ashamed of their bodies, of their sex, everywhere, but as I said because the development in Egypt was slow we stayed with the shame for a long time.

Bigsby: So it must have been odd, to say the least, that in training to be a doctor you were suddenly confronted with naked male bodies and for men, who had been taught that women should cover themselves, to suddenly be confronted with female ones. Did you feel any sense of embarrassment?

Saadawi: No, I was not embarrassed at all but I remember when I was in the final year in medical college, and we were making rounds in the hospital, there was a boy patient who was supposed to be naked in front of us. The boy came from a village and he was ashamed to undress in front of us, especially girls and students. He was reluctant, almost refusing to obey the professor, so the professor slapped him on the face and the boy submitted and took off his clothes. I was very much offended. I hated the medical profession for that. I felt that the medical profession was very inhuman and fails to see patients as people. Even now I don't go to doctors because they are very inhuman, even to colleagues. What about that poor boy?

Bigsby: Once you had qualified as a doctor and went out to practice what did you learn about the society you were moving in?

Saadawi: I learnt a lot, though I hated the profession and wanted to be a dancer. I wanted to be a dancer when I was a child but this was a taboo. I loved music. I wanted to play the piano but then this also was a taboo. It was my parents who wanted me to be a doctor, a lawyer or something very serious, but I loved writing so I combined writing and medicine. I never regret having gone into the medical profession because it opened my mind to reality – death, disease, suffering, inhumanity, poverty, especially poverty. I specialised as a chest surgeon at the beginning, working with poor people who had tuberculosis. Many of the patients who were under my supervision didn't complete their treatment because they had to go to work in order to feed their families. I started to make a link between poverty and disease and that sent me to politics and economics and this was dangerous because if I had stayed only as a medical doctor I could have been a very rich person, like my colleagues, and never gone to prison and never had any problems, but simply to link health to politics, to poverty, to economics, to colonialism, to history, to religion, made me dangerous because then I was exposing the system. So they had to fight against me.

Bigsby: Didn't you get into trouble for drawing attention to the prevalence of bilharzia at one stage? How did that come about? Why would you get into trouble for that?

Saadawi: Because the government is not interested in the people, not in Britain, not in the United States, not in Egypt. There is a contradiction between the interests of the government and the interests of the people. So you feel that you cannot be silent.

Bigsby: But bilharzia is a medical condition.

Saadawi: But it is very much related to poverty. Every disease is related to political, economic and social conditions, even neuroses, psychosomatic diseases. I became a psychiatrist after that. You cannot separate the body from the mind, the spirit from society. That is very important because medical doctors don't study sociology or politics. Medical doctors deal with the patient as an isolated phenomenon, as an organ separate from society. They split the organism into heart, spleen, intestine, lungs, the nervous system, so they lose a holistic vision of that human being. And bilharzia is like that. Rich people do not have it. In Egypt most of the peasants do because they are working in the field and the water and because they have low resistance and suffer from exhaustion. We do not become diseased because we are strong. We have an immune system. That is why we do not have tuberculosis. But the minute we lose our immune system we become sick. When we do not eat well, when we do not sleep well, when we are exhausted, when we are sad, when we are depressed, when we are oppressed by religion, like women for instance, we become ill. I notice that many women develop not only psychological but physical diseases in addition to depression because of religious education and how they are afraid of God or hellfire or something. So you cannot separate it.

Bigsby: You graduated in 1955. The following year, 1956, Britain, Israel and France conspired to invade the Canal Zone following Abdul Nasser's nationalisation of the Suez Canal. What did you do in 1956?

Saadawi: I volunteered to fight. I took off my white coat, my doctor's coat, and I became a guerrilla fighter. I was trained to shoot and to kill. The whole health unit was transformed into a military camp and we were trained to fight the British. This was not terrorism. I say this because when people in Palestine fight against the Israeli occupation they are called terrorists. The resistance in Iraq, fighting against the American invasion, are called terrorists. They don't call George Bush, who invaded them and killed them for the oil, a terrorist. So the whole world is upside down. There is something wrong with this world in that people who are killers are forgiven just because they have power. The International

Criminal Court never punished any of the big leaders in the world, but they punished minor dictators in Africa or Asia or Latin America. When I was a young doctor I was enthusiastic and because I was very aware that health cannot be separated from economics or politics, I felt that fighting was part of my work as a doctor.

Bigsby: Your writing is partly polemical, partly autobiographical, but you also write short stories, plays, novels. You started writing very young.

Saadawi: Yes, thirteen years of age.

Bigsby: What were you writing then?

Saadawi: When I was thirteen I was in high school. The teacher in the composition lesson told us to write a story from our imagination. So I was happy because I was living in the imagination all the time. I went home and wrote a story based on my life, but I disguised myself. The teacher took the story – it was maybe thirty, forty, fifty pages long – and after two weeks he brought back all the stories. Some girls he gave an A but he gave me zero and in red ink he wrote, 'This girl is eccentric. She needs a lot of education in religion.' I was scared. I was thirteen years of age and he was ruining me. So I took this story home and hid it in my drawer. I stopped writing, though I loved writing. I felt I was no good at writing. I had no talent. One day, when I was in school, my mother was cleaning my room and found the story. She read it and when I came back she told me, 'Oh, you wrote a beautiful story. This teacher is stupid.' My mother saved me. I am a writer because of my mother. She saved me from the opinion of the teacher who was very traditional and narrow-minded and this story was not published until maybe thirty years after that. I published it because I kept it and for me it is precious because it is the first story I wrote in my life.

Bigsby: Eventually, Nasser made way for Anwar Sadat and it was under him that you were sent to prison. Why was that?

Saadawi: Because I believed him. He came to Egypt and he said Nasser was a dictator and now we have democracy and freedom, and I believed him. I was naïve and landed in prison because I started criticising him. I wrote two articles in one of the opposition newspapers in Cairo that were established under Sadat. I criticised him and when I went to prison the General Prosecutor interrogated me because of those articles.

Bigsby: There are lots of things that interest me about your time in prison, but one is your determination to write. How did you manage to keep this secret from the guards who were told to be careful in case you did write?

Saadawi: There were twelve women in our cell from different parts of the political spectrum, from the extreme right Muslim fundamentalist women to the extreme Marxist left. I was in the middle, the independent writer. Every day the jailer came to me and said that if they found paper and pen in my cell it would be more dangerous than if they found a gun. So I decided to have paper and pen that day.

Our cell was very near the prostitutes' cell and one of the prostitutes helped the jailer clean the cell and bring us bread. Some of the prostitutes had read my work. They were young women and were educated. So I told this one that I needed paper and a pen by any means. We were not allowed toilet paper in our political cell but the prostitutes were because nobody feared the prostitutes politically. So they could write because nobody feared them. The next day she brought me a whole roll of toilet paper and her eyebrow pencil. For three months, every night after the jailer had gone away, I sat on something very uncomfortable and wrote with this little pen on toilet paper which tore when I pressed the pen hard, but if I didn't press the letters were not visible. So I had to be careful and I wrote the whole book. I didn't feel the prison because I was writing. I felt free because of the pleasure of creativity. I was very happy in prison because I was writing and when I write a novel now, and I am not in prison, I imprison myself in my room. So what is the difference?

Bigsby: There seem to be two different kinds of fictional writing you do. One is expressed in very simple language, almost as though you are writing it for people who are not necessarily sophisticated, but *The Fall of the Imam* goes in the other direction. It is extremely lyrical but extraordinarily sophisticated in its structure and its use of language. Do you see two different kinds of writing, one reaching out for a broader public?

Saadawi: It is a matter of mood. When, in prison, I met the woman in *Woman at Point Zero*. I came back home and felt that I had to write about her. She had an effect on me. She haunted me at times and I wanted to get rid of her, so I wrote about her. When I finished the novel I was released from her. When you are a writer you do not think much about who will read you. You think about how you have passion, you have an urge, you have something and you want to get it out, and it comes out in different ways according to your mood. Sometimes I am in a very scientific mood. I am the doctor. I am the psychiatrist. I do not make much of a distinction between fact and fiction as I do not separate the body from the mind and the spirit. They are one. But sometimes I am more oriented to reality, to facts. That is why *Woman at Point Zero* is very simple. It was read by students in primary schools and understood. *The Fall of the Imam* is a very difficult novel and many people didn't like it. They preferred *Woman at Point Zero*. I prefer *The Fall of the Imam* as a writer. It came like a nightmare. It was the effect of Sadat. In fact the central figure in *The Fall of Imam* is Sadat, because he called himself the Imam.

Bigsby: A number of your books were not originally published in Egypt. They had to be published elsewhere. It must have been difficult knowing that you couldn't initially publish the books in your own country and that the criticism would not be literary. It would be religious or political criticism. How difficult was it for you to maintain the idea of yourself as a writer?

Saadawi: It is very frustrating. I can say that not a single novel of mine in Arabic was published complete. Part of *Memoirs of a Woman Doctor* was cut. All my novels were censored. Some were totally censored, completely destroyed. At best they were partially cut, paragraphs that were hinting at some religious or sexual taboo. We have three major taboos, the power of politics, sexual problems and religion. Those are the three main areas we should not touch. But if you do not speak about politics, religion or sex, what are you going to speak about? In fact it is frustrating when the book comes out and it is not what I wrote. They cut the best part of it because the best is really that which touches on politics and taboos. They cut these parts and they changed the titles. For instance, I have a book called *God Dies By The Knife* and even though the publisher was in Beirut, and Beirut is much more liberal than any other country, the publisher changed the title. He told me, 'I cannot put *God Dies By The Knife* for a title in Arabic.' He changed it to *The Death of the Only Man on Earth*. It has something, but it is not *God Dies By the Knife*.

Bigsby: In the early nineties you were under threat and there were guards outside your house. Now you are under threat again in two very strange ways. Firstly, you have been accused of apostasy, and because under Islamic law it is not possible to be married to an apostate there was pressure put on your husband to divorce you. Secondly, you have written a play which is itself now the cause of further problems. You are between two trials at the moment. Are you going to go back to Egypt to live through that trial?

Saadawi: No. All my life I wanted to go back to my country. That is where I struggle, where I am inspired by reality. I cannot write here in London because I don't suffer here. You need some suffering to write. I am also a political activist because this inspires me too. I was very keen to go back to Egypt all the time and I returned all the time but this time I don't think I can go. I am waiting for a verdict because there are many cases against me. They want to withdraw all my books from the market. I have forty-five books in English and Arabic, and five are censored, including the play *God Resigns*. They want to withdraw all my books, even from homes and from the market and to destroy them because they don't want any people in Egypt, any man or woman, to read Nawal el Saadawi. But people do read me, so that is the struggle.

The other case involves an attempt to withdraw my Egyptian nationality, to take my passport so that I will not be able to go back to Egypt. If they take my Egyptian nationality away I cannot go to Egypt, of course, and after that I will be threatened physically because when the courts condemn me this means an open invitation for people to shoot me. So I will not go back. But this is not the problem for me. I don't believe in what they call identity politics, this postmodern identity politics. They ask who are you? Are you African? Are you Muslim? Are you Christian? Are you a Jew? Are you British? I don't believe in that. This is false. This is division. People are divided by nationality, by religion, by gender. You are a woman. You are a man. I am against divisions. We have to undo all divisions.

What is the difference between you and me? My background is Islam, your background is Christianity. So what? You are British. I am Egyptian. We are fighting for justice, freedom, love, equality, beauty and creativity. We are similar, so we need to celebrate our similarities rather than confirm our differences. I feel at home here. When you listen to me I feel at home. So my home is not in Cairo. My home is anywhere there are human beings. So I say the best identity for us is the identity of a human being, so that we can unite and come together.

Even in prison I was very optimistic and told my colleagues that Sadat will die and we will come out. Optimism is very important. Hope is power. Despair kills us. It diminishes your power. So even when you are in prison, or even facing death, when you have hope you struggle much more powerfully and effectively than people who have despair. So I believe in the power of hope. Those who are not active – who do nothing and stay at home and say that everything is black, nothing will change – are pessimists and this is a weakness. I am always active, either writing or travelling or talking or doing something. You have to be active all the time. And you must have a progressive group with you. You cannot fight alone. We need collective power, collective struggle. There are a lot of progressive people everywhere, secular people.

I am very much against a religious state. I am very much against a Jewish state in Israel, or a Christian state anywhere, or an Islamic state anywhere because when you have a religious state it means discrimination between people according to religion. It means racism, it means the inferiority of women. So I am in favour of secular movements. I am in favour of feminist movements, real feminist movements which connect women's issues to political and economic issues at the global and local level. When you are surrounded by, and working with, progressive groups, men and women, then you have hope in the future.

I will tell you something from my experience. Progressive people are greater in number and power than traditional conservative people, but what happens is that the right-wing, the conservatives, have power, economic power, political power, media power. I am censored by the BBC. I am censored by CNN. I cannot speak on Egyptian television, Egyptian radio. So we have power but we do not have the media, we do not have the money. How can we compensate? We must unite, because unity is power and that is why I am against divisions between people. But they divide us under the name of so-called diversity. They divide us under very good names, but I am very hopeful.

We are all born creative. I do not divide people into writers and readers. We are all writers and all readers. We are all creative but we lose our creativity through education systems, through religious education, through fear, through oppression.

Bigsby: How did the BBC censor you?

Saadawi: Many times. The BBC is very subtle. They called and said they would like to record an interview with me but would like to have a chat before we do so. So they chatted with me and the woman didn't like what I said and so didn't tape it. Sometimes they take me to the studio and waste my time. They record an interview and it is never broadcast. This has happened many times with the BBC and with all the media. So there is a very subtle censorship in Europe and in the United States. In Egypt the censorship is crude, but here it is subtle.

Bigsby: You have been nominated for the Nobel Prize several times?

Saadawi: Yes, I was nominated several times, including this year. I will tell you something, though. I am not in favour of the Nobel Prize, or any prize. Those prizes are political. The best writers never had a prize. My main prize is that I write a good book and people read it. The world is prize-minded. I am not dreaming of the Nobel Prize. I am dreaming of finishing this novel before I die.

In Conversation With Jane Smiley

- 6th October 1998 -

Jane Smiley, born in Los Angeles in 1949, was educated at Vassar and the University of Iowa. Her first novel, *Barn Blind* (1980). Other novels include *The Greenlanders* (1988), *A Thousand Acres* (1991), which won a Pulitzer Prize, *Moo* (1995), *Horse Heaven* (2000), *Private Life* (2010). She is also the author of *Thirteen Ways of Looking at the Novel.* For more than fifteen years she taught at Iowa State University.

Bigsby: *The All-True Travels and Adventures of Lidie Newton* is set in the past. What is the pull of history to you as a writer?

Smiley: I think the pull has been specific rather than general. I started it because of the Oklahoma bombing. There were plenty of people writing about survivalists and right wing extremists groups in our own day but what I felt was interesting was that these were not new and that there was a certain strain of resistance to change in American history that had always been fully armed. So that was the pull for this book. And then there was another slightly different one too. I had set out, a long time ago, to write one example each of the four major genres – epic, tragedy, comedy and romance. The one that was least congenial to me was romance, which is why I put it off to the end. But I had read somewhere that all nineteenth century American novels were romances so I thought, well, I can now do my romance and wrote what I think turned out to be an anti-romance, which I define as a narrative in which the protagonist sets out on a journey and sees many wonders, sees many amazing things. Obviously anybody heading into Kansas in 1855 is going to have a romantic journey and see many amazing things.

Bigsby: You said that you set yourself to write one in each of these genres as though that were a perfectly rational and normal thing to do.

That is an incredibly calculated view of a literary career. Why did you set yourself to do that?

Smiley: Probably because I was a graduate student.

Bigsby: You wanted to show off?

Smiley: The first novel I wrote that I was truly, truly, truly engaged in was *The Greenlanders* which is an epic based on an epic European tradition and I think that once I had thought about writing *The Greenlanders*, which happened very early in my career – I conceived of *The Greenlanders* before I had written any other novels – I thought, okay, it will be fun to write an epic and it will be fun to write a tragedy, it will be fun to write a comedy, so I have got to write a romance too. It was great fun. I have always seen my writing career as an opportunity to learn how to write and so I didn't want to write the same thing over and over again because I wouldn't learn how to write anything else. So I guess I wanted to learn how to write all those things.

Bigsby: You said that this book was spurred by an act of violence and that you then went back to a period of violence. What surprised me in reading it was that it wasn't more violent because that was an incredibly violent period. You do have John Brown but he is off stage, and the killings he was involved in were horrible.

Smiley: I guess there are two parts to that question about the level of violence. The level of violence in Kansas in the eighteen fifties seems low to us but it seemed high to them because they came from an extremely civilised world in some ways. Much violence was done to slaves, much violence was done in some parts of cities to the urban working classes, but the average American lived in a world where most people died in childbirth, or of childbirth, or through disease. Lidie sometimes says in this book that she can't believe they aren't shooting each other more because they are talking in such an inflamed way about things. But Kansas was where the barrier was broken, where the veil was rent. People back in the east were quite shocked at what was going on in Kansas. I think the question about John Brown is quite a separate one. The people of Kansas and the people of Lawrence, who are still very deeply committed to their abolitionist roots, have never fully admitted that they knew that John Browne killed the five southerners that he killed. Certainly it is known that Brown's supporters in New York and in New England were prevented from knowing this so that when he went back after killing those people to get more money from them he was able to play upon their ignorance to get their support.

For me the conundrum of the killings has to do with the people around him who knew for sure what had happened, because the rumour mill was very active, but allowed their knowledge to slip into rationalisation and denial very quickly, within days. Then the retribution taken against Brown they picked up on as a way to sustain their loyalty to the abolitionists. But you only had to see him walk down the streets to know what he was capable of. Everybody knew he had these pike things with him, which were the weapons that he killed the slave owners with. So that is what interested me, not so much did he do it or didn't he do it, but who knew about it and what did they say about it? And it is still very quiet. People still don't talk about it much. One of the things I discovered when I was doing my book tour, which began in Missouri and Kansas this spring, was that these issues are pretty much still alive there. The rivalry between the University of Kansas and the University of Missouri is, on the surface, just a football rivalry but really there are still burning hatreds there and that has fascinated me.

Bigsby: That story, the clashes in Kansas and Missouri, the John Brown story, the civil war, Quantrill's raiders, indeed the whole westward movement is conventionally presented as a male story. You have told this through a woman. Did you go back and find that those women's stories were there, available to you, or did you have to construct them?

Smiley: There are many, many memoirs of women settlers in Kansas and so there are lots of primary sources about that. One of the best is by the Governor's own wife, Mrs. Robinson, Sarah Robinson. She published her memoirs as a justification for Governor Robinson's actions before the election of 1856, but there were other women who went out, many of them. Their accounts are quite touching. They went out thinking something good was going to happen but their whole families were wiped out and they ended up in Michigan with nothing. So there are plenty of sources, plenty of women's primary sources, plenty of men's primary sources, especially correspondence from eastern newspapers whose reporters came out to Kansas to see what was going on. The primary source material was coming out of my ears so I did not feel at all hesitant about portraying this as a memoir of Kansas because there is this body of memoirs.

Bigsby: And that raises the question of research and the role it plays with you.

Smiley: I do a lot of research. I get to a point, probably half way into the research, where I feel like I am ready to write. I never quite know when that is going to be. The book I am writing now is about horse racing [*Horse Heaven*]. I was standing in my kitchen, on the 2nd February, though why it was on the 2nd February I don't know, and I pushed the toast down in the toaster and I was looking at the toast and I thought, 'Oh my God, the time has come.' I ran into my office before the toast popped and I started. That is the most distinct the moment has ever been. So I do a certain amount of research and then I start writing the book. Then, if I don't know something I will research it, if I have the books, or I will make it up, if I don't, but I always know where I made it up and whether it needs to be fixed or not because those parts have a little less authenticity even to me than the parts where I really know what is going on.

Bigsby: And do you find it easy to find the right language? I am talking now about the historical novels and especially *The Greenlanders*, where you went back to the fourteenth century.

Smiley: Yes, because the language is so distinct from ours, so it is like walking into a room and closing the door. You are inside the room. You are inside the language. You kind of click it on and you are gone. It takes about fifty pages to work yourself into it but that is an eleven hundred page manuscript and so it is a trek. It is like an actor who has an ear for languages. They work out a few things in their mind and then they put themselves in that space. That is how it has always been to me.

Bigsby: And you found that as easy with this book?

Smiley: Yes. Remember, I was reading a lot of primary source materials so that sets you up, but every book has a different language. The one that was most intimidating for me, but also turned out to be fairly easy, was the comic language when I did *Moo*. I was very afraid I wouldn't be able to have the kind of stylistic precision and lightness that a habitual comic novelist would have.

Bigsby: You didn't list a campus novel as one of those you were going to write but you wrote one.

Smiley: Well, no, that was a comic novel. I thought, I can do this because somehow the rhythm of it, and the ironic tone, spoke back to me and said, yes, this is the groove. It was really fun. Every book is written in an alien language because it is alien to the last book you wrote, at least it is for me. So, beginning any book is a matter of finding the language to write it. The book I am writing now, about horse racing, begins with four breedings, and they had to each be distinct because eight horses breeding isn't inherently very interesting. Actually, it is really interesting, and one of my favourite things to watch, but I consciously gave each breeding separate characteristics. One of the stallions in question is a very vicious one, which some of them are, and he is also a self-abuser, which some of them are. So when I began the horse book, writing about that particular stallion and what causes him to be so vicious, from a lyrical point of view rather than from an objective point of view, that was what got me into the language of that novel. There is always somewhere I can pinpoint where the language clicked.

Bigsby: Has winning the Pulitzer Prize proved an advantage or a burden?

Smiley: I have found it to be a wonderful monetary advantage. As far as other potential disadvantages, there haven't been any because I was firmly embarked upon my work by the time I won it so I was not deflected in any way. Also, when I won it I was four months pregnant so I wasn't really available for that kind of media blitz that could have been a temptation. By the time the child was old enough the media blitz was over.

Bigsby: When you start a novel do you have a set plan or do you find that the novel takes you places you didn't know you were going to go?

Smiley: That has varied from novel to novel. The tightest plan I had was for *A Thousand Acres*, which of course follows *King Lear* very closely, though not scene by scene. So I knew what that plan was and I knew that the trick to getting to the end was more or less figuring the internal logic of the play, which is hard and taxing to do. So I knew what that would involve. Other books have had looser plans. *Duplicate Keys*, which is a murder mystery, had a pretty strict structure. It didn't have a real plot plan but I knew, for example, where I had to start building to the climax, what chapter the climax had to occur in and how many pages it would take. Other books have been looser. I find with the horse racing book I have no idea what is coming. New characters show up all the time.

The horses are always doing things I didn't expect them to do and I think that since it is a comic novel that is essential because the wit is basically improvisation. If you have rehearsed your joke ahead of time it is going to be flat when you tell it the second time. So I sit down every day with the horse racing book just waiting to see what will happen, and it doesn't always come easily. Sometimes I have to go and stand in the shower for a while and then it will come, or take a nap, or something like that. But almost every day with this book I sit back and look at the computer screen and say, wow, where did that one come from, and it has really, really, really been the most fun I have ever had precisely for that reason.

I have always loved sitting down at the computer or the typewriter and going at it. I never had any rituals that enabled me to do it except drinking a cup of tea or diet coke or something. I would say it hasn't been nearly as difficult for me as learning to ride a horse, for example, but maybe the key to that is that very early in my writing career, even in graduate school, I stopped judging my own work and learnt early on that judgement wasn't going to get me anywhere. I had a pattern. It was to overestimate while I was writing it and underestimate it when I was reading it through, and as soon as I realised that was my pattern I didn't pay any attention to myself at all. I just kept on going. I think that for most writers the fear of being judged is the most terrifying fear.

In Conversation With Alexander McCall Smith

- 17th November 2009 -

Alexander McCall Smith was born in Bulawayo in 1948 in what was then Southern Rhodesia. He studied law at Edinburgh University and went on to teach law at Queen's University, Belfast. While there he entered a competition and a children's story won. He then went on to write a succession of such before, in 1998, he published *The No. 1 Ladies' Detective Agency* which marked the beginning of what would swiftly become a highly popular series of books, to be joined by other series – *The Sunday Philosophy Club*, *44 Scotland Street* and *Corduroy Mansions*. For many years he was Professor of Medical Law at Edinburgh University.

Bigsby: To date, *The No. 1 Ladies' Detective Agency*, which began in 1998, has sold twenty million copies and been translated into forty five languages. *44 Scotland Street* has sold a million copies, and yet you used to be a respectable professor. What went wrong?

McCall Smith: Well, I did write in my spare time when I was a professor. I suppose that, as most of us do in this life, I wanted to have my cake and eat it, but I realised that I couldn't. I would have to make a choice so I decided I would devote myself to writing, which is, of course, a naïve decision because you think that you will become a full time writer. In fact you don't. You go around having conversations and spend a lot of time travelling. You spend a lot of time in airports. I am an expert on American airports if you would like to discuss any.

Bigsby: There will be a new book by Alexander McCall Smith every month for the next eleven months. I find that quite breathtaking.

McCall Smith: Four or five of them are paperbacks.

Bigsby: So it is a mere six or seven.

McCall Smith: I find this line of questioning very embarrassing.

Bigsby: Well perhaps that's enough about the present for the moment, so let me take you all the way back. You were born in Africa, in what was then Southern Rhodesia. What were your parents doing there?

McCall Smith: My father was a public prosecutor in Bulawayo, which is where we lived at the tail end of the British Empire. As a boy I remember looking at the atlases in school and they were all coloured in the imperial red, which was the British Empire. Looking at it today, what effrontery, what extraordinary arrogant self-confidence this country must have had to do that, but there it was. So I was born into that.

Bigsby: It was a colonial lifestyle.

McCall Smith: Yes, it was. If you read Somerset Maugham, it was quite like that. We had tea on the lawn. People have tea on the lawn in other countries, but tea on the lawn in those circumstances carried some business with it. In many respects it was an unhappy society, deeply abnormal in one sense. There was something wrong, obviously, but on the other hand there were aspects that weren't so bad.

Bigsby: So you were sitting in the middle of Africa eating British-style food?

McCall Smith: Oh yes. I remember as a boy that we kicked off the day with a breakfast which consisted of porridge and then eggs and bacon and tea. Then lunch would have been soup followed by a main course. Dinner would have been soup followed by roast beef, every day, in the heat.

Bigsby: Your mother had a particular thing about tomato sauce.

McCall Smith: Tomato sauce was a big treat. It was almost contraband in our house because my mother had a theory that excessive consumption of tomato sauce caused, as she put it, juvenile delinquency. Now of course we laugh and say how unsophisticated. We go through life and think that everything our parents said, and particularly, I suppose, everything our mother said was wrong. We believe that into our twenties, and then gradually this awful realisation comes that some of the things that our parents said might be true. Even some of the absolutely outlandish theories that parents had were suddenly demonstrated to be true by research, in this case into behavioural difficulties and diet. Everybody now accepts that if children have too many coloured drinks, or the icing on the cup cakes at the birthday parties is too heavily coloured with e numbers, then they go manic. Our children would come back from parties terrifically high. She also felt that tomato sauce was somehow connected with excessive amorousness.

Bigsby: Did you have much connection with Africans themselves?

McCall Smith: Not as much as we should have. Those societies were abnormal in many respects.

Bigsby: So it was a master/servant relationship?

McCall Smith: Alas, alas, there was a lot of that, and you can look back on that with regret. I regret, for example, that I didn't learn an African language properly. I picked up smatterings. That is a matter of great regret to me. But we are born where we are born. We are born when we are born, and most of us, as we go through life, look back at the world as it was when we were younger and say, what a different place it was. The world changes so quickly. We could look back at Britain ten years ago and say it was in some respects a rather different place. And of course if you look at a photograph of yourself twenty years ago you look back with embarrassment at what you were wearing, or do you say that those bell-bottom trousers were terrific?

Bigsby: How old were you when you went to Britain?

McCall Smith: Eighteen. I spent my entire childhood in Africa.

Bigsby: And was Britain the place you had been led to believe from seeing it from afar?

McCall Smith: Yes, I think so. Those were the days, the late sixties, of Carnaby Street and Swinging Britain, but they rather passed me by. This country had obviously changed a great deal but there was still a Britishness about it. The more you travel, the more you see certain characteristics in your own society that make it what it is. I think this is a very tolerant country and rather fun. I think there is an easy-going feeling to it still, and certain positive British attitudes are still there.

Bigsby: You went to university and spent some time in Italy. Was that just a place to you or did that have some significance?

McCall Smith: I went to Italy as a student. I spent a short-ish time in Siena as a postgraduate student sitting at the feet of a very great Italian professor of the history of law. And of course Siena is a marvellous place to go as a student. It has a magnificent student life and all these trappings of Italian civic identity. I was there in the time of the Palio di Siena, which is this wonderful chaotic horse race where horses are taken into the chapels to be blessed and to have holy water thrown over them. The people marched through the streets with the banners of their particular Contrada fluttering above them. What a wonderful experience it was. I fell head-over-heels in love with Italy, as I think virtually everybody who goes to that part of Italy does. Italy plays such an important part in our romantic imagination and who could be anything but seduced by the country. I still love it and I still go there, not as frequently as in the past, but occasionally. I was a visiting professor in Trento some years back, which I enjoyed, and I am an honorary graduate of the University of Parma.

Bigsby: So while celebrating Britain there are other loyalties to other places that mean something to you?

McCall Smith: I find that I like just about everywhere I go. I don't know whether there is a sort of emotional promiscuity there but I am really very, very taken with so many countries. I love Australia and I am very happy when I am there. I love India. It is curious, but every country I go to I think to myself, I could live here, I really do, and I look at the property columns wherever I go. I was in Alabama in the United States a couple of years ago, in a place called Mobile. It is a wonderful place. It is an undiscovered New Orleans. Everybody goes to New Orleans but in fact they invented Mardi Gras in Mobile. There are these gorgeous oak trees which grow above the street to produce a lovely closed avenue. We went past this beautiful white-painted southern mansion with quite a large yard, with Spanish Moss hanging off the trees, and there was a sign which said "For Sale" so I said, 'Please stop the car. I want out.' They put little boxes in front of these houses with a leaflet so you can go and get particulars of the house. So I nipped out and got one of these and we drove off. It was a wonderful seven-bedroom house which was for sale for three-hundred and eighty-thousand dollars, which at that stage was about one-hundred and ninety-thousand pounds, for which one might get a one bedroom flat in this country. So I was terribly tempted to move to Mobile.

Bigsby: You became a lecturer and you have written a fair number of academic books concerned mainly with medical law. And you haven't entirely given up on that, have you, because you were an adviser to the government at one stage on aspects of biomedicine.

McCall Smith: I was on various committees. I suppose I wouldn't dignify myself by saying that I was a government adviser. Well, I was, technically, but they never listened or, rather, they listened very attentively, but didn't necessarily do what I thought they should do. I was on a government commission for four years, which I enjoyed very much, and then I was on the UNESCO International Bioethics Commission, which was very interesting because we met in various parts of the world dealing with the international dimension of bioethics.

Bigsby: There came a time when you went back to Africa, to Swaziland. Was that what triggered something in you?

McCall Smith: Yes, it did. I had tried to put it out of my mind in a sense but I went to Swaziland. I had a sabbatical, and we had a particular link at the University of Edinburgh, for which I worked, with Lesotho, Swaziland and Botswana. I went to work in Swaziland and it was a wonderful experience. It is a very pretty, small country entirely surrounded by Mozambique and South Africa. It is the last absolute monarchy in Africa, the last real functioning non-constitutional monarchy. At that time the king was in *The Guinness Book of Records* for having the largest number of wives at the same time of any ruling monarch. He had one hundred and forty two wives. He had several buses for them so that when they were in port the king would arrive in a large black car that the American government had given him, followed by buses bearing the wives. I went to a ceremony and saw the king. He had two sorts of outfits, one was a wonderful leopard skin with red feathers sticking out from his head, and the second was European court dress. Nobody knew, his ministers didn't know at any particular time, what the king was going to be wearing and if the king was wearing traditional clothing and the ministers were wearing European court dress they all had to rush into their cars and do a quick change. Nobody knew until the door opened and the king got out as to whether they would need to go and change their outfit.

I remember Malcolm Rifkind, who had been Foreign Secretary, going on behalf of the British government to represent them at the funeral of this great man, who was in many respects a very wise king. Kings of

Swaziland are buried in a cave in a sacred mountain, and nobody can go to the sacred mountain. So you say farewell down at the bottom and then the king is carried up, but the king is buried sitting on a chair in a glass-fronted coffin. Malcolm Rifkind said that the king had received a very particular decoration from the Queen, a very clear condition of which was that on the death of the recipient it was to be returned to Buckingham Palace. But he was wearing it when he was carried up into the caves. However, I am sure they took a decent view of that.

Anyway, I really enjoyed Swaziland. I had some wonderful experiences there, including a marvellous encounter. I used to go into Manzini to have lunch and I was coming back from there – I had a little VW Beetle car – and a man in his sixties came up to me and said, 'You remember me, don't you.' Of course I didn't want to say, 'No,' so I said, 'Yes.' and he said, 'Could you give me a lift back up the valley?' So I said, 'Yes, jump in.' I gave him a lift, dropped him off and he introduced himself as Mr. G. This is a very common name in Swaziland so that was no surprise. The following evening I was sitting in my study in the house I had. I had a study with no curtains. There was a bougainvillea outside, but no curtains and it was dark. I was sitting at this table near the window, with the window to my side, and suddenly I became aware of a very creepy sensation. I realised I was being watched. I turned around and there was Mr. G. looking at me through the window. It gave me a tremendous fright, so I went to the door and he came up with a story about how he needed to borrow some money from me, which happens in Africa. There is a lot of lending of money takes place. So I gave him the money because he needed it, he said, for a funeral. That is usually the reason why people need to borrow money, and so I gave it to him and off he went. He came back a couple of days later with another story. So I said I would give him something but this would be the end of it.

In the meantime, I had allowed somebody to live in what had previously been the servant's quarters of this house, one of the secretaries in the university. She was running a house of ill-repute in my garden, but I felt that it was inappropriate of me to raise this issue. After the second visit from Mr. G. I told her I had been visited by this man called Mr. G and I described him and told her I had given him money. She said, 'Just give me more description.' I gave her the description and she said, 'But that is Mr. Albert G, the murderer.' Then she said, 'Next time he comes you call me,' and indeed he turned up a few days later and I called her. She came out of her establishment in the garden, wearing only a towel wrapped around her – she was a fairly traditionally built lady – and she made for Mr. G and began to tell him that this was not the conduct that she approved of and that he was exploiting me.

Bigsby: I am no longer surprised that you are a storyteller. Did you always want to write? While you were advancing in your academic career was there a bit of you that had always wanted to do this other thing?

McCall Smith: Yes, I am sure there was. I think most of us in our lives eventually do the thing that we really want to do though some of us never quite get around to it. Some people are late developers and don't really do what their heart says they should do until much later.

Bigsby: And you started with children's books. In fact you still write children's books, but was that what you wanted to do or was that what you could publish initially?

McCall Smith: That was what I found myself publishing. I don't think that was what I really wanted to do. At any stage I don't think I ever said to myself, 'I am going to write children's books.' What had happened was that there was a literary competition in Edinburgh run by Chambers the publishers who, as you know, do the great dictionary. It had three categories and I entered the novel and also a children's story because I thought it would give me more chance, and indeed I was fortunate enough to be one of the winners of the children's story category. That led to my finding an agent and then a publisher and thereafter I was encouraged to write more of those. So I wrote thirty plus children's books over the years, and I quite enjoyed it. Quite a number of them are still in print and one of the series I still keep going. I had one published last year in that series and I will probably do another one.

Bigsby: Did *The Number One Ladies Detective Agency* begin as a short story?

McCall Smith: It began as a short story, yes. I wrote a short story about a woman who at her father's death bed says that she will start up a business with the proceeds that he leaves her. I had no idea at the time that I wrote that short story that it would change my life completely. I think there are many such examples in all of our lives where we make a decision, or we do something. We may go to a party and meet the person who we are going to marry. That was one such moment for me, but I don't remember the actual setting of pen to paper. I do remember finishing that story and I do remember finishing the book, when I made it into a book, but I don't remember the precise moment that I started.

Bigsby: Do you remember the moment when you suddenly realised what it was becoming?

McCall Smith: Yes, I remember that very clearly because what had happened was that I think three books had been published in this country and they had been imported by Columbia University Press in New York and distributed through their reps, mostly to independent booksellers in the United States. What happened was that these books started to catch on through word of mouth and they found that they wanted to order more of them from the small publisher in Scotland who was doing them. He really couldn't cope with the demand at that stage and subsequently became much bigger. He continues to be one of my publishers, but at that stage they found it a little bit difficult to deal with the demand. Then *The New York Times* did a full-page article about the books and that is the point at which the Random House Group, who I think are the biggest publishers in the world, said that they would like to buy the books.

I think I was planning to go to the United States anyway – I can't recall the exact circumstances – but I thought that I would go and meet my new editor. So I went to New York and I had an appointment at their offices and went along thinking that I would have about half an hour, because prior to that stage in life nobody had given me more than half an hour. Anyway, I went in and they didn't quite have a red carpet out but metaphorically that was the case. They were wonderful. They took me round and introduced me to all the various members of staff and then they did something which really made me realise that they meant business. They took me to lunch.

In New York you don't have lunch any more. Lunch is a very old-fashioned thing in New York because everybody is so busy. Lunch is now illegal, but we went off to lunch and they had actually hired a restaurant. They had the whole restaurant. I had never met anybody who could take more than one or two tables and they had the whole restaurant. They had all these people, their publicity people and their sales people, sitting along this table and looking at me in what I thought was despair because, obviously, they were wondering what can we do with the merchandise of this guy. But they were great and we got on very well and we then went and had meetings. So I was about three or four hours in their company and I remember going out onto the street in New York thinking, my life is going to change now. Something has happened. That was the exact moment. Going out into the street. I walked around the corner and bought myself a new pair of shoes.

Bigsby: Shoes are going to crop up in your work.

McCall Smith: Shoes come up a lot.

Bigsby: Did there come a moment, as the series became more and more successful, when you realised that you don't necessarily own these characters?

McCall Smith: Yes, that is very interesting. I realised that quite early I think. It was a realisation which came as a bit of a surprise to me and I didn't worry about it. I think it was readers saying how much this series meant to them. It became apparent to me that my characters had become part of the lives of rather a lot of people. I do, however, remember some examples of extreme, not expropriation, I wouldn't call it expropriation, but extreme embracing of the characters. I was in California and I went to a party. It was a reception before a talk I was going to give, and they had all the citizens of the town at this party. These two ladies came up to me and said, 'Your books have changed our lives.' So I felt rather flattered and said, 'Well, thank you very much.' And they said, 'Yes, we bought a van' – and you know there is a tiny white van in the stories that is important. These wonderful ladies had bought a van that they painted white and they had a number plate for it which was TWV, tiny white van 1, and they drove around the town pretending to be the character in the books. And then I had a letter from a man in New Zealand which said that he and his wife played the parts of the characters and drank bush tea, but they did it twenty-four hours a day. They were the characters.

Bigsby: Once there was a film version of this, made for television, could you keep the figure as you had seen her in your mind separate from what you saw on screen?

McCall Smith: Yes. I have seen the television series and I do keep them separate because, interestingly enough, I never had any idea of what my characters looked like, of their faces. It is a curious thing. I just don't see their faces. I don't have a conception of what they look like other than in very general terms. I know that Precious Ramotswe is traditionally built, so she is a large woman, and I know that she has got a pleasant smile, but that's it. I went to Botswana to visit the set when Anthony Minghella was filming the feature film and people said we are going to take you to meet the person who plays her. I went to the set and I was very interested to meet her, because obviously she is playing a character that I had spent a lot of time with, but there was no sense of my judging whether she was right or wrong in terms of appearance. She seemed to me to be absolutely fine. All the characters I have seen in the films are fine, but I don't now see those people, those actors and actresses, when I write the books. I am not thinking of faces.

Anthony Minghella was shown the first book at quite an early stage by a person to whom I had sold the film rights and he said, 'Yes,' he wanted to do it. He was quite fond of it but it was tremendously difficult to get the film organised. It was a very long, complicated process. When they were making the film they were haemorrhaging a million dollars a day every day. He went out to Botswana and made a terrific effort to get to know people there and he was very much appreciated by the people of Botswana because he was so courteous and so interested in them. They really responded well to him and I found that a very touching story. Here was one of the most famous film directors in the world going to Botswana and he really bothered with everybody.

When he was making the film his driver, who he had just had for a week or ten days, died. He had a heart attack. Anthony Minghella dropped everything and went to the other end of the country to the funeral. They noticed it. It really meant a great deal in that particular culture. There were a lot of people in Botswana who were very, very distressed when Anthony died. He realised that this was very important for people in Botswana because this was the first time that somebody was going to portray their country, of which they are justly proud, and he fully understood the responsibility of presenting a positive picture of the country. He understood Botswana, so that is how he came to get involved. But before the film was made for years I used to meet these film people for lunch once a year and they would say, 'We are just about to start.' This happened every year. So as far as I was concerned the film industry was all about lunch and I have decided next time I sell a film rights I am selling them directly to a restaurant.

Bigsby: That series appeared when there was a renaissance of Scottish writing, but it wasn't like your kind of writing. On the street where you live, or just around the corner, one of your neighbours is Ian Rankin and another is the author of the Harry Potter series. But the renaissance was really to do with a kind of harsh realism.

McCall Smith: I think you are absolutely right. That was the expectation. The general expectation was that contemporary Scottish literature was very gritty and in-your-face. That was what people expected. They wanted a sort of head-butting literature which engaged with the reader in a very direct way and also literature which focused on the bleak. Somebody else, I didn't make up this term, used the expression contemporary Scottish miserablism. And it was. There was a lot of miserablism around. If you were a Scottish writer you were just, by definition, miserable and the more miserable you were the more you were celebrated. I suppose there were people who were so miserable that they couldn't write anything, and they were regarded as being the very best.

Bigsby: So you are an antidote?

McCall Smith: I wouldn't really like to describe myself in those terms. I don't like saying my work is of a particular sort. I think probably what people said was that it was in a more positive register and not particularly nihilistic, and I have never denied that. All I say is that I work at that end of the spectrum and I think that literature is quite properly a broad church, to mix my metaphors, composed of different parts of a spectrum. I think that it is perfectly alright to be positive, and I can justify it philosophically, in that I can say that we obviously must be aware of the bleak and we must be aware of the essential horror of human existence, but we don't necessarily need to dwell on that entirely. A lot of people actually say that that is the job of literature. They ask me, 'Where is the social realism? Why aren't you writing about the problems?' But they don't say that to painters. People engaged in the plastic arts aren't told that they are using too many bright colours, and they don't say that to composers. Composers aren't told to get into the minor key. They are allowed to compose the occasional thing in a major key.

Bigsby: We have been talking as though this was the only series you have written but that is a long way short of the truth because there are many other series. I am interested in a couple of them, for a special reason, *44 Scotland Street* and *Corduroy Mansions*. *44 Scotland Street* appeared every day of the week, except Sunday, for about six months over a five-year period in a newspaper. You were, in other words, writing the book even while it was already appearing?

McCall Smith: Yes, and I am doing that now. I am doing *Scotland Street* at the moment and *Corduroy Mansions*.

Bigsby: And there is a sequel to this which is now on *The Daily Telegraph*, on-line?

McCall Smith: Yes, on-line, and then it appears in the Saturday print edition and *The Scotsman* appears Monday to Friday.

Bigsby : Presumably in writing a serial you are potentially open to the response of the readers of the early part of the book?

McCall Smith: Yes, I am, and with *Corduroy Mansions* and *The Dog Who Came in from the Cold* at the moment, if you look at the website, you will see that we get sometimes twenty, twenty-five comments a day from the readers, and I do read them. So occasionally I have used a suggestion that the readers have come up with, or I can see if sentiment is going in a particular direction. For example, at the moment I have got a character called Terence Moongrove who has been on a voyage of self-discovery for many years which has got him as far as Cheltenham. He is a great exponent of sacred dance and the theories of a Bulgarian mystic. He is a really pretty hopeless character and I am realising now that opinion is very divided on Terence. Some of the readers think he is an extreme waste of space, while others say they love him. I have always been quite fond of Terence but I have now realised that not everybody is, so I might shade it a bit as a result of that. I am just getting people to realise that Terence, at heart, is a rather sentimental, mystical type, and actually really quite a nice man.

Bigsby: You write five thousand words a day, is that right?

McCall Smith: That would be a particularly productive day.

Bigsby: You need a thousand for the newspapers?

McCall Smith: Yes. This morning I wrote two chapters of *Corduroy Mansions* when I was in a hotel room in Nottingham. I have to because if I don't we run out and, touch wood, I haven't yet let one of these newspapers down. I came close to it once in *Scotland Street*, when I was on the Queen Mary II with my wife going round South America. It was the original free lunch. We didn't pay for this. For three talks on this ship they took us on this wonderful cruise, which was tremendous. As we went round the Horn we lost email communication with headquarters and were down to just two episodes, so I was really worried. Then we steamed into Chilean waters, email came back up, and we were saved.

Bigsby: Do you get up at five o'clock in the morning still?

McCall Smith: I do, yes, and I find that those hours are quite useful for writing. Then I go back to bed and I will get a very good hour of sleep, the rather tired sleep you have when you go back to bed about seven o'clock and sleep until about eight. I find that is very refreshing. I also get a great deal done then.

Bigsby: There is a book of yours, *La's Orchestra Saves the World*. I gather you like the cover. I don't, because it seems a bit whimsical and I found the book moving. It seemed in a different mode.

McCall Smith: It is, yes. It is different. It is a stand-alone novel. There is no possibility of a sequel to that. I wouldn't say it is a sad book but there is a feeing of loss in it. I am writing about a period which revealed some very fine aspects of the national character. There were an awful lot of people during the Second World War who suddenly found that they rose to the occasion when history presented them with the need to do so, whatever it was that they had to do. La, a divorcee living in Suffolk, found that she had this role working on the land on a farm. She went and helped with the hen house and this was allocated to her as her contribution. At the same time she formed a little orchestra which took airmen from the nearby airbase, who played musical instruments, and the locals, and they played their way through these very dark days of the Battle of Britain.

The other thing that I wanted to talk about in that book was the heroic role of the Poles and the rather bad way in which the Poles were treated. In some respects this country was good to Poles but in other respects it wasn't. Of course their whole country was sold down the river, and I hadn't been aware of something until about two years ago. It had just passed me by. I hadn't realised what had happened in the Victory parade, at the end of the war, in London. All the countries that had participated in this endeavour were represented except the Poles. Stalin said he didn't want the Poles and the Polish servicemen stood on the pavements and wept. It is only recently that we have redressed that. In the sixtieth anniversary laying of wreaths, they put Poles at the front, and so these men were able to go and put their wreath down as an act of apology, in a sense, for that. I wanted to talk about that and I did. The Poles actually made a terrific contribution to post-war Britain and in Scotland many Polish servicemen stayed and did very well, so I felt quite strongly about that.

Bigsby: The other thing about it is that music brings a community together. You have done something rather similar to that in constructing an opera house and writing an opera for it.

McCall Smith: I set up this little opera house called The Number One Ladies Opera House in the bush. The idea was to have a stage for local singers who might want to perform and who liked doing opera and hadn't had the chance to do very much, because in Botswana they are very, very keen on singing. There are lots and lots of amateur choirs. A lot of people go at the weekend to choir competitions. It is a marvellous tradition and of course they sing like angels. So we set up this little opera house in a converted garage. It seats sixty people and it has been great fun. I wrote the libretto for an opera called *The Okavango Macbeth* with a composer in Scotland called Tom Cunningham. He and I have written a number of pieces together. The BBC came out and covered it, and we had the world's press there.

The first couple of nights it took a little time for word to get out but word got out and I think the last six or seven of the ten performances were sold out. People were giving standing ovations and the singers had such a terrific time because they were all amateurs. They were students and they were paid proper professional fees, so this was great for them that they got proper payment. At the end one of them came up to me and said, 'This is the best thing that has happened in my life.' They got a terrific kick out of it and said, 'Let's take this on tour.' People do want to perform it elsewhere and we are looking into a number of possibilities.

In Conversation With Tom Stoppard

- 17ᵗʰ November 1997 -

Tom Stoppard, playwright, screenwriter, was born Tomáš Straussler, in 1937, in Zlin, Czechoslovakia. From there the family moved to Singapore, Australia and then India before coming to Britain. He left school at the age of seventeen and went into journalism, with the *Western Daily Press* and then the *Bristol Evening World* where he worked as a drama critic. He wrote radio plays in the early 1950s. His first play, *A Walk on the Water*, later re-titled *Enter a Free Man*, was written in 1960 but not staged until 1968 by which time *Rosencrantz and Guildenstern Are Dead* had established his reputation, winning awards in Britain and a Tony and New York Drama Critics Circle Award in the United States. Ahead lay a series of award-winning plays including *Jumpers* (1972), *Travesties* (1975), *Arcadia* (1993), *The Invention of Love* (1997), *The Coast of Utopia* (2002), *Rock 'n' Roll* (2006). In 1997 he was knighted for services to drama.

Bigsby: Your new play, *The Invention of Love*, has at its centre the figure of A. E. Housman. Housman also gets a mention in an earlier play of yours, *Indian Ink*. In a 1994 interview you said that there is a play somewhere about translation. Do I infer from this that the ideas behind *The Invention of Love* were circling around in your mind even at that time.

Stoppard: Yes, I think you can safely infer that, but it is not a very self-conscious notion of mine, that I save up ideas and stack them like airliners waiting to land. I am the kind of writer who is really surprised and grateful for a sense that here is something to write about. That doesn't happen very often with me. I don't have a drawer of ideas waiting to be used. I write a play and when I have finished it I have got nothing and the search for a play is very much to do with rather abstract or almost ethereal notions, like one ought to be able to do something with the idea of translation, and I hoped to with this play about Housman. On the whole I am quite glad that I end up with rather too many things jostling about trying to get into the same play and I tend to leave one or two of them out in the end. I am glad about that because it suits my temperament in some way rather more than perhaps trying to get some kind of attenuated version of a single idea and trying to body it out. I like things jostling about, colliding, and sometimes it is really quite difficult to say, for me as well, what two elements in a given play are supposed to have to do with each other.

Bigsby: That sounds like a prescription for the creation of metaphor.

Stoppard: Metaphor is central to any discussion about my plays but it is not a phrase I use very much. I think I can only safely speak of mine. It may not be true of other playwrights but for me I often get going because I am attracted to something which seems to me to be a really good metaphor for something and the search for what that something might be is what results in a play.

Bigsby: Can you say something about the metaphor in this particular play. Is there a parallel between Housman's attempt to reach back to some kind of original text before it was corrupted and the notion of there being an original meaning to existence before it was corrupted. Is that the metaphor that you wanted to follow or not?

Stoppard: I remember saying, or writing, that plays are often thought to be the end product of an idea or a set of ideas. That kind of play I have never been able to write. In some sense the ideas are the end product of the play. Picking up the point you just mentioned I suppose one could say I can think of a speech in this play about Housman and if I were working with you here, if you were teaching me how to study them, I would say that was a key speech. In fact, as you have perhaps implied, it is a speech which takes the terminology of classical textual criticism, which is a terminology that speaks of recovering texts from the corruptions that have made them nonsense as scribe upon scribe, generation after generation, have tried to copy them faithfully and failed. There is a speech in the play where Housman relates this to the meaning of life as something of which there might have existed an autographed copy and we are trying to recover what it said. As he himself points out, if there were no such autograph then there is no solution. Somehow they knock over rows of dominoes, don't they.

I only want to say, and I will try to be succinct now, that would appear to me externally to be a kind of speech which was always going to be there, which perhaps preceded the play as a thought, but my experience is exactly the opposite. These very almost over appropriate conjunctions seem to arrive by post, in some mental letter box. Some postman, whom I have never met, just pops them through when I need them and they just lie on the mat and I pick them up and open them and put them in the play thinking, thank God, hurray.

Bigsby: Let me ask you a simple, straightforward question and that is why Housman? In *Indian Ink* he is referred to as a dry old stick, and in some ways he is a dry old stick, so why place him at the centre of a play.

Stoppard: I did classics until the age of seventeen and much, much later, perhaps ten or even twenty years later, I experienced a deep sense of regret for having lost touch with Latin particularly. I didn't know that A. E. Housman was not only a classical scholar but *the* classical scholar of his generation. He was *the* superb Latin scholar and I think that those two facts alone, a poet and top classical scholar, had some sort of chemistry which made it worth my while. That is understating it. It made it imperative to look further. I didn't know he was homosexual. I just knew him as the author of *A Shropshire Lad* and I should say that it is quite a step back – I don't know how many minutes or days – but I already had a sense that there was this great play to be written about this man with a cruel mistress who was writing about Copernicus. I began to see that there was a kind of deck and you could shuffle things. I think probably I was saved from a glib play because there was no real correspondence between Houseman's emotional life and the emotional lives of those poets he was studying.

Bigsby: There is an aspect to the play, though, that is particularly interesting. Its title is *The Invention of Love*. Partly that is to do with the beginning of love poetry, tracking back in classical terms to when love poetry began, but it is also about Housman himself. Because of its humour I think people have a model of your work which assumes that you can cut your characters and they don't bleed, but he does bleed. The play is surely a love story, and not the first one that you have written.

Stoppard: It is a love story. Very briefly I should explain that he fell profoundly in love with a fellow student when he was at Oxford, when he was perhaps nineteen years old, and remained devoted to Moses Jackson who was a hearty heterosexual. He had nothing against poetry but he liked athletics and had not the slightest reciprocal interest in Housman but this devotion, on Housman's part, lasted for most of his life, one might say the whole of his life, and was never replaced. So it is not only a love story, it is a tragic love story. I don't know if one could ever hope to do justice to a life like that. I think that *The Invention of Love* is a work of fiction that does tell the truth about Housman but could not possibly tell the whole truth or anything like it.

Bigsby: A central tactic of the play is that there are in fact two versions of Housman, one very old, on his deathbed, and the other one, young, fresh off to university. Was that there from the very beginning?

Stoppard: Yes, it was. Let's talk about what the word *beginning* means. It got to be there pretty soon after I got to the top of page one, but getting to the top of page one was preceded by about three or more years. The thing is I knew nothing about anything when I began. I vaguely remembered some Latin. I didn't know what it meant to be a textual critic. I had never heard of people who were absolutely central to Housman's life, like Richard Bentley, a classical scholar who was around about the time of John Milton. I knew nothing. I was reading for three years, though I was doing other things as well. I have always thought about the subject in a slightly impersonal way, thought about it in terms of the metaphors within and the ideas it suggested rather than, 'This is what happened to him. In this year he did that and in next year he did that.' Within five minutes of starting to actually write the play I realised that this was impossible. It had no dramatic structure. The play would last three or four days and it was impossible. Then one started looking around for ways to deal with what is important to one in a way that somehow gave a truthful sense of a life which you could not possibly deal with sequentially or fully. The best reviews were for a scene between the old Houseman chatting with the young Houseman on a bench for twenty minutes and I had no plan to do that when I was starting to write the play. That was just a lifeline. I had no drama. I had no theatrical events and then this saved me.

Bigsby: But that scene is quite demanding. It is about a sixth of the entire play and it is concentrated. I suspect people have an image of you and your work which leads them to expect that when they go to the box office they are likely to be asked for their degree certificate or at least their A level certificates. A Stoppard play is likely to make demands on the audience. Are you aware of that yourself and does it give you pleasure or pain? I know you had conversations with a director about this subject, the subject of what demands you can make on an audience.

Stoppard: There is no such entity as the audience. I suspect that the people in this room are the ideal audience for the plays I write, but on the other hand they are not the complete spectrum. It is a tough one. Just in case anybody entertains the notion for a moment I will dispose of the idea that I set out to do any such thing as what you have described. To get the steam up to write anything you have to really be turned on by it. This is what I like. I have to like something a lot to be able to do it. You don't read and research for three years to produce ninety pages or so – a tiny thing, a play, novelists would sneer at such a work, barely a novella – unless there is a degree of necessity which impels one to do it or encourages one to do it. And believe me what the theatre does not need is plays where you have to have a quick course in something or another before you can really like them. That would be an impossible and absurd way to look at what I do.

Bigsby: But it is true that you had these conversations with Peter Wood in which he places himself in the position of an unknowing audience feeling too great a demand is being put on their understanding.

Stoppard: I am completely in agreement with that. I am completely uninterested in a play which fails to be comprehended. Everything I have written works as comedy on one level or another. They are all comedies in a sense. This one may be a farce or maybe a comedy of manners or ideas and it is true that we do talk about why we can't get this laugh, but what I would like to say is that laughter is the sign of comprehension. It is the only reason it is important. Silence can also be a sign of comprehension, but not when a joke is being told.

The Invention of Love has been directed by one of half a dozen great directors in this country. It has been acted by several of the best dozen. It couldn't have a better cast. I am suppose to be good at what I do. There are perhaps two or three or perhaps four jokes in that play which they don't even get. They miss. They go to the next field, they are so far off target. We have no bloody idea what is going on. We have had lots of shows now to figure it out and I still have no idea. To me there is something which fails utterly to be comprehended. If it was comprehended they would laugh. And that is what's so great about theatre. It doesn't yield all its secrets.

Bigsby: Let me take you back a little. *Professional Foul* and *Indian Ink* are set in Czechoslovakia and India respectively. You were born in Czechoslovakia. You were raised until the age of nine or so in India. Is that simply the happenstance of production of those two plays rather than a nod in the direction of your origins.

Stoppard: I think happenstance is closer. I think I intellectually felt referential but not biographically. I use what I have got and I don't have that much. One of the writers, perhaps the writer, I know more about than any other who every lived is Ernest Hemingway and for the last thirty years I keep thinking I have got to do something with this but I have never worked out what. There is something in his prose and his life which appeals to something deep in me. I don't mean I have got a hero worship for him. I am also aware of what a flawed person he was. When I was in my twenties works like *Waiting for Godot* and *Look Back in Anger* had the expected affect on me, the affect that you would expect, but actually, really and truly, as Housman would say, what knocked me completely sideways was the short stories of Ernest Hemingway and I have never absorbed that, never managed to express it in what I write. He had a theory about writing which depended on what you left out and it worked for me. I felt that his prose did indeed convey that kind of compression and I copied it a lot. I wrote some of my own but it didn't last long.

Bigsby: You were brought up in India but then you came to this country at the age of nine and went to a sort of grammar school cum public school, I don't know how you would describe it, and then left at the age of seventeen. You did not go to university, which would probably surprise those who see your plays. Are you pleased you didn't go on to university, or is there any way in which you regret it? You set several of your plays at universities or have characters who are professors, although you are, perhaps, rather scathing about them at times.

Stoppard: I think the most I can be accused of is an affectionate smile at some forms of behaviour but I really don't have enough superior ideas myself to be able to write down towards even a fictional professor. I am rather in awe of them and the answer is yes, I do regret not having been to university. I regret it all the time and this is simply to do with a sense of my still trying to catch up all these years later. I am over-estimated in every possible way and one of the ways is that I am thought to be, on the whole, for a playwright, an erudite sort of person who has picked up a lot and knows a lot of whatever. I know a little about a lot of things but I feel that I missed those three or four years where I would have done the reading which I still hope to do now. I also like the social life there.

Bigsby: You became a reporter and then you started writing for the theatre. You said at that time, which was in the fifties and beginning of the sixties, that if you wanted to be a writer then you wanted to be a playwright because of what was going on in the theatre. On the other hand things were going on in the novel too and you wrote a novel yourself. Did you feel that it might be the novel side of you that was going to take over?

Stoppard: No, I never felt that. I did write a novel but I did it for the reason one does many things in one's life. Somebody asked me to and so I did. I published two or three short stories and I was asked to write a novel.

Bigsby: Don't I remember that the reviews of your first novel appeared at the same time as the reviews of *Rosencrantz and Guildenstern Are Dead*?

Stoppard: That was a coincidence. Actually my novel and *Rosencrantz and Guildenstern are Dead* were reviewed in the same Sunday papers and I would like to write a book of some sort but not in fact a novel. I am not quite sure what it will be.

Bigsby: What was it about theatre that drew you and continues to draw you.

Stoppard: It was something internal and something external. Just to dispose of the external, it was hot and rather exciting and if you wanted to get noticed it was like a short cut, I don't know why. In 1959, which is when I think I started trying to write a play, if you could get a play on for one night at the local theatre you had more critical attention lavished upon this work than a novelist publishing his tenth book, or a novelist publishing his first book for that matter. There was something got distorted at that moment in quite a healthy way. It was probably a corrective and it is still with us but it is surely the novel now which attracts the young writer, though curiously, surprisingly and gratifyingly, there are a number, not a huge number, but a useful number of writers in their twenties, thirties, who still think that what they want to do is have a play, which is wonderful and very reassuring since one has been told on all sides that the theatre has actually been moribund for years.

Bigsby: But is it the communal aspect of theatre, actually getting involved in rehearsals with actors, directors, that is part of the attraction to you?

Stoppard: It is now. Rehearsing is a pleasure. It is an activity in itself that is quite distinct from ever opening the play to an audience. I imagine it is rather like being at university in a way in the sense that it is a form of study. It is a combination of study and practice, which is good in itself. Clearly we do it for an ultimate purpose. It has a function, but it is great. I like people, what else can I say. It is scary as well. You can't hold your gains in theatre, by which I mean that when you do film for the first time, if it hasn't struck you before, you are completely bowled over by the absolute sublime God-given benefit of the bloody thing staying the way you left it. In the theatre, if one took these things seriously, and sometimes one does too seriously, one has the sense almost of tragedy, that you wrote something and you are there that night and it is absolutely pitch perfect and somehow the right audience is there in the right frame of mind and you think, well, that was a completely unrepeatable experience but if you come back tomorrow night, forget it.

Bigsby: You are there when the original production takes place, and therefore have an element of control, but when it is done abroad, in another language, presumably it can get away from you. There are writers who patrol the boundaries of their art quite rigorously. They will get teams of lawyers to move in if there are major alterations. What is your attitude to the transformation your work has undergone?

Stoppard: The whole area of foreign language versions is one that I would prefer not to think about. *Arcadia* goes into rehearsal this month in French for the first time. I can read French but not well enough to be a critic of the translation. Word play is a killer for a translator I would think. I am told that the French *Arcadia* has actually got quite a few things in it that I never wrote in any language and I am catching up on that situation slightly late. The answer is that I am culpably distanced from the problem. I pretend it doesn't exist.

The second act of *Travesties* begins with what I thought was a deliberately dry and unfunny monologue that roughly takes the history of socialism from the publication of *Das Kapital* to *To The Finland Station* of 1917. The first act was full of parody and song and dance and jokes and all such fun and but then I thought it would be quite nice to hit them with a lecture at the top of act two as a sort of anti-joke. I thought I would get away with it because the person giving the lecture was a very attractive woman who was a librarian. It didn't work at all and in the end I cut it down to about a paragraph, but when the French production of *Travesties* was due the director called me up and said, is there anything he should know. I said, 'No, good luck and don't feel you have to do all of the lecture.' And he said, 'Oh, but it is magnifique.' And I said, 'No, no believe me. I have been there. Just take it down. Use what you can. Use the last paragraph. We had terrible trouble.' He said, 'No, no, no, I completely disagree,' and he went off. So weeks and months went by and the thing opened and I heard it was okay. He phoned up and told me what a good time he had had and how the audience loved the whole thing, and I said, 'What about the lecture?' He said, 'Ah, c'est magnifique.' I said, 'You mean you cut it.' 'No, we use every word, absolutely.' So I thought, this is the sort of audience I deserve.

Then I went to Paris to see it and it was completely true. It was uncut. He had kept the whole thing but he hadn't mentioned that she was naked. You could have heard a pin drop. People were riveted, which is actually not an un-instructive anecdote because theatre is an equation between what you it looking at and what you are listening to. It is chaos mathematics. In every eddy there is a smaller eddy working away and however small you get there is another one and the interrelations between the components of this event we call theatre, the components existing on every conceivable scale. Even the inflection of one syllable of one word in a sentence alters the mix that night. Believe me, it does. So the interrelationships between these half-understood elements, which exist on every scale, perhaps explains why there is still a theatre. Television didn't kill it, videos didn't kill it. They didn't do anything. Books seem to be healthy. People aged twenty-one want to write plays, not that many but enough. Maybe in the end it is not about social behaviour, it is about something really deep.

Actually, I am a complete tart for the visual effect. Believe me, 'the wordsmith Stoppard' doesn't have anything against the other bits. I like the other bits.

Bigsby: Can you explain your motivation for adapting plays from languages which you do not yourself speak.

Stoppard: Without exception, fatal obligingness is what accounts for these adaptations, without exception. I have never ever volunteered to do one. I have never ever found a foreign play that I wished to adapt or translate. I write a full length play, a proper play of my own, maybe every three or four years and in spite of what I have mentioned in passing about reading three years for Houseman, that was an exceptional case. On the whole a play occupies a year of my life and I have nothing to write for two or three years. I very much like the part of the job that is offered by adaptation. Somebody else has invented the plot and the characters, which I find very difficult, and I am asked to write dialogue, which I enjoy very, very much. In every single case a director has found the play he wishes to direct, or a theatre has found the foreign play that it wishes to present, and they are looking for somebody to put it into English. You might well ask why there are so many translations of Chekhov. The official answer has to do with something called personal vision, but the true answer is that directors, out of vanity, wish to work on their own text, a text that has not been worked on before. In my case I have always been approached and if I am not busy, and I like it, I do it.

Bigsby: Do you make an effort to see the various productions that are put on of your plays?

Stoppard: No, I don't. When I was young I thought it was extraordinary, and also discourteous, the way that people didn't seem to want to visit and revisit their plays in different places and different forms. Then I realised that somehow it has gone, unless I am working on a show, and that does happen, an old play being done somewhere. Then I can get reinvigorated and reinterested and also change it in small ways. But actually being told, 'Look, *Jumpers* is on in Liverpool. I bet you can't wait to go up there and see it,' the answer is, 'Yes, I can wait actually.' I don't feel like that about them. Sometimes by social accident one does see them and it is wonderful, not always, but it can really stimulate me into doing something but I have got a bit lazy in the last ten years or so. In *The Fugitive*, with Harrison Ford and Tommy Lee Jones, there is a line which I think is one of the great lines in the last ten years of cinema, though I don't see a lot of films which might explain this. Harrison Ford has not killed his wife but people think he has and he is on the run and this policeman is chasing him. There is this wonderful moment where finally the policeman gets within ten yards in this quarry and there is nowhere to go. In fact he is on the edge of a huge drop. Harrison Ford turns round and says, 'I didn't kill my wife.' And the policeman says, 'I don't care.' And I thought, 'Yes, that's it. Norman Mailer has written a biography of Jesus Christ and I don't care.' I am just not young any more. I don't have time.

In Conversation With
Graham Swift

- 4th October 2000 -

Graham Swift was born in London in 1949 and educated at Queen's College, Cambridge and the University of York. His first novel, *The Sweet-Shop Owner*, appeared in *1980*. His second, *Shuttlecock* (1982), won the Geoffrey Faber Memorial Prize. This was followed by *Waterland* (1983), which was short-listed for the Booker Prize which he subsequently won with *Last Orders* (1996). This was followed by *Tomorrow* (2007) and a non-fiction book, *Making an Elephant: Writing from Within* (2009).

Bigsby: Your new novel, *Last Orders*, takes the reader on a strange journey with a curious cast of characters, including one who is dead throughout.

Swift: Whatever else *Last Orders* is, it is the story of a journey, a very peculiar journey, a journey which four men undertake in a car in the course of a day to dispose of the ashes of the fifth man to whom they were all close in one way or another. There was a time when I was thinking of calling it, in a sort of facetious tribute to a writer friend of mine, and indeed a genuine graduate of the creative writing school here, *The Day of the Remains* but I settled on *Last Orders* partly out of tribute to that solemn phrase which can greet us at about ten to eleven of an evening, but mainly out of tribute to the last orders, last wishes, instructions of the dead man in the novel. He is, or was, a man called Jack Dodds, a butcher from Bermondsey in South East London. Incidentally the novel is written in a language which at least reflects the language of that part of the world, south east London, where I come from.

The book is set in 1990 and Jack has died quite suddenly in his late sixties but he has left behind this mysterious request that his ashes should be taken and scattered into the sea off the end of the pier at Margate and, indeed, soon after his funeral these four men meet up to carry out this wish. Significantly, they are not joined by Jack's own widow, Amy, but although she is absent from the journey she does have a pretty crucial role in the novel. Of the four men in the car three are contemporaries of Jack himself, that is to say men in their late sixties, approaching seventy. There is one younger man in his forties called Vince. He has a special relationship with Jack but has been an apprentice butcher, has been in the army, and is now a dealer in second hand cars and because of this he provides a special car for the journey, a blue Mercedes, and acts as the driver for the day.

Of the three older men, one is called Ray Johnson. He is really Jack's oldest and closest friend. They go back to when they met in the war in North Africa, and that is about fifty years from the time of the novel. Ray is the son of a scrap merchant. He has worked in insurance but the real vocation of Ray's life is betting on the horses, at which he has been successful enough to earn the nickname of Lucky Johnson, and his interest in horses goes a little bit further than that because Ray is a small man just as Jack is a big man and Ray has nursed all through his life this unfulfilled fantasy of being a jockey.

Next we have a man called Lenny, Lenny Tate. Lenny is still working in the fruit and vegetable trade. He, too, as it happens has had his unfulfilled ambitions in life. Lastly we have a man called Vic, Vic Tucker. He is one of the few people in the novel who is content with what he does, which is ironic given that he is an undertaker and has undertaken Jack's own funeral. So those are the four men. But there is, of course, a fifth man in the car and that is Jack himself and although obviously, being dead, he is absent from the novel, I certainly hope that he is present as well partly because we go back in time into Jack's life. In any case Jack is quite literally present in the form of this collection of ashes in a little plastic jar and really quite early on in the writing of the novel I realised that this little jar of ashes was going to take quite an active part in the novel.

Bigsby: If the novel, as a genre, has a habitual tense, it is the past tense yet much of this novel is in the present tense. Why?

Swift: I don't know, but what I do know is that it is wonderful to use. Something happens when you use the present tense. I guess in a way it is obvious. You get the feeling that it is happening right now. You have this feeling of immediacy. I write about the past, but I do like to make it present and I feel myself looking for ways in which to use the present tense about past events. In *Last Orders*, because of the way it is constructed with different characters telling their stories, that immediacy was very possible. That is one of the reasons I enjoyed writing the novel.

Bigsby: The present tense is the tense of the theatre, of spoken language, and this is very much a novel of the spoken language. Were you speaking aloud as you wrote? Could you hear a voice?

Swift: Yes, I could, but it wasn't as though I rehearsed it. In fact, surprisingly in some ways, the language of the novel came to me very quickly and immediately. I suppose that is partly because it is the language where I come from. I have heard it all my life but I was aware that what I had to do was construct a novel which used an appropriate language. It was a piece of artifice, so I worked with the language in a way which the language of the streets can't actually do. For example, a large part of the novel is internal monologue and when the characters have their internal monologue they use what they would in speech, plus some little extra thing which allows them, now and then, a little bit of poetry but I had to be very careful that I wasn't creating something implausible. I was making something that would authentically register what is going on inside these characters partly in the voice that they would use. I think generally I do have a great faith in people's language but what is in there doesn't all come out. What a novelist can do is bring it out for them, but the last thing I wanted to be was condescending.

Bigsby: I remember you once saying there is an oddity that writers who deal in language very often begin a book with an image, but did this book begin with language?

Swift: I think it probably did. I never really know the point where it began. You suddenly know that you are in it but my hunch is that it began with the voices. It began, possibly, with Ray's voice and when the voices happen the characters emerge very quickly.

Bigsby: Did you have that cast of characters ready when you wrote the first sentence or were they generated by the text?

Swift: I think they were coming in the pub door pretty smartly. This is a mystery. I struggle and labour over a character and even get to a point when I say this character is no good and throw it away, but I think in *Last Orders* the core of characters, those men, were a bunch pretty early on. I am always amazed. I don't spend a lot of time analysing the creative process but I am amazed how fast the imagination will sometimes work once it has got hold of something it relishes. In hindsight, I can see that Jack was always there and for some reason he was always a butcher, don't ask me why. He was always going to be a butcher. You think of a butcher. You think of a shop. You think of a street, a high street. You think of other shops, so before I knew it I had Vic across the street, an undertaker, and I had that interplay between a butcher and an undertaker. Then, by association of street and shops, all those characters were there very quickly and they would all go to a pub. So I had my first scene pretty fast.

Bigsby: You would think that this would be a difficult novel to film because of these multiple viewpoints. But you chose not to do the screenplay. Why ?

Swift: Because I don't know if I am any good at screenplays.

Bigsby: But you would only find out by doing it.

Swift: True. The second reason overrides that. I had written the novel, and I think a lot of novelists would say this, when it comes to it being filmed you don't want to go over the same ground. And there is an argument for it benefiting from a fresh eye. I was offered the screenplay and after some thought said no. In fact the director of the film wrote the screenplay. I have an element of consultation over it, not a lot, and I think you have to respect, especially if it is the director who has written the screenplay, their vision. I have been filmed before. *Waterland* was filmed. It was a mixture, partly successful, partly not, which on average is not bad. I think once you say yes to being filmed then in the end you have to take the rough with the smooth.

Bigsby: But presumably the multiple viewpoints become one viewpoint in the film?

Swift: In the novel Ray does rather predominate but even so I think it would be hard to say that there is only one central character and only one narrator in the novel. It is a shared experience and I think that translates directly into dramatic terms. Firstly, you have to get out of internal monologue. You just have your characters and you give them reasonable equality, dramatic quality. There are certain things which the film is likely to focus on, particularly the relationship of Amy and Ray, though the novel does that anyway. I think Amy will be important in the film but I don't think that is the problem. I think the problems are how do you externalise the internal stuff and how do you deal with the jumping around in time that the novel does. There are obviously cinematic conventions for doing that, flashback and so on, but they aren't automatically straightforward. What a novel or piece of prose can do in a paragraph, or even in a sentence, film can't do so easily in visual terms, not at least without risking complicating things, muddling things.

In Conversation With
Amy Tan

- 30th November 2005 -

Amy Tan was born in Oakland, California, in 1952. Her first, highly successful, novel was *The Joy Luck Club* (1989), subsequently made into a film and translated into 35 languages. It was followed by, among others, *The Kitchen God's Wife* (1991), *The Bonesetter's Daughter* (2001) and *Saving Fish from Drowning* (2005). She has also written children's books and non-fiction, including *The Opposite of Fate: A Book of Musings* (2003), an autobiography.

Bigsby: Your most recent book takes us on a literal and metaphoric journey. Could you say something about it and how it relates to your ideas and your approach to writing?

Tan: I find it difficult to talk about *Saving Fish from Drowning* because writing a novel for me has a very deep personal meaning and I don't think it is a meaning that I can transmit to other people unless you have lived my life. I believe that when a book is in the hands of the reader it becomes a different book. It is interleaved with your experiences and your emotions and that is the meaning of the book.

I will say that this book begins with a rather preposterous set of circumstances. There is a note to the reader and in it I claim that during a surprise thunderstorm I dashed into a building that turned out to be the American Society for Psychical Research and that there I found, much to my surprise and luck, a pile of about nine-hundred pages that was the dictated rantings of a ghost named Bibi Chen, delivered to a psychic. I claim that when I found this I thought how wonderful to have this ready-made material that I could simply polish, especially because Bibi Chen was somebody I knew in San Francisco. She was a society woman who gave a lot of money to the arts. We would see each other at various Asian fundraisers and she talked about a story that many people will remember, the story of eleven Americans who went to Burma and subsequently disappeared. It was a story that was headline news for weeks and weeks. I claim that it was fortunate that I had actually known this woman, Bibi Chen, and that I was able to get this first-hand account.

According to this foreword she had been found dead in her shop window, a very garish kind of death with blood all over the place. I asked my friends if they remembered Bibi Chen and the store – they lived in San Francisco – and they said they did. I asked if they remembered the story of the eleven Americans who went missing in Burma and they said they remembered that, too. I thought, 'How amazing,' because this was a fictional foreword. It was in the great tradition of fictional forewords. One of my favourite books is *Lolita* by Vladimir Nabokov and there is a fictional foreword there by a sociologist who talks about this being a moral warning to people about the evils of paedophilia. It was written tongue-in-cheek by Nabokov who hated any kind of analysis and the application of sociological aspects. The difference of course is that his foreword included the name at the very end. I chose not to include the name because I was examining for myself the nature of truth, where we find truth, and whether we question it, because in looking at truth we also set out our beliefs and our beliefs influence what we do in the world and in particular how we justify our actions, what our intentions are. For example, when you come across ambiguity in your life, and you have to decide between one course and another, you often find reasons to justify your decision and often that depends on what your beliefs are and where you got your truth. So, to me, it was this continuum, or maybe this confused spiral and swirl of things, that leads to what you do. And what we do as individuals often affects other people and therefore what happens in the world.

I often ask myself, if I have certain intentions, and they are good intentions, and then something else happens and it is not so good, do I blame myself? Do I take responsibility? What is my moral response? Is it simply guilt? Is it a feeling that I should do something? The flip side of that is that if I had no intention and something good happened as a result of something I did, could I take credit for that? After I wrote *The Joy Luck Club* women, especially, came up to me saying that because of the book they had mended their relationship with their mother or their daughter and they thanked me for that. I didn't feel I could take credit for it. People thought it was being modest, but I just honestly didn't think that it had been my intention. I had written this book for very personal and perhaps selfish reasons because I was confused. I didn't know that much about my relationship with my mother and I was seeking to understand something and discovering it along the way. I also thought that my relationship with my mother, and the stories there, were very peculiar and only particular to my family, so it came as a surprise that people thought it reflected their own relationships.

I then took this question of intentions into other areas of my life. I think I ask these questions in part because my father was a Baptist Minister by avocation and he was an electrical engineer. He was a man who questioned his actions, his beliefs and his intentions all the time. I came across his diaries later in life, after he had died, and I saw that he was tormented about many questions, including how his beliefs had affected what had happened, and how God's will had led to certain consequences. His son, my brother, took ill when he was sixteen and was found to have a brain tumour and my father, with all the strength of his faith, believed that if his faith was strong enough a miracle would happen and God would grant him his prayers. Instead my father developed a brain tumour about five months after my brother was diagnosed. They both died within a year and it caused me, as a young person at that time, to question everything that had been handed to me as truth in a package that I was not supposed to question, just simply take as my own. So I became interested in asking where truth comes from and what questions I should ask myself. That is why the book begins with a fictional foreword that many people have taken to be the truth.

Bigsby: But you were also, surely, interested in a political question?

Tan: I was interested in a very personal question having to do with going into Burma where I had been invited on an art expedition. It was a lovely place to go. I had a great interest in art and also in Asia, the confluence of history and art and cultures. I had often felt that perhaps there was an immigration of ideas and sprites and animus notions that had trickled down from China, China being such an influence for so many cultures. Then on top of that there was Buddhism that had come from India and had made its way over to places like China and Japan but also upward into Bhutan and down into Burma. I wanted to see how those had changed. It was going to be a fascinating journey. But then I discovered that going to Burma was controversial. I thought it had improved over time after the military regime had overthrown the democratic elections and placed the opposition leader Aung San Suu Kyi under house arrest. But then I discovered that she was still asking for a boycott.

My tendency was to go with what I felt was politically correct, to honour this woman because, after all, she had won the Nobel Prize for Peace. So I found myself thinking I must boycott going to Burma. I then thought to myself, if I go to Bhutan instead of Burma was that really going to help people, joining in on this boycott? I then learned there was another side to this, which is that nothing much had changed in the fifteen years or, at that time, the ten years that had passed between the overthrow of the legitimate government and the military regime taking over, and that people, including many, many Burmese, were asking that people should come not only because they were impoverished and had grown increasingly so over those ten years, but because when people were there they were witnesses and they would treat the people better if other people were watching.

There was another side, or course, with businesses saying that one should be actively involved, as they had been in China, a constructive engagement, that the helpful benevolent big brother, big sister, would guide the errant younger brother or sister toward a more enlightened path. And I realised that actually what I didn't have was any understanding. So I decided to write about it because discomfort for me is a perfect place to begin a book. It is the reason why I began the other books, *The Joy Luck Club* and the *Kitchen God's Wife*. They start off with discomfort and confusion and chaos, and all those pieces of my life that don't quite make sense, that don't quite have the meaning I am looking for.

Bigsby: Did you do any research into the situation in Burma?

Tan: I had never wanted to read stories about the military regime, about people suffering, being tortured, I have to admit. I knew the books were out there but I knew I couldn't write a book like that. But in still wanting to examine the questions I thought how could I seduce myself into writing about this? So I chose the vehicle of comedy, something that would be entertaining enough that I would stay with it. I chose a narrator, or rather the narrator chose me.

Bigsby: Was there also a personal dimension to the book?

Tan: Around the time that I decided to write this novel my mother died. She had been ill with Alzheimer's disease and she died in 1999. When I was about to begin this book I felt sad, of course, that I didn't have her there as my inspiration, my source, my news. She had often served, inadvertently, as the inspiration for stories I hadn't even thought of as a result of remarks she made. But it was as though I heard her say to me, and perhaps she did, that she could be part of my stories, she could be the narrator. I said, 'You're right. You can be the dead narrator,' and I loved the idea of the dead narrator because I have always loved the first person but in this story I wanted a third-person narrator. Mostly third person narrators can be fairly objective. They know what you are thinking and your motives and what you do and the secrets of the past and they have that all-knowing sense. I wanted somebody who was right up there, very close to the details, and yet I wanted that point of view that was very opinionated, particular, had a particular voice, because I have always loved the first person for that. The choices seemed to be rather limited. One might be God, but usually He wouldn't have opinions and that would be inappropriate. Perhaps I could have somebody who was demented and thought they were omniscient and talked in the first person. Or I could have a ghost. So that seemed very good, to have a ghost, but what would be the set-up of this ghost. And then I thought who would be this voice? Well, my mother had already volunteered for that. I thought, this is perfect because my mother as the voice conveys all those qualities that I am looking for in observing what happens in a story.

Bigsby: And the voice is central to you?

Tan: The voice is the thing I look for at the beginning of writing any story. I have to determine what it is. It is not diction. It is not vocabulary. It is not necessarily the broken English that somebody might think is the voice I am looking for in my stories. It is a way of observing the world. It has to do with the narrators' point of view, their beliefs, and often their beliefs in how things happen in the world is a question I ask myself. My mother had been somebody who always insistently asked that question, especially when things went wrong, especially when people fell ill or when they died. And so my mother, fortunately for me, or unfortunately for me, when I was a child, believed in everything.

She didn't believe in God's faith as my father did. Well, she believed in God's faith, but she also believed in fate and in curses. She believed in ghosts and bad luck and the propitiation of bad luck. She believed in karma. I remember once she said to me that she felt that she and I must have known each other in a past life and that she must have done something terrible to me because why else had I come back to torment her so. She used to seek advice from the other world after my father died through a Ouija board. She believed I could communicate with these ghosts, that I had this talent because I had lied when I was four years old saying that I didn't want to go to the bathroom because there were ghosts in there and ever since that age, and from that lie, she believed that I had the ability to talk to ghosts.

After my father died she would have me in front of the Ouija board, which was blasphemous to the Baptist religion. She would say things that were very, very poignant such as, 'Do you still love me? Do you miss me,? and then I would have to point to the right answers that she wanted to hear, which was of course, 'Yes, yes.' She would often then go into all these practical matters like, 'Should I invest in IBM or US Steel?' Then I would have to put USS or IBM or whatever. That was how she did her investment strategy. I would just make it up. I do have to say that at the end of her life she had quite a nice portfolio of stocks which I had to thank myself for. She would also say things like, 'Amy treats me so bad. What should I do? Send her Taiwan school for bad girls?' And I, of course, spelled out the answer, 'No, no.' That was I think my foray into realising the power of the word, 'No.'

I could change the course of my life by making up the answers, a kind of fiction. This mother, with all her beliefs, and the fact that none of these beliefs were, in her mind, in contradiction with one another, was perfect for my fiction because I could impose that upon my narrative, explanations that came from every direction according to what seemed to apply at the time.

When you write a novel you are in essence putting into it some notion of cosmology that is your own because the narrative is ordering what happens – the concatenation of events, the characters, their backgrounds, who said what, who did what to another person that leads to what happens. This is in effect an expression of your mini-cosmos of beliefs. And so I get to choose not just from randomness or anything like that. I get to choose from my mother, this virtual pot-luck of beliefs. In fact that's what I did. I threw them all in there. She doesn't accept that her death was a freak accident. She can't accept that that is the way she is going to go down in history, or at least in her obituary, and so she wants to find an explanation for how things happen. Of course from my mother's point of view a lot of bad things happen because you didn't listen to your mother.

That is what happens in this novel. These tourists, these friends of hers, did not follow her itinerary for the trip on the art expedition to Burma. So things begin to happen. It seems to be fate in some cases or a karmic retribution for ignoring her plan. They go off and eat at a restaurant that hasn't been vetted by her and that causes them to pick up a little visitor along the way, a bacillus causing a kind of dysentery. I have never been on a trip, by the way, where at least one person did not get this malady. I also put in cultural beliefs that were not that of these various people on the trip. In Burma there is a belief, among many of the people, in disturbed spirits who died in violent and often premature ways. They are not necessarily malevolent but they are very irritated and if you don't propitiate them and give them offerings and a certain amount of respect they can come out of wherever they dwell – a tree, a doorway – and cause a lot of havoc and bad luck. In my book it is not just one belief, it is everything. It is bad luck mixing with spirits. It is freak accidents mixing with karma. I thought this is a good way to explain how things happen because I think often we don't know. We like to take a rational and scientific notion of what happens in the world but I often find, for myself, that there aren't really any good explanations and how do we know for sure. So I let myself be open, as my mother was, to all possibilities.

It is a wonderful way to look at the world if you are a writer. It is not a good way to look at the world if you are a doctor or minister or the captain of the plane I am on. In this book, through this voice, I examine the nature of truth, where it comes from and what I should believe. I examine the way I look at suffering, a matter that bothers me greatly. I look at the question of moral ambiguity and how we make decisions, along with the feeling that we can never really completely control the outcomes. So if we can't control them, and have irresolvable situations, what can we do?

Bigsby: You are the daughter of immigrants. Both your parents left China, but scarcely under benign circumstances.

Tan: My father left earlier than my mother, in 1947, but I think everyone saw the writing on the wall. He had a scholarship to go to MIT, probably one of those indemnity scholars from the Boxer Uprising. My mother left with the idea that if she didn't get out then she would never get out, and so she left her daughters behind. So, yes, I would say that was under extreme and unfortunate circumstances.

Bigsby: How much did you know when you were growing up about the existence of your abandoned sisters?

Tan: Nothing. I didn't know anything about them until after my father died. I didn't know my mother had been married before. My mother was the wife of a Baptist minister and after my father died – this may be a distortion of my memory just as I have distorted other people's memories – my mother told me about these daughters when we were having a terrible fight and she said, 'I wish you weren't my daughter.' I said, 'I wish you weren't my mother.' Then she told me about these daughters and I pictured them as these girls, of my age, who spoke beautiful Chinese and would have been completely obedient to her. I imagined she loved them more than me.

Bigsby: In fact you didn't know her real name until right at the end?

Tan: There was so much I didn't know and I learned over time. Practically the last day of my mother's life, when she was unconscious, my sisters were around, the entire family, and we were beginning to write her obituary. I had to put down, 'Wife of John Tan.' I had to put down the father's name of the other daughters, my abandoned sisters, but I couldn't because my mother hated that man so much she would never say his name. She only called him *that bad man*. I couldn't say, 'Married *also* to *that bad man*.' So I put down what I thought was her maiden name and my sisters, said, 'No, no, that wasn't her name.' I said, 'What do you mean?' And they told me her name. It was a lovely name and I couldn't believe that here I was, somebody who wrote books about her, based on her life, and I didn't know her name until the day she was dying.

It was the same with my grandmother. I didn't know her name. They told me her name when I started to write this obituary. It was such a powerful moment for me, not just because my mother was dying, but because it was a name that her mother had given to her the first day of her life and this was the last day of her life and it was only now that I was hearing what this name was for the first time.

Bigsby: There is something about the children of immigrants in that they can fall into the role of being literal interpreters, certainly cultural interpreters for their parents, and they can also feel ashamed of their parents because they are not fluent in the language, don't quite understand the culture, can't read it. Did you feel any of that?

Tan: I did. My mother's English was one that never improved over the fifty years that she lived in the United States. In the beginning I just felt that because she didn't speak perfectly her thoughts were equally imperfect, that she was in fact a little stupid because people who spoke well were intelligent. I think that my culture became a scapegoat in many ways. You are growing up and your friends don't like you, or you are not chosen to be part of something, and you start looking for blame. It was very easy to blame my culture and my mother. It was something that I naturally rejected when I was growing up.

Bigsby: And you present your mother in your books in a benign and bemused way, but actually there was another edge to it, wasn't there, because you got harried around the country at her whim because she didn't want to stay in one place?

Tan: She wanted to move a lot whenever she was unhappy. We ended up moving – I think, not counting the last year I was in high school – twelve times in the first fifteen years of my life and because we were moving I often left behind the friends I had just made. She would get unhappy and you knew it was almost a matter of time before she would say she wanted to go back to China or elsewhere. She wanted to move and my father seemed to always acquiesce. If I ever got angry at my father it was because he gave into her. I think it was also her way of moving up in the world. The last year of all that moving was because my father and brother died and she believed that we were cursed and would all die. Or she thought that where we lived was bad and we had to leave that place if we were going to save ourselves. She sold everything.

This sounds like a joke but my father died in February and probably shortly after that, maybe the end of February or March, as she was cleaning the kitchen, and my younger brother and I were nearby watching television, she picked up this can of Dutch cleanser, old Dutch cleanser, and suddenly she said, 'Holland is clean. We are moving to Holland.' By June, she had sold the house, the car and the furniture and with three suitcases and a duffle bag we moved to Europe.

Bigsby: Is this how you ended up at school in Switzerland?

Tan: We ended up in Switzerland because she couldn't find a place to live in Holland. She didn't know where we were going to live. She didn't know which city, or which school. She certainly couldn't speak the language. She could barely speak English. We couldn't find a place in Germany so just kept going south, downward. She had a handbook of English-speaking schools and we stopped in a town. 'Do you have an opening?' 'No.' Or they had an opening but there was no place to rent.

We ended up in a resort town in Switzerland. Because it was a resort town they had furnished apartments and there was a school that happened to have two openings for day students and that is where we ended up for the next nine months. I look back and I think it was the most wonderful thing that could have happened to us and that my mother was crazy. Who takes two angry teenagers to a country where you don't know the language or anybody there?

Bigsby: You went through a wild period in your teenage years. Was that a consequence of this real trauma? You said that your father and brother died and that that made you re-evaluate, but the trauma must have gone beyond that. Was that what lay behind this disorganised period in your own personal life?

Tan: I think it was natural to feel angry and rebellious and reject everything and I tried all the things I had resisted doing. I was the good minister's daughter who believed in everything and had never done anything. I wasn't perfect but I tried to follow everything that was expected of me and so I rejected it all, found my first boyfriend and got into a lot of trouble. There is a Cliff Notes version of my life which says that I had a relationship with an older German man who had close contacts with drug dealers and organised crime. In fact he was twenty-two and friends with a couple of Canadian hippies who sold hashish from time to time, but I don't remember them being that organised about it. I went from being the good minister's daughter to smoking cigarettes laced with hashish. I actually thought it was legal because everybody did it so openly. So I was raising my skirts, wearing eye makeup, having a boyfriend and getting arrested for drugs. My mother hired a private detective who found all this evidence and arrested me. She was dangerous, you know. She could change fate. She had all of them arrested and deported and I had to appear before a magistrate and swear I would never do anything bad ever again.

Bigsby: There was an Amy Tan writer before the Amy Tan writer that we know of. You worked for IBM?

Tan: I was a business writer. I wrote for a lot of high technology companies, not the kind of technology where you say, insert A into X and then take Z and put that in with C after you have opened B and then suddenly the VCR will play. Mine was more corporate messages to employees on how to get them to work harder and faster and longer by paying them the same money. That was what I did. It was a kind of fiction.

Bigsby: But you began to pay the price for doing that?

Tan: My friends called me a workaholic. I said, 'I'm not a workaholic,' but I was working ninety hours a week, billable hours. I was a freelance writer. Billable hours means I also had additional hours that I couldn't bill. They said I should see a psychiatrist. So I went to this psychiatrist and sat there crying my eyes out and talking about things but discovered one day that he was asleep. I was horrified, but I assumed it was a technique, a very clever technique because he must be saying that I am not confronting my anger or expressing my anger to people. He was waiting for me to get angry and say something. I didn't say anything. The next time he fell asleep again. Again I thought it was a technique. The third time he did it I realised that he was bored and was asleep. I am frugal and didn't like paying a lot of money to go to therapy even if he had been awake and I certainly wasn't going to pay money to watch him sleep so I decided to quit the therapy and take up jazz piano lessons and write fiction and see if any of those things stuck. Guess which one stuck. I thank the psychiatrist for falling asleep because if he had been a really good and awake psychiatrist I might still be there happily paying my money and getting insights into myself as he continued to be very silent.

Bigsby: Was it around that time that you went to China with your mother?

Tan: I started to write and I had an experience. I thought my mother had died. I got a phone call that she had had a heart attack and I got this message four days late. She had been in intensive care they said. I went to the phone and called to find out what had happened but in between hearing this and going to the phone I had said, 'Dear God, or Buddha, or whoever rules the universe, if she lives I promise I will get to know her and take her to China. We will meet the daughters.' I got on the phone and went through all these different transfers and then I heard her voice, and I just said, 'Are you OK? I heard you had a heart attack.' She said, 'No, I didn't have a heart attack. I had a fight with a fishmonger and it made me so mad it gave me a pain in my chest.' Then we talked for a while. She was so happy I had been scared. Then I hung up and I thought, 'This is great. I can go back to having a good time.' Then I heard this voice. Whoever is ruling the universe said to me, 'You made a promise!' So I had to take her to China.

Bigsby: When James Baldwin went to Paris he said that for the first time he felt really American. When you went to China did you have a similar feeling?

Tan: I had an expectation that I would feel very Chinese. I had a worry, in fact, that I would go there and would blend in for the first time, that I wouldn't stand out, as opposed to how I felt when I was growing up in the States, being the only Chinese girl in the school. And I also had this fear that when I tried to leave China they would say, 'You are one of us. You can't go.' But my mother said, 'No. The minute they see you walk, the minute you open your mouth, they will know you are not Chinese.' She was right. I had never felt more American in my life and it wasn't just the way I looked. I did have a lot of people staring at me because I was wearing my hair differently, and all kinds of external things. It was because of my assumptions about the world. I think that going abroad is a wonderful way to realise what your identity is. I certainly felt that way the year I was in Switzerland but it was a greater shock to me being an adult and being there as a Chinese person in China.

Bigsby: And your mother goes on being an influence in your work even after her death?

Tan: I started *Saving Fish From Drowning* around the time my mother was diagnosed with Alzheimer's, and that was around the same month that my editor was diagnosed with cancer. My editor was like a second mother to me and I ended up going to New York to live with her. I would go back and forth between the two of them so that the book was about memory and I didn't want to finish it because it seemed that when I ended the book they were going to die. Something else intervened. I got very ill during that time and I couldn't write that much anyway, but they both died in 1999 – my mother on November 22nd and my editor December 7th – two weeks apart. I had to start the book all over again because I think when a person dies you become a different person in a way, you see the world differently, so I was a different writer and I had to write about memory in a different way.

Bigsby: And in the run up to writing the book there was another problem to do with memory because you yourself were suffering from an illness which at first you must have assumed might be a recurrence of what your mother had gone through?

228

Tan: I had been bitten by a little insect in 1999, a tic, and it turned out that I got something called Lyme disease. It is a bacteria, a very clever bacteria. It went very quickly into my brain and I had all the symptoms. I had a rash. I had the flu the next day. My feet started turning numb. I couldn't move my arms because of joint problems but no one knew what it was. I went for four years before I was diagnosed. Your own immune system, if it is healthy, can fight off most of the symptoms for a while, but by the middle of 2001 I couldn't really think that well. I am in a joke rock band. At the end of 2002 I was given a new song to sing, *Material Girl*, not terribly deep, not terribly difficult, and I practiced the lines for thirteen hours and each time at the end I could not remember the first line.

To learn that you have no short-term memory is a frightening thing. People would say things to me and I didn't remember them. I would ask the same thing again. I looked at things I had written and didn't recall them. It was a very, very frightening time and I thought I had Alzheimer's. Finally I was diagnosed with this disease and started to get proper treatment. It is a disease, by the way, of which I will probably never be completely cured but I am under excellent management and I have gotten rid of the brain clog and the achy joints and stiffness and a lot of the exhaustion and fatigue. I am left with peripheral neuropathy and seizures. I am left with sixteen lesions in my brain.

In Conversation With
Colm Tóibín

- 12th October 2009 -

Colm Tóibín was born in Enniscorthy, County Wexford, and was educated at University College Dublin before living in Barcelona for three years, a fact which led to two books, *Homage to Barcelona* and a novel, *The South*, both published in 1990. The latter won the Irish Times/Aer Lingus First Fiction Award. He worked as a journalist and travel writer, publishing several travel books. Among his novels are *The Heather Blazing* (1992), winner of the Encore Award, *The Story of the Night* (1996), winner of the Ferro-Grumley Prize, *The Blackwater Lightship* (1999), *The Master* (2004), which won the Dublin IMPAC Prize among others, and *Brooklyn* (2009), winner of the Costa Novel of the Year Prize.

Bigsby: You come from Enniscorthy, County Wexford, which is a small town of nine or ten thousand. What sort of a place was it to be growing up in?

Tóibín: My father was a teacher and was involved with Fianna Fáil, which has ruled Ireland more or less all the time since independence. Our local representative was the Minister of Finance who was living outside the constituency. My father was his representative in the town. He was involved in many activities. I remember he bought the local castle, which had been lived in by Walter Raleigh and Edmund Spenser among others, and set it up as a museum. I remember people coming into it with metal tops of pipes from the 1798 rebellion which they had either in their houses or had found somewhere. Or they had coins, or anything. So everybody knew you. If I go to the graveyard now it is very strange because I can walk through it and see the parents of everyone I knew, all the graves there in a row. And you could almost tell people, if you met somebody, 'Oh, I know where you are going to be buried. Is there room for you there because so and so is there? So where are you going if you don't go there? Well, you could go over there.' So it was intimate in that sense.

Bigsby: It is a small town but it has a castle and a cathedral and it is fairly heavily invested in history. On the other hand, is there a part of Ireland that isn't?

Tóibín: Yes, I think the difference is that the name Banville is not Murphy or O'Connor. The Banvilles would have been Huguenots. My name doesn't have an 'O' before it or a 'Mac' because the 'T' is a 'D' apostrophe, from the Norman invasion of 1169. That quarter of Ireland which is Wexford would have been a mixture of races. The land is good, or at least it is better than land elsewhere in Ireland. There is really no bog land. It is very fertile, which is one of the reasons why Raleigh and Spenser were so interested in it. It was beautifully wooded at a certain point. There was an Elizabethan plantation, a Norman invasion, Huguenots came, and there was the original population, so you had not only a cultural mix but a degree of wealth in the place. That meant that even during the years of the famine they could commission Pugin to design the cathedral.

Bigsby: Yours has, historically, been a basically Republican family.

Tóibín: I think one of the reasons why the 1798 rebellion took place in County Wexford is that the ideas of the French Revolution and the American Revolution had seeped through to the local Protestant intellectuals who joined forces with the locals, at least for a short time, in attempting a revolution in the name of the people. In that part of Ireland you have got the sea on two sides so that the port of Wexford town would have been a busy one where ships would have gone out to America, into South America even. I can trace back a grandfather and a grand uncle who would seize any opportunity they saw to infiltrate a group of people to cause a revolution in Ireland. This came with its ironies. For example, when my grandfather was interned in 1916, after the rebellion, he was interned in Wales. All the people he was interned with were English-speaking, but all the guards were Welsh-speaking, and he found that a bit strange. So there was a lot of talk about freeing Ireland.

The last battle of the 1798 rebellion was fought on Vinegar Hill, which we could see from our house, and certainly that sense of being brought up on a battlefield was there if you were interested in it. All the ballads named the town and it gave a sense of importance to the place, which I have to say on a Monday night, when it was raining, the town didn't often yield in the same way.

Bigsby: You went to a Christian Brothers School, and I always assume that at a Christian Brothers School the intention was to create the next generation of priests. Was there ever any pressure on you in that direction?

Tóibín: Oh, no. That might have been more true out in the countryside, in farms of a certain sort, but in my house my mother was really rational and sensible and forward-looking. She would have laughed her head off at the idea of one of her children being a priest, at the pomposity of such an intention. She was religious, but she would have seen none of that nonsense.

Bigsby: When you were twelve your father died, and you say something strange in one of your books. You were going to go to the school where he was a teacher and you were afraid that he would teach you. So when he died, for a moment you felt a sense of relief, and, in fact, his death doesn't seem to have really hit you profoundly until much later in life.

Tóibín: That was 1967, when people knew nothing about those issues, children's grief, trauma, at least they didn't where I was from. The attempt was to get back to normality as quickly as possible. I was cheeky and stupid. Well, I wasn't completely stupid but teachers picked on me, didn't like me. Therefore I wondered what my father would do with me, because it would be so embarrassing. And then there was what the others might say about him. So I was dreading the fact that he would teach me. Then he died, so that didn't occur. That I understood later is a typical mechanism that you use to obliterate how you actually feel.

Bigsby: Later you went to a psychiatrist and effectively broke down as suddenly all of that past, your father and your relationship to him, seemed to overwhelm you.

Tóibín: Yes, I worked then with a psychiatrist in Ireland, who is still one of the wisest people I know, and he explained something to me that I didn't understand, what most people still don't understand, which is as follows. When traumatic experiences occur we block them or manage to forget them. His experience as a clinical psychiatrist is that what we do is not have the experience but do everything not to have it. We go on through our lives with this experience not actually experienced and his job, in therapy, is not only to get you to unblock it but to get you to have it for the first time. This happens with rape victims, with abuse victims, with victims of trauma, but it also happens with victims of grief. We don't often mention victims of grief because everybody goes through grief, but he was saying people don't go through it, that if something happens to you as a child in a house where there is silence afterwards, where you deal with it by carrying on as best you can, then what you have to do is have the experience. I found this to be true, though I hadn't known it before. I didn't know anyone else who knew it and I hadn't read it anywhere. Very strange.

Bigsby: You went on to a college which later was subject to some scandal, but that wasn't something you registered while you were there, I presume?

Tóibín: It was terribly funny. Afterwards, St. Peter's College became notorious, and it was the most unlikely priest with the most unlikely students. I am sorry for smiling and laughing about it because it did have an awful affect on people, but a friend would call you up and say, 'Guess who is in court tomorrow, Father X.' I said, 'Father X, that is the last thing you would imagine.' I found it all very liberal and I sort of liked it all. It is very useful for a novelist in a way. It was all going on in front of my nose. It was almost like Agatha Christie or one of those Alan Ayckbourn plays where there is always one fellow who never gets told anything. Well, I was that fellow because I certainly didn't know. If it had occurred to me that you could have sex in the school with the priest I would have been in there straight away, but I should say that wasn't what they were looking for. It was about power and abuse. Some of them were very handsome but that wasn't the issue, I think, it was power and abuse of power.

Bigsby: When did you first start writing?

Tóibín: In my house, if I got sent into a room on my own from the age of twelve in the evenings to learn Latin and things, I just wrote poems. Because I was seen to be writing, or making myself useful in the room in some way or other, no one minded. There was a funny magazine run by Capuchin Friars which had two pages of poems, so I sent some poems and, from the age of about thirteen or fourteen, they actually published them. They would send me a cheque. Luckily, I don't think anyone could find them now.

Bigsby: And you were still writing poetry when you went to University College, Dublin.

Tóibín: Yes, right through.

Bigsby: Why did you stop?

Tóibín: Life is more interesting than literature. When I ended up in Barcelona in 1975, the last thing I wanted to do was write because life took over. There was a revolution going on, albeit a quiet one. There were demonstrations all the time. There were riots in the street. I was in the Mediterranean for the first time and I was twenty years old.

Bigsby: You arrived there at a very interesting time, a couple of months before the fall of Franco. You were learning Spanish only to discover that you should have been learning Catalan because suddenly a language and a culture that had been suppressed re-emerged.

Tóibín: It was an absolutely fascinating idea that you were busy learning Spanish and then when he died you discovered that everyone you wanted to talk to and meet was talking Catalan to each other. They would talk Spanish to you if they had to but the language that had been underneath the society for all those forty years was Catalan, so I had to turn around and try and learn that.

Bigsby: You were there for three years. You said you ended up in Barcelona, as though it was an accident. Presumably it wasn't?

Tóibín: No, someone just said you could get work there and the minute they said it I went home and said that I had been offered this wonderful job in Barcelona, which was a lie, so I went there.

Bigsby: Out of that time in Barcelona came *A Homage to Barcelona*, which is a non-fiction book, but also a novel, *The South*, in which there is a woman who has left Ireland behind and in a sense left the history of Ireland behind. But ironically there is this other history waiting for her, which is Catalan history. Are there parallels do you feel between the Catalans and the Irish?

Tóibín: Yes. The Spanish Civil War had marked people and places in the same way as the Irish revolution had marked people and places, and what that left was not only a change in leadership but the use of violence. For the people who use it, who might feel victorious, it has a bad gnarling effect. Both places were, I felt, locked into history in a way that other places were not. There was a novel that I was interested in, Nadine Gordimer's *Burger's Daughter*, where somebody comes out of South Africa into the South of France and cannot believe that the people there can live freely, that history and politics are not affecting their daily lives. The death of the dictator affected how people walked in the street, how people did everything they did in their lives, and seeing that first hand, and having the memory of it, or knowing about it from Ireland, certainly mattered to me. It was something I thought I could dramatise. Somebody attempting to paint the landscape as pure, without knowing that a lot of the landscape was a battlefield or had been a battlefield, or that things had happened other than clouds, would be an interesting subject. Franco died in November and by the summer it was clear that what was coming was democracy, and that it was coming in the most miraculous way. It was coming through politics and that was a dream at the time.

Bigsby: When you came back you worked as a journalist for a while and said that in some ways, for a writer, working as a journalist is better than doing a creative writing course.

Tóibín: I remember one day, when I was in Texas, which is not far from Mexico if you fly, saying to some of the students that there were riots in Oaxaca at that moment – they were actually baton charging people in the streets – and that there were certain students in that class who could really benefit from being baton charged, that it might help people's prose style, a baton charge. It would also give them all something to write about.

Bigsby: You said something interesting about your approach to writing fiction and non-fiction. You said that when you are writing fiction you write longhand. I presume, therefore, that means that when you are writing non-fiction you are on the computer or typewriter. Why is that?

Tóibín: I don't know. It is almost that I like to be able to touch the words. Often with non-fiction you are writing for a deadline. There is something more official and less personal about it. But with fiction you try to get things out of yourself. It is closer to your blood and having actual ink – I wouldn't use a biro – matters. I don't know why that should be.

Bigsby: In your novels the fictional world is often overlaid on the real world and I recognise aspects of your life. What are the ethics of incorporating real people into your fictional world?

Tóibín: I got a letter from a student I had taught in Stanford in the States and he said, 'I have got a book coming out, finally' and he named the publisher. It was Random House and it was a pretty deal. He said, 'I want to thank you very much for your help with it.' I said, 'I didn't help you at all with it. You didn't ever listen to me and you were as good when you came as when you left. Congratulations on your book.' He said, 'No, you don't understand. It was something you said.' What I said when I came into the group one day was that, 'I have a short story. If this short story is published the couple the short story is about will read it. The woman will realise something about her husband she didn't know before and when she realises that there will be a lot of trouble between them. They could even break up. Now what should I do? Should I publish the story or should I put it in the drawer?' They all said, 'Oh, Jesus you can't publish the story. You can't do that. It would be an awful thing to do.' They said, 'Are they friends of yours?' And I said, 'Oh, yes.' They said, 'You would do that?' And I said, 'What would you all do?' And all of them said they wouldn't do it. They said, 'No,' if you were friends and if it was a secret they just wouldn't do it. I said, 'Get out of here all of you. All of you are losers. You shouldn't be here. How did you get in here in the first place? You are going to be no good, all of you. You are useless. You can all write but look at you. You are all stopping yourselves.' I was almost joking but I was trying to push them harder towards being really personal in what they did, or just not saying, 'I can't write that because...' Anyway, he was listening to me more carefully than I thought he was and he ended up writing a wonderful book about his mother, all about her, seemingly.

Bigsby: That edges me towards *The Story of the Night*. You went to Argentina because of the trial of the Generals and the disappearances and you did write about it as a journalist but a novel came out of that as well. You once said that you didn't think you would be able to write about the English but there is an English person at the centre of this book, or, rather, his mother is English and there is much English about him.

Tóibín: Well, it is a sort of parody of Englishness, isn't it? It is Englishness in Argentina. If you ever see the English abroad like that they are trying to be English but they are not quite.

Bigsby: The central figure is gay and becomes ill. He has a mother and that presents him with a problem, which is going to recur in your work, namely the difficulty of exposing an aspect of yourself, particularly to your mother. Did you choose that moment to introduce a gay character out of a feeling of obligation or was it the pure logic of writing that led you to him.

Tóibín: You don't choose. It is a funny business. I hesitate to say that the subject for a novel chooses you, because perhaps that is too easy, but whatever happens in the strange months before you actually start writing is mysterious. It is certainly never a deliberate choice. But there were a few things around my mind. One was that I had covered the trial of a General. I had sat there every day while people described the torture in those years in Argentina and the disappearances and people who had been tortured. It seemed to me that there was no need for a novel about this. There was a need for a lot of journalists or people who would write non-fiction books to describe what happened in those years, but to try and invent some of them was – I don't know if sacrilege is the word – not something I would do. I have never seen it done successfully about the Argentine situation. What interested me were the years afterwards when democracy had come back to Argentina and when people had to suddenly face the fact that this happened on their watch. This happened while they were in the city and they all tried not to notice, or they were all in a way impelled in various ways not to notice. There was a drama surrounding that issue of silence, that issue of not actually experiencing things as they are happening in front of your nose. That is what interested me. I obviously knew more about it than I even knew I knew but then what happened was that I was exposed to England really for the first time because I had published two novels in England. I was coming across people in England who were ten or twenty years ahead of Ireland in their thinking and their attitudes.

Some of it was quite odd because one day I was talking to someone who had worked on my first novel. She had been involved in *Spare Rib*. She had been an early feminist in London and I mentioned that I had this story in my head about a gay man in Argentina and she said, 'Colm, are you never going to write about being gay? Are you going to go through your whole life like that?' I was really shocked by the question. I said, 'Well, you know novelists create metaphors for themselves?' And she said, 'I know, but are you always going to do that?' She was looking at me like a psychiatrist, almost. She wasn't accusing but nonetheless was saying, 'Are you joking that you think you can go through your life as a novelist without dealing with the elephant in the corner?' So, as a result of that conversation I went back to Dublin with the story in my head and wrote the first chapter of that book.

Of course what came immediately was the difficulty of that, coming from a small place and suddenly having a little revolution going in myself. In one of my books a son says, 'If I had been in the IRA it might have been easier for them to accept.' He was joking but nonetheless there was that sense that if I had been politically weird everybody would have just said, 'Colm is politically weird. That would be normal because your grandfather was, that comes in the blood, but being sexually weird…' They wouldn't have thought about that before. I discovered this was a dramatic subject and, having avoided it, I suddenly went for it. I didn't just do it once. I did it twice.

Bigsby: In both of those books there is the dilemma of a character telling his mother that he is gay. Was this something that was difficult for you to do?

Tóibín: There was the business of coming out in Ireland versus coming out in America. Seemingly, if you are gay in America you just one day wake up and tell everybody at a party. In Ireland, you don't tell your grandmother or your aunt. She mustn't know. So things are done gradually. It works like that. I am not going into pure autobiography because I am saving that up if you don't mind. You are making your point pretty well.

Bigsby: *The Blackwater Lightship* really isn't so much about the gay character, who is dying of AIDS, as the people around him who interest you because they have a real dilemma. It is a fractured family but in some senses the pieces seem to come together because of necessity. It is almost like the reforming of a family rather than the breaking of a family, because it was already broken.

Tóibín: Yes, I had been looking at Electra and the rage of a daughter against her mother, a daughter who effectively wants to kill her mother. I wondered what that would look like if you could bring it into a more domestic setting. I had seen a few productions which had been very powerful so I wondered if there was anything I could do with that. But then I left it aside because there wasn't anything I could do with it. Actually I was writing the book before I realised that I was actually dealing with that and once I knew that I started to work on that more.

Bigsby: And that is the real tension of the book, rather than that between the mother and the son?

Tóibín: But I should say also that the landscape where that is set is oddly more important than some of the characters or the ideas, how those waves crash and what those cliffs are like on the east coast of Ireland.

Bigsby: Then came a book about Henry James, in the same year that David Lodge wrote his. Do you have any explanation for the fact that two writers should choose the same subject, not just the same person but the same period of his life?

Tóibín: I think there are two, maybe three reasons, but I will just give two. The first one is that in the years before we both wrote the books a number of books came out about Henry James which changed our entire view of him. All you had to have was a subscription to the *TLS*. In the previous five or six years a lot of stuff was coming which was looking at James again, studying his silences and secrecies. James became a great subject for people in those few years. That is the first one. The second one is when all the trouble started I looked up David Lodge on the internet just to see if there was anything I could find in the background that would make him write the book and there was, I thought. I have never said this to him but both of us were sent away at key moments of our lives. When my father was sick I was sent away where I didn't know anybody. It is a time I have never forgotten and have never stopped writing about. I go over and over it. And I noticed in one of the interviews that he said he was, too. At the age of seven or eight we were moved to a strange place where we never knew if we were going to get home again. He said in an interview that it was something he had never recovered from, which is what I would say about it. If you are looking for a metaphor for that it might be James's removal to England and Alice James's removal to England and their exile there, their aloneness there. I did wonder about that.

Bigsby: James, as you say, was someone who had more than one country, and who moved between them, and that lies at the heart of your new novel, *Brooklyn*, in which a young woman goes to America in the 1950s. I was surprised to learn, from something you wrote, that significant numbers of Irish were emigrating at that time. Now, of course, Ireland itself is experiencing immigration and not handling it terribly well, something, presumably, that lies behind this novel.

Tóibín: Very few actually went to America in the fifties but great numbers went to England. Then I noticed the Polish people, the Nigerian people, the Chinese people coming into Ireland in the nineties and Ireland said, 'This is not what we do. We go to you.' People became very uneasy about what they called non-nationals in the country. I started to watch Polish people with their own shops, their own newspapers, their own hair cuts, and thought, how strange it must be to be here. So the whole thing began to preoccupy me. Also I found myself in Texas, and it is not normal. It is very far from the sea. It is very flat and you feel that nothing has ever happened there, not that I could see anyway, and nothing certainly happened while I was there. I longed to go home. It was the first time that had ever happened. I longed for things like Irish bread. I hate Irish bread. I longed for Irish newspapers. I hate Irish newspapers. It was homesickness. I was crossing the days off. So all of that got mixed up into the novel *Brooklyn*.

Bigsby: There is a character called Father Flood who helps the girl at the centre of the novel to go to America. Did you base him on anyone or were you trying to redress the balance with the versions of priests that we have had more recently?

Tóibín: I think there was certainly some of that involved. I felt that if you put a priest into a novel now the reader would expect something to occur and therefore, dramatically, the novel would work by not doing so. The other thing is I was very concerned about the demonisation of a figure like Eamon Casey. I wasn't concerned about him before he was demonised. I didn't like him before he was demonised. But once he was demonised I took an interest in him and disapproved of the way in which at one moment he was a great figure of authority and reverence and the next minute everyone hated him. I just didn't like how quickly that happened. Eamon Casey had been the Bishop of Galway and it was found that he had fathered a child. Later on, when the real abuse was revealed, it turned out to be the healthiest thing he had ever done. But he worked with emigrants in London. He set up emigrant centres and worked tirelessly all those years before he came back to Ireland. Many priests did that for Irish emigrants in the English cities and the American cities and I just thought that it would be good to put that into a book, the fact that such figures existed and did that sort of work, tirelessly and selflessly. It was partly to redress the reader's expectations but partly also that it was true, that it was there and it certainly needed to be said.

In Conversation With
Claire Tomalin
&
Michael Frayn

- 14th November 2007 -

Claire Tomalin, literary editor and biographer, was born in London in 1933. She worked in publishing before becoming literary editor of the *New Statesman* and *The Sunday Times*. Her first biography, *The Life and Death of Mary Wollstonecraft*, was published in 1974 and won the Whitbread First Book Award. Subsequent biographies were of Shelley and Katherine Mansfield. *The Invisible Woman: The Story of Nelly Ternan and Charles Dickens* (1990) won the James Tait Black Memorial Prize and the Hawthornden Prize while *Samuel Pepys: The Unequalled Self* (2002) won both the Whitbread Biography Award and the Whitbread Book of the Year. In 2006 she published *Thomas Hardy: The Time-Torn Man*.

Michael Frayn, playwright and novelist, was born in Ewell, Surrey, in 1933 and is a graduate of Cambridge University. He has been a columnist for *The Guardian* and *The Observer*. His first novel, *The Tin Men*, was published in 1970. Among his ten novels are *Headlong* (1999) and *Spies* (2002), which won the Whitbread Best Novel Award. His plays include *Donkey's Years* (1977), which won an Olivier Award, as did his farce *Noises Off* (1982). Later works include *Copenhagen* (1998), which won a Tony Award, among others, *Democracy* (2003) and *Afterlife* (2008). His philosophical thoughts were published in *The Human Touch: Our Part in the Creation of a Universe* (2007).

Bigsby: Claire, when you were growing up you were an avid reader, mostly of poetry and Shakespeare but, rather surprisingly, at the age of thirteen you saved up money to buy a book on medieval nunneries?

Tomalin: *Medieval English Nunneries* by Eileen Power, who was a great woman historian.

Bigsby: Did you have another career in mind at that stage then?

Tomalin: She was one of my idols. She died tragically young during the war. I did save up to buy that book and I met an old school friend about a year ago who said, 'I remember you were so boring carrying that great brown book about medieval nunneries around in your satchel all the time.'

Bigsby: Didn't that strike you as rather strange?

Tomalin: It seemed to me absolutely normal. The other book that meant a great deal to me was J. E. Neale's biography of Queen Elizabeth, which was one of the great historical biographies. I still have that. My *Medieval English Nunneries* got chucked out by some one.

Frayn: It was probably me.

Tomalin: No, long before you. I think it was my stepmother, but I don't blame her. It was just that I had too much stuff.

Bigsby: And the *Bible,* which I remember you describing as a series of biographies?

Tomalin: Actually, it is very interesting, and to the point of what we are talking about today, because in quite a lot of the *Bible* you are not sure whether it is biography or fiction, whether King David is this wonderful Philip Roth character, or whether he is actually someone who was around.

Frayn: I think the current opinion is that he was fiction, that he was not a real character. It is such a wonderful picture of a human being, though, that whether it is fiction or it is not, it is a most amazing piece of writing.

Tomalin: But it makes you see that all writing is story telling. It is just slightly more tightly corseted if it is biography, if it has to be fitted in to what facts you can manage to scrape up. You take the corsets off, I believe – I have never written fiction – to write fiction.

Bigsby: It is very interesting to me that there you were as a teenager reading biographies while you, Michael, were writing a novel.

Frayn: I think what I was mostly reading when I was young was Arthur Ransome, and the first book I attempted to write was certainly a children's novel about sailing, complete with illustrations of sailing dinghies. This was despite the fact that at that time I had never seen a sailing dinghy, which I suppose does say something about the power of fiction. I spent a lot of my youth pouring over ordnance survey maps trying to decide which of the lakes in the Lake District the lake described in *Swallows and Amazons* was, but of course what I couldn't take in, and a lot of people can't take in about fiction in general, is that it was a fiction. It is probably more Coniston than anywhere else but it is also a bit like Windermere, and it is fictionalised. People never believe this about fiction. They think that with fiction you just simply put your friends and relations in and change their names. You make people with dark hair have light hair and so forth, and that sometimes does happen, but I have to say sometimes writers of fiction have confessions to make. They do tell lies. They make things up.

Bigsby: Sometimes people resent it when they discover that something is only a fiction. They want it to have this level of fact in it somewhere.

Frayn: Fiction covers a great many different kinds of activities and I think some fiction is simply reality with the names changed and some, at the opposite extreme, is just pure play. It doesn't have any particular relation to the world at all. Some fiction has a moral purpose and some fiction has a historical background but you can have every kind of different story. At one end it is very close to biography and at the other it is pure fantasy.

Bigsby: You, Claire, were a reviewer and then moved on to become a literary editor. You Michael, were a reporter and a columnist, but those were very different days from the journalism of today.

Frayn: I worked for *The Guardian* first of all and then *The Observer.* They were very unlike the general run of newspapers in Fleet Street. They had a very different ethos. In most newspapers in Fleet Street you could be hired as a reporter in the morning and fired before you had even got into the office. It was that sort of work. *The Guardian* prided itself on never firing anybody. I had just been touring around Germany with a novel of mine called *Towards the End of the Morning,* because it had just been published in Germany, and I had been trying to explain to people what *The Guardian* was like in those days. When I joined it, and worked in the reporter's room in Manchester, I wouldn't say we were behind the times. We had accepted some modern innovations. We had accepted the telephone. In fact we had not one but two telephones in the reporter's room, not on the desks in front of the reporters where they might have disturbed reporter's thinking, but kept in a soundproof box at one side of the room. If you wanted to use the telephone, as reporters sometimes do when they are writing articles, you had to queue up for the telephones just like people queuing up for the phones in the street outside.

We had accepted one other modern technological innovation and that was a typewriter. All the reporters had typewriters. They had those big Victorian constructions weighing about half a ton. The trouble was that this technical innovation had been imposed upon the last earlier piece of technology for making marks on paper, which of course was using a pen and paper, and the typewriters were placed on writing desks that were sloped for writing by hand. If you type on a typewriter it vibrates, and if you have a vibrating machine on a sloping surface it gradually works its way down until it falls in your lap. I can tell you from painful personal experience that having a heavy typewriter fall in your lap is very, very painful and I sometimes wonder with hindsight that any of us were able to have children after that. That is what *The Guardian* was like.

Bigsby: And then, Claire, came Rupert Murdoch, which fact led to you leaving *The Sunday Times*.

Tomalin: Oh, yes. I left when they went to Wapping, but I wanted to leave then anyhow. I was not a proper journalist, as I was often told when I was at *The Sunday Times*. I was just a literary editor and real hard journalists were quite different sorts of people. Despite Michael's sad story about the typewriters slipping down, they are very tough people. They go out and they confront the world and I think Michael believes this is very essential. If you are a literary editor you never confront the world. All you confront is probably a drunken contributor.

Bigsby: But you had the ability to intervene in the culture because you had the power to decide what was going to be reviewed and what was not?

Tomalin: Yes, though much more when I was at the *New Statesman* where I first went to work for Anthony Thwaite. That was a lovely, lovely place to work and I was his assistant before later I became literary editor. Because the *New Statesman* was not owned by some rich proprietor and didn't aim to have a huge circulation you could actually discover people and print the sort of poetry you wanted to print and print the sort of articles you wanted to print. It was a marvellous education, really, having the freedom to do that. *The Sunday Times* was the big thing. The editor was always saying you must use famous people to write the reviews and I was saying we make the people famous by giving them the chance. I crossed swords rather a lot, particularly with Andrew Neil who thought that books in any case were a sunset industry and wouldn't be lasting for much longer.

Bigsby: One thing I noticed, in looking at *The Times*, *Telegraph* and *Observer*, is the number of biographies that are reviewed, rather than works of fiction. Why is that do you think?

Tomalin: One reason is they are much easier to review because if you have a nice biography to review all you have to do is give your account of what has been written in it, adding your own touches. A work of fiction is very difficult to review. It is like reviewing poetry. You have to spend a great deal of time thinking about it, finding a way of saying anything intelligent about it, but a biography is very easy to review.

Bigsby: Your first biography was of Mary Wollstonecraft, which came about when you wrote a piece about her and were then approached by publishers, but I am interested in how you arrived at your other subjects. The sub-title of the one you wrote about Dickens, and his relationship with a young actress called Ellen Ternan, is *The Invisible Woman*. Was there any sense in which part of you was reaching out to people to describe aspects of life that had not been described, particularly women's experiences?

Tomalin: Absolutely. That is what I was trying to do, and what I enjoyed doing. I was always interested in history – remember *Medieval English Nunneries* – and I thought history had been insufficiently written through the eyes of women. If you look at Trevelyan's *English Social History* I think there are three entries in the index which say "Women" and that is the whole history of the British Isles. It seemed to me that there was a gap. E. P. Thompson talked about trying to rescue the working classes from the condescension of history and I thought, 'Yes, yes, you can do that for women too.' And so I did after Wollstonecraft. I wrote about Mrs. Jordan, the great actress who was more or less written out of history because of the fact that she bore ten grandchildren to King George III. These seemed to me very interesting projects. What has happened, I think, is that there is now a huge thriving industry of feminist biography and that pleases me very much. It was over thirty years ago I started writing and in the bibliography at the end of my *Mary Wollstonecraft* there are lots of books I listed by very minor eighteenth and nineteenth century women. I think now, thanks to feminism, every one of those women has got her own biography written by somebody.

Bigsby: That raises the question of why Thomas Hardy? What was it about Hardy that compelled you to move in his direction?

Tomalin: Each book you write is a new departure, a new adventure, and some of them are linked. When I researched Ellen Ternan I was researching the history of actresses and that led on to my next book, *Mrs. Jordan's Profession*. But it doesn't always happen like that. As the years go by what has really motivated me with each of my books is that I have been curious about a subject. I have read a lot about it and have only done it if I felt there was some question that hadn't been answered, or some approach which I felt was different from the approaches that had been made before.

A biography is only a personal approach to one person, one period of history. I felt brilliant books had been written about Samuel Pepys, but I felt he had primarily been written about as a naval administrator and I wanted to write about him as a great writer, and a writer with an extraordinary gift of standing aside from himself when he wrote about himself, and of writing about himself dramatically. It seemed to me there was a space there for writing a book that was different from others. As to Hardy, my experience is that although I have always loved his poetry, he is better known in England and America as a novelist. One of the things I wanted to do was to bring Hardy the poet to the forefront. I have always been interested in Hardy. He seems to me an extraordinary figure, someone who wrote great poetry in his seventies.

Bigsby: I was sent by the BBC to do a programme about Edith Wharton. We went to her house and I interviewed all the biographers, the screenwriters etc. and went back to the hotel. That evening the producer pushed a piece of paper underneath my door and I opened it and it said, 'What is the story?' I thought, the story is that she was born, got married, had an affair, wrote those books, went to France and died. Then I realised that the producer was right. You are looking for a story, and everyone's story of these writers is going to be different. There is a story you want to tell that you think has not been told.

Tomalin: I think you are right. Michael often says to me, when I am thinking of writing something, 'What's the story?' and I think that it is right. You have to be a bit careful, though, not to invent the story.

Bigsby: You've written about disappearing into the nineteenth century and not being very good company when you are writing about that period. On the other hand several of your books have maps at the front, along with an acknowledgement to Michael for walking with you. You walk the territory where the person lived, but often things have changed, been transformed. What is it you are getting in touch with?

Tomalin: When I went out to Huntingdon to look at Pepys house at Brampton I found it was extraordinarily not transformed. You could do the same walk that Pepys used to do, from his uncle's house into Huntingdon, going past the great house of his cousin on the way, and I was absolutely knocked sideways. The schoolhouse was still there, the great house was there, the path. The huge meadow in which Pepys heard the milkmaids singing as they brought the cows in in the evening was still there. There were no longer milkmaids and there were different cows. I think walking the territory is important. When I was working on my first book the historian Richard Cobb said to me you must go over the territory of your subject, preferably on horseback, but if you don't want to do it on horseback you could bicycle or you could walk, but you must do it at the same pace and at the same height or level as your subject. I thought he was a great historian and that was very good advice and I have tried to follow it. I must say Michael has been heroic because it is much nicer walking with someone sympathetic. I am a bit impatient and I tend to cut corners but occasionally Michael says, 'Have you really spent enough time here? Are you sure you have looked at everything you should look at?'

Bigsby: Michael, do you walk the territory at all when you are writing a play or a novel?

Frayn: If there is a real background to it, yes, certainly. I wrote a novel called *Spies,* and that is entirely fictional in its background, but it is based on an area of the suburbs of London that you and I both know very well. I did a lot of walking around looking at that. The last couple of plays I have written had a historical background and I did a lot of walking around Copenhagen and various other places. I went to Germany a great deal to look at the background of *Democracy.* I saw where Willy Brandt had worked.

Bigsby: Are we getting closer to somebody's life by being in the same space they were, going to Salzburg to see Mozart's house?

Frayn: I am a bit baffled by that. That is a sort of heritage business, the recreation of what the house was like when somebody lived in it. I think it is very nice. It makes a museum thing. I am not sure that it really helps much if you are researching something.

Tomalin: I am not sure. When I was working on Catherine Mansfield I went to the house she had lived in on the side of Hampstead Heath. The house has been completely changed but they very kindly let me go in and just stand at the windows. It seemed to me that to be there, and to look out at the same sight, pretty well, and the quality of the light was important. I don't think that is just sentimental. I think with Jane Austen it was very, very important to walk around Chawton, even though the house has gone, to walk up to the church, to have the same sort of physical experience that she had had.

Frayn: What struck me in the Mozart house, much more than the house itself, was looking in a glass cabinet at a Mozart manuscript. I scarcely read music at all but I suddenly realised as I looked at these hand-written notes on a bit of paper, these faded ink marks on paper, that I was actually looking at *The Marriage of Figaro*. *A* wonderful moment. The house itself, though, didn't say very much.

Bigsby: You once said, Claire, that you preferred truth to fiction because it is more interesting to inhabit other people's lives, but I would have thought the point of fiction was precisely to inhabit other people's lives?

Frayn: Indeed, and you no doubt try to do it if you are writing biography, but you can't. There is no record that you can consult of what went on inside people's heads. You have to try and work that out from what they said and what they wrote and their relationships with other people, whereas in fiction, if you want to, and you don't have to do this, you can simply say, 'He thought this,' and, 'She decided that,' which implies that the writer has absolute access to the thoughts and feelings of the character.

Tomalin: I think when I said that it was apropos of *The Invisible Woman*. When I was working on that book David Lodge, a wonderful novelist and friend, said, 'Why don't you fictionalise it, Claire? Why don't you make it into a novel?' I thought about this and I wrote some letters, imaginary letters. I never dared to try and write a Dickens letter but I wrote letters between Nellie and her mother and Nellie and her son, and they are quite fun. Then I realised that this wasn't what I wanted to do. What was interesting to me was how difficult it was to write this story because I knew so little and the difficulty was what made it an interesting project. That is why I gave up. I don't think I would have a gift for fiction, alas.

Bigsby: You gave that up but you did write a play?

Tomalin: I just wrote a little play about Catherine Mansfield because somehow it seemed to me there was one incident in her life that lent itself to drama. It was great fun doing it, but it was a very slight, forgotten thing.

Bigsby: The more I read your novels and plays, Michael, the more I feel the importance of the fact that you read philosophy at university. Is there any truth in that?

Frayn: Yes, I think so. I hope it is rather concealed behind the fiction. I can't imagine anyone would read the books if they thought they were just going to get a philosophical lesson but I did slightly come out of the closet with my last book, *The Human Touch*, which was a fairly straightforward account of what my philosophical views are. I have been writing it for about thirty years but I have assembled it at long last into a book. Whether that is of any interest to anyone I don't know.

Bigsby: It begins with the paradox that the universe exists independently of the human mind but at the same time the universe only exists because of the human mind, because it is perceived as existing. One of the characteristics of the human mind is the desire for order. We look at the stars and shape them into constellations. You are given a Rorschach test and you say a whale, very like a whale. It seems to me that you play with that quite a lot, with the desire for order and structure as opposed to entropy and anarchy.

Frayn: Yes, I think they are in probably everything I have written. It turns largely on the effort we all make to make sense of the world around us, and to understand each other as people, to make some estimate of each other's feelings and motives. None of these things are given. To everything we bring our own readings. We bring our own understandings to the world in front of us and see things in terms of those understandings. Then, of course, those understandings are modified by what we see. It is very difficult to go around the back of that process and examine it. All we can say is that we sometimes find our interpretations do have to be modified. But what the interpretation is, and exactly what we are bringing to the interpretation, is very difficult to look at.

Bigsby: And that makes me want to reach out for Heisenberg, not just because he is a character in *Copenhagen* but because of his uncertainty principle, the notion that the observer changes the thing that is observed. In *Copenhagen* Heisenberg goes to meet Niels Bohr and we don't know why. Was Heisenberg working with the Nazis to develop the atom bomb or was he trying to prevent work on the bomb? Was he trying to find out how the west was doing? What were his motives? Out of this comes the sense that it is unknowable. In the end you can't know. There were two people present and even the people present wouldn't have known their motives.

Frayn: The play is indeed about how you can understand, whether you can ever know what people's motives are and whether you can ever really know what your own motives are. There is a curious parallel to the uncertainty principle and I used the idea of Heisenberg and Bohr because Heisenberg had introduced the uncertainty principle into physics in the 1920s with Bohr and suggested that we can indeed establish that we can never know everything about the behaviour of physical objects. I suggest in the play that there is a parallel with human beings.

There is a curious parallel with the uncertainty principle that has emerged from *Copenhagen* itself – and I know that Claire has discovered the same thing – that if you tell a story, if you give an account of something, it does actually change what you give an account of. It happened most dramatically to her. But, in the case of *Copenhagen*, there was so much argument about the play in America – a lot of people thought I had been too soft on Heisenberg – that somebody mentioned the existence of a letter that Bohr had written to Heisenberg in 1957 disputing Heisenberg's account of the meeting, a letter which had never been sent and which had been placed, on Bohr's death in 1962, in the Bohr Archive in Copenhagen, embargoed for fifty years until 2012. As soon as the thing was mentioned, everyone then speculated what was in the letter. The Bohr family very sensibly decided to release it early and you can, I think, still find it on the web, not only the letter but the many drafts that Bohr wrote, and indeed he does disagree with many things about the meeting. What has been less noticed is that the Heisenberg family then released a letter written by Heisenberg.

One of the problems about what happened at that meeting is that all the accounts of it came much later and there are a lot of problems associated with memory. Both Bohr and Heisenberg were trying to remember what had happened fifteen, twenty years earlier and people's memories of earlier events always differ. Bohr's letter was first drafted in 1957, about a meeting in 1941. The interest of Heisenberg's letter is that it is absolutely contemporary. He wrote it during the week he was in Copenhagen with Niels Bohr and he wrote it in three bits. He doesn't actually mention the conversation, probably because he thought the letter was going to be opened by the Gestapo. He knew he was under surveillance by the Gestapo. One thing it clears up is whether he ever went to Niels Bohr's house, much disputed by many people. As soon as he got off the train from Berlin he did go to Niels Bohr's house. He went on a Monday. In fact he went back again on the Wednesday and from internal evidence, although he doesn't mention the endlessly disputed conversation between the two men, it almost certainly occurred at some point during the meeting on the Wednesday.

Only one thing has ever been agreed by both Bohr and Heisenberg, and everybody else who have ever written about the meeting, which is one of the central points of the play, and that is that, whatever got said at that meeting, it wrecked the friendship between Bohr and Heisenberg, which had been very close. They had worked very closely in the 1920s and remained very close friends and whatever got said at the meeting in 1941 we all agree wrecked their friendship. What the letter makes clear is that Heisenberg went back to Bohr's house two days later, on the Friday, and it was a particularly nice evening. He says, 'Niels Bohr read aloud to me and I played him the Mozart A major piano sonata.' In other words, the one thing we thought we knew about that meeting turns out not to be so. What sense can you make of this? I don't know the answer, but I think the only sense you can really make of it is that history is not what happens at the time. It is what you make of events when you look back on them afterwards. When Bohr and Heisenberg looked back on that conversation, their feelings about it, and their memories of it, changed as the circumstances of the German occupation in Copenhagen got worse, as the full extent of the Nazi crimes at the end of the war was revealed, as the whole question of the morality of using atomic weapons and Bohr's rather peripheral part in that, and Heisenberg's attempted part in it, became a matter of debate. Their feelings and their memories of that meeting changed. My writing about that meeting, saying it wrecked their friendship, has actually changed the record and made us understand that it didn't actually change and wreck their friendship at the time. It was in hindsight that it did. But Claire has got a much more dramatic application of this principle.

Tomalin: Well, no. It is much less dramatic. Two things happened after *Pepys*. The great, adulterous romance of Pepy's life was with Deb Willet, who was the companion to his wife. She leaves at the end of the diary and Pepys is full of grief for her. She moves out of history. A brilliant young woman academic, by the name of Kate Loveman, was doing some research on Pepys' reading matter and she somehow got into some parish records and tracked down what happened to Deb Willet. It is absolutely fascinating. Deb marries a clergyman very soon after the death of Elizabeth Pepys and they come to London. Pepys finds this clergyman a job as a chaplain on one of the ships of the husbands of various other of his girlfriends. It was so thrilling, so extraordinary, and so clever of her to find this, and to add this extra marvellous flourish to the story of Pepys, though I am afraid Deb Willet dies young, like Elizabeth leaving one daughter, little Deb, who we haven't been able to track down.

The other thing which I think Michael thinks is more dramatic is that after I published *The Invisible Woman* I got a letter from a very respectable person who said that in his family there was a story that Dickens had collapsed not at Gad's Hill but in the house in Nunhead where he used to visit Nelly. I looked into this at great length, and very carefully. I consulted with many people and was very uncertain about it, but for reasons I explain in the postscript to my book I decided in the end that it was a possibility and I give my arguments for it. But it was an amazing thing to happen. It rested on the fact that no one was actually there when Dickens allegedly collapsed at Gad's Hill except his adoring sister-in-law, Georgina Hogarth, so that all the accounts of what happened came from her and it is generally agreed that she would have done anything to protect his name. I think it is possible that Nelly actually brought Dickens back from the house where she lived to Gad's Hill.

Bigsby: What I am drawing from this is how complicated the job of a biographer is because you have been talking about the unreliability of evidence, even when the evidence originates from the people themselves. Your play *Democracy*, Michael, features a spy working for the German Chancellor Willy Brandt. A spy, by his nature, is a construction. He is putting forward a simulacrum, but then so is the politician. It is what Willy Brandt did. You, Claire, are dealing with people as a biographer, many of whom deliberately constructed a persona. They would destroy letters and documents. Here you are, as a writer, going back and trying to penetrate that. Add to that the dilemma that the past, which people tend to think of as inert, finished, done with, a completed project, is anything but that and you have a problem. We are back with the paradox that the universe is independent of the human mind but only exists in the mind. The past is independent of the human mind but also a product of it. When you travel back you are a time traveller. You already contain the past as well as the present. A biography of Jane Austen written in 2007 will not be like one written in 1920. It is not just because the person is different, but because everything that surrounds them is different. How do you find your way through this morass of problems?

Tomalin: I think you do have to be very modest, and I was a bit crusading about Mrs. Jordan and poured scorn on the professor who had edited her letters. I thought he had missed out all the most important bits and skewed the picture. I did actually say I realised that in the future somebody else will think I have skewed the picture in another way. I have brought in the things that I thought interesting and important and this is why I again say that I think a biography is only an approach. I wanted to call my book on Jane Austen, *Jane Austen, An Approach*, and of course my husband wouldn't let me. Publishers loved the idea that this is the definitive biography, which of course doesn't exist. The heroic people are those like John Forster, in the case of Dickens, who lays out the ground and on whom in a sense we all depend. Forster just gave up. He wrote three volumes, and the first two are absolutely magnificent. In the third he says absolutely nothing because he knew that Dickens was protecting his life during the last twelve years and didn't want anything said about what he was doing.

Bigsby: So, is there an ethics to biography? You said you wouldn't write the biography of a living person. Does ethics disappear as soon as they are suitably dead?

Tomalin: Not at all, not at all. I was talking to Valerie Grove last night, who has just written a biography of John Mortimer, and I was so impressed by her account of the anguished interviews when she would say to John, 'I would really like to have those letters, John' and he would say, 'Oh, I don't know about that.' I thought she had a lot of fun and she obviously persuaded him to reveal much, much more than another biographer would have persuaded him to reveal. It is very interesting. It made me think that perhaps it would be fun to write about a living person.

Frayn: It is also important to note that it is not only the biographer's interpretation which is an issue, but the letters that the biographer uses which are themselves interpretations. They are accounts of events as seen through the eyes of the person who wrote the letter and even if you think of the most objective sources that modern historians like to use – tax records and so forth – they are interpretations of what happened. You can't actually get hold of the world except through the way people see it and the way people have seen it.

Tomalin: Many people ask me do you think Pepys's diaries are true? Well, you have to look at the context which is what you do when you are a biographer. You spend as much time looking at the context as looking at the person and the documents from the person.

Bigsby: The trouble is there is no end to context. Can I ask you, Michael, why have you in recent years been drawn more to the past and to biography in your plays? Obviously *Copenhagen* and *Democracy*, but your new play is equally drawn to biography and the past.

Frayn: Yes, it is a rather freer approach to biography. I think one of the things I have been impressed by is the way Claire works on things. I have certainly taken research much more seriously as a result of seeing the absolute scrupulousness with which Claire works. Claire actually likes research. I don't. I feel I am cheating somehow, that I should actually be making things up rather than doing research. So in the past I have rather skimped research but I have done much more thorough research for the last few projects I have done. Also, you don't know why you do things. New stories come into your head and where they have come from and why you want to do that story rather than some other one, I don't know.

Bigsby: Can you lift the curtain on your new play, going to the National next year?

Frayn: I can tell you that the source of it was going to a conference on biography with Claire, where Claire was speaking. I was just going as her arm candy and the conference was held in a place called Schloss Leopoldskron, outside Salzburg, this absolutely enormous baroque palace built by one of the Prince Archbishops in the eighteenth century. I discovered while we were there that it had been owned by Max Reinhardt, the great German producer and director. This was astonishing. The theatre is a very uncertain profession and to see that somebody had actually done well enough to buy a complete baroque palace I felt was rather encouraging. He also bought it when it was more or less derelict at the end of the First World War and poured love and treasure into it to restore and furnish it suitably with renaissance and baroque furniture and pictures.

At the same time as he lived there he also lived in a wing of the former Crown Prince's palace in Berlin and had an apartment in the Hofburg, the former Austrian Emperor's palace in Vienna. So he did pretty well. I was very taken by this, and then I discovered that in 1938, when Austria was taken over by Nazi Germany, it was stolen from Max Reinhardt. He lost everything he had put into it and I began to think about this story because the conference was not strictly about biography but how you told other people's lives.

Bigsby: Claire, what about the ones that got away, the subjects for biographies that you considered but decided not to go ahead with? Are there such?

Tomalin: Yes, there have been four in the last year. I began to think maybe I could write about H. G. Wells, and I am re-reading all his early novels, and re-reading all the science-fiction. I have been looking at existing biographies and finding out where the papers are and talking to Patrick Parrinder, who is the great expert on Wells. I thought, 'I am really going to do it and I am really going to immerse myself,' but then, as I went on through two marriages, I thought I can't do this man. There are too many women in his life and it just gets very boring, and not only that. He actually becomes coarser in some way and his writing deteriorates. Patrick Parrinder said, 'No, no. He writes very well again at the end of his life.' I didn't just give up because he broke my rule about not having too many love affairs, but somehow I saw why I had that rule. There is something monotonous about it.

Frayn: There is a novel to be written, if somebody hasn't written it already, about someone arranging his or her life so that it is suitable for biography, declining the advances of someone and saying, 'I can't have an affair with you because I think it would overload.' I did have a friend when I was on *The Guardian* in Manchester, an extremely ambitious man who arrived and started working but hated it and immediately wanted to leave. I said to him, 'I suppose you will be resigning and going back to London,' and he said, 'I can't resign until the year has changed because in my *Who's Who* entry, when I get one, it can't just say *The Guardian* 1958 because it looks as though I have been sacked. It has to say *The Guardian* 1958 – 1959.'

Bigsby: How serious are your comic plays?

Frayn: I think they are rather serious plays. *Noises Off* is, after all, about some people who are trying to put on a play and everything goes wrong and it gets desperate. When the play was first done it contained a pastiche of an English sex farce and when it was a success in London people said, 'Oh, well it works in England obviously because everyone knows about an English sex farce. It couldn't be done anywhere else.' It has now been played absolutely everywhere in the world where they do plays, including countries who had never seen an English sex farce and I had to ask myself why does it work. I think it is because we all, inside us, have this terror of appearing in front of other people and feeling that we might not be able to go with the performance. This extends not only to sitting in front of an audience but to life in general. We are all presenting ourselves to other people all the time and I think we do all fear that at some point the performance might stop. It does happen. People do have breakdowns and can't face other people. They do sit down in the corner of the room and can't do anything. I think why people laugh at it is because of this serious fear that we have inside ourselves and the great relief of seeing it happen to some other idiots.

Bigsby: Can I ask you a Donald Rumsfeld question Claire? There are the known unknowns, but more alarmingly there are unknown unknowns, the things that you don't know you don't know when you are writing a biography. Blake Morrison wrote two memoirs, one of his father and one of his mother. He thought that his father had had a relationship with another other woman. His father was dead, though, and the other woman wasn't speaking very much. It was not terribly clear. He published these books and then afterwards, about four years ago, he found that not only was there an affair but there was a child. He had a half-sister. There is something like this in the Dickens book. Is it destabilising, that nagging fear that you don't know what you don't know?

Tomalin: Yes, his son Henry Dickens said that there was a child who died. I think there was a child and the child died and then Nelly wonderfully had her new life with her children. Yesterday I was brought actual letters between Ellen and her sons written later. They were loving, adoring letters. You could see they absolutely adored each other. I think I will do a little bit more on this because we have also discovered that Ellen translated a travel book from French in the 1890s. She was really clever. She was really somebody.

Bigsby: So you get a chance to revisit your biography?

Tomalin: Yes, and my publishers go mad because then I say can we have another appendix to *Mrs. Jordan* because I found out this or I found out that. As for finding unknown half-brothers and sisters, it seems to me half the people I know now are finding that they have them. I would love to find I had some more brothers and sisters. It would be marvellous.

Bigsby: How do you mediate between the objective view and the fact that inevitably there is a subjectivity involved in writing?

Tomalin: I don't think I am entirely objective. As I have got older I have got more and more sympathetic to my subject. I was quite tart about Mary Wollstonecraft. How I dared to be I don't know, but I did once or twice say I expected more of her, which I would never say now and many, many women have said to me, 'How could you forgive Hardy for being such a hopeless husband simply because he wrote the wonderful poems after Emma died? That was too easy for him.' Actually, I think one has to see that people are complex and that the poems are great. They are wonderful and they are a testament of love, even though he failed to show that love during his life. I feel it is more important to understand people than to tick them off. But I can see you have to watch yourself so that you don't sink into sentimentality. When I was working on *Mrs. Jordan* I had lunch with my publisher and I said, 'She had these ten children and they were all beautiful, intelligent children,' and he said, 'They can't all have been beautiful and intelligent.' I said, 'Yes, they were,' and I could see I was sinking into sentimentality all too easily. Writing is all a balancing act, trying to tidy up your thoughts all the time.

Frayn: A viewpoint very much again in one of the plays of Dickens. The world is full of very different sorts of people, some nice, some nasty, some beautiful, some ugly, but everyone is a grandchild and all grandchildren are beautiful, intelligent geniuses.

Tomalin: A definition of a genius is someone with a grandmother.

In Conversation With
Rose Tremain

- 24ᵗʰ November 2010 -

Rose Tremain, novelist, short story writer, radio dramatist, was born in London in 1943. She was educated at the Sorbonne and the University of East Anglia where she would subsequently teach creative writing on its famous MA programme. Her first novel, *Sadler's Birthday*, appeared in 1976 and was followed by *Letter to Sister Benedicta* (1978), *The Cupboard* (1981) and *The Swimming Pool Season* (1985). Her breakthrough book, however, was *Restoration* (1989) which won the *Sunday Express* Book of the Year Award and was made into a film. Later novels include *Sacred Country* (1992), winner of the James Tait Black Memorial Prize for Fiction, *Music and Silence* (1999), winner of the Whitbread Novel Award, *The Colour* (2003), *The Road Home* (2007), winner of the Orange Prize for Fiction, and *Trespass* (2010). She was awarded a CBE in 2007.

Bigsby: You aren't the first writer in your family. Your father was also a writer, of sorts?

Tremain: Yes, he had what I think you would call a chequered career. He was a playwright and I remember that when I was a little girl a great reverence was given to the days of noisy typewriters. We could hear him tapping away in his study and my mother would say, 'Be quiet, be quiet. Dad is working.' So I grew up with the idea that writing was an honourable thing to do but that it was also a risky thing to do. My poor old dad had a play that was going to migrate from Watford into the West End. It was going to star an actress who in those days was very famous called Margaret Leighton. At the last minute, just before this play started, she was offered a very juicy film part so she turned down the theatre role and the play never made it. I don't know how long he had been at it by that time but he drifted away and he also then drifted away from my family.

Bigsby: How old were you then?

Tremain: I was ten.

Bigsby: And was that a trauma to you or was that just something you took as part of life?

Tremain: It became in every way traumatic for me because what my mother decided to do, having been abandoned by my father, was move out of London where we lived and send me and my sister to boarding school. She moved to the country and we eventually settled down very well there. She remarried and this story has a happy ending, but at the age of just about eleven I was sent to boarding school where I knew nobody. So I had lost my school and my school friends. I had lost my dad and lost my house. I also had a nanny who was very involved in my upbringing, and that of my sister, who I absolutely adored and of course when we were sent away to school there was no more role for a nanny so she was sent away, too. So, suddenly, from having had a rather wonderful, not spoiled but very stable childhood up until that time – and I was doing well at my little school in London and had a lot of friends – I suddenly found myself completely disorientated and that is the time I started to write.

Bigsby: You mentioned your mother and you said things worked out happily but she didn't have a very happy upbringing and didn't she later nearly go blind?

Tremain: She did, which was a really terrible thing to watch because reading had been very important to her, reading and playing bridge, and she couldn't play bridge any more. That was more traumatic than not being able to read because the RNIB furnished her with talking books and they were her lifeline. She belonged to a generation of women who had it really tough. She was born in 1913, so she grew up during the First World War. In the Second World War she lost both her brothers and was part of a generation where the role of women was completely defined, or completely undefined. The possibilities for her realising any gift she might have had were non-existent. She was sent to boarding school at an even younger age than I was and grew up as this person who felt in some way both unloved and unlovable. I think in a way she managed over the years to be a reasonable parent to me and my sister but she was very much confined by this Edwardian upbringing she had had and her world, in a way that was very frustrating to me, was very limited. I think she found it just really difficult to understand some of the lines that I have taken in my books. I tried not to mind about this but I suppose in all of us there is the charred remains of someone who wants to please the parents and having totally been unable to please my father, who wasn't there, it felt quite important to please my mother who was not very pleased by what I wrote. She found it too challenging, too difficult.

Bigsby: And when your father re-entered your life he was dealing with a daughter who was now a success at the very thing that he had largely failed at. Did he find that easy to take or not?

Tremain: He was awful about it, really. He invited me to lunch and I thought, well maybe this is the beginning. I was grown up by then and very much into my own life. I was married, with my own child, and I thought, I can be very grown up about this and perhaps have a proper adult relationship with my father and indeed with my half-siblings, because he had a new family who I didn't know. But it turned out, in the course of this lunch, that he had written a novel by that time, and really all he wanted to do was to pick my brains about literary agents. So it was difficult. I struggled on for a while, and I often say this to people who seem to have been haunted by the things that the parents do to them all their lives, you can, I think, by some act of will, change your patterns of thinking, certainly patterns relating to any idea of being the victim of something. You can change the internal landscape as you can your external landscape. I have to say – and rather embarrassingly not really until my forties – I just decided I am not going to be hurt by this anymore. I am going to forge my way out of it and not think about it, and when my father died about five years ago I can truthfully say I didn't feel anything except possibly just some sense of relief.

Bigsby: You are very resistant to the notion of writing an autobiography but you were briefly tempted, were you not, to write about your mother? Why was that?

Tremain: Yes, I was. When my mother died in 2001, really for the reasons I have just given, I did feel that she was part of that generation of women who had, by accident of history, had a terribly raw deal just to find out who they were, to become rounded and good and clever people. She was not stupid. There was some quite vibrant intelligence in my mother and when she died I just toyed with this idea of possibly writing a little memoir, not of my own life, although of course I would have come into it to a certain point, but of my mother's early life and particularly the fact that my poor grandparents had lost both their sons. There were only three children in the family and they had lost both their sons and were left with my mother who was the one child they really didn't love. This was manifest to me in my childhood.

I used to go and stay with my grandparents which for us, because they had a farm in Hampshire, was a paradise, really, but I think even at a young age I picked up that there were huge tensions particularly between my grandmother and my mother. And I thought I would like to rescue her from this feeling of unlovedness. I have to say that that didn't continue all her life because, having got over my father leaving, she married my stepfather who was very different to my father who was clever and sulky and difficult and moody. My stepfather was not clever but a very amiable man, very jolly, very sweet to us. I think he was probably just what my mother needed. He didn't play very good bridge, but in all other respects he was lovely.

Bigsby: Let me take you back. You have gone to boarding school. What was your boarding school experience like and where did the idea of writing occur to you?

Tremain: It was before school, just before. My sister is a very talented artist, and I grew up with this thing of my sister being the one with talent. My parents were so proud of my sister's artistic skills that they used to do this slightly pretentious thing of having a Christmas card designed by my sister, Joanna, every year. I grew up in a decade when we hardly knew my parents, let alone the friends of my parents, and so the friends of my parents used to come and look down at me and some would say, 'Oh, are you the talented one?' and I had to always say, 'No, no, that is Jo.' That is why I started writing. I wanted to put words to the pictures that my sister made and we had a slightly lovely few years, which continued on into boarding school, of collaboration, of doing picture stories. I would write a story and she would illustrate it and it would get published in the school magazine. It started there, and then at my boarding school, where literature was highly valued and we had a very adorable and charismatic teacher of English called Miss Robinson, Ida Robinson.

It was so cold in my school that she used to have to teach wearing her fur coat. It was in the days when you could still wear fur and I can see her now standing in this ratty coat, which she seemed to wear winter and summer, staring out of the window and sometimes stopping a lesson to just make us look out of the window at what she was seeing. It was in a rather lovely park in Hertfordshire and she used to be amazed by the qualities of light and the arrival of spring or the arrival of winter and she would make us stop and look at this. She was very inspirational in helping our reading but also in helping me with the stories. The thing about boarding school is that you have got a lot of free time and you need to fill that in some way, and the way that was most enjoyable to fill it was by writing plays and putting them on. So I became a playwright for about five years, and the star and designer.

Bigsby: When you looked forward to what you were going to become was it always a writer that was in your head?

Tremain: It sounds so pretentious to say that doesn't it, but I think it was. I also realise that the difference between writing school plays and being a grown up writer was immense and that it would take years to come round to that stuff where I could write what I wanted again. So I was fully resigned to many years of teaching, researching or whatever. I had lots and lots of day jobs and funnily enough when I was here at UEA [University of East Anglia] as a student, although I used to show one or two things to Angus Wilson, which was really the reason I came here, I don't think I was writing very much. There was too much else going on.

Bigsby: Before you even got to UEA you went to a finishing school and to the Sorbonne?

Tremain: I did. I was sent to a school in Switzerland. I don't know whether it called itself a finishing school, because I am not sure in what way it finished us, but it did help us to learn French which I think we all spoke with a very bad accent. It was an international school and we were only allowed to converse with each other in French. I learnt to ski very badly. Then I was sent to the Sorbonne. The so-called finishing, from the year in Switzerland, in fact stood me in good stead because by the time I got to the Sorbonne I could speak really quite passable French so I was able to enter into the classes on philosophy, literature and history. It was only a year. It was like a pre-MA and that was a wonderful time.

Bigsby: Was that when your engagement with, indeed your love of, France really began, because that is evidenced in a number of your novels?

Tremain: I think probably that all of us, beyond our homeland, have one other beloved place. It might be the United States. It could be anywhere in the world. It could be Africa, it could be Poland, it could be anywhere, and it just happens that mine is France. I think that if you have a language you can get deeper into the culture of the place and if you have it you don't feel so much like an exile. The other thing I owe my mother is that for one part of her own education she had a happy year in Paris, not so freewheeling as I was as a student, but she had enjoyed it very much and had learned quite passable French. When we were quite little she used to take us on holidays to France, so I grew up feeling that France was the next place. I can't remember how soon I actually managed to go anywhere else. I think one year, because she had some friends there, we were taken to Portugal for two weeks, but always we went to France, to Brittany.

Bigsby: You said you came to UEA in part because of Angus Wilson. The creative writing programme wasn't really underway when you arrived but he was giving lectures. I can remember going to lectures packed not only with students but with faculty who wanted to hear him talk about Dickens.

Tremain: He was the most fantastic lecturer.

Bigsby: How has he become invisible as a writer?

Tremain: I find that such a disturbing subject because at the time I first knew him in the sixties he was at the height of his fame, and he was a man who liked fame. I don't think this is a terribly bad thing. Some people put it on like a wonderful garb, like the clothes that Angus used to wear, the ties and the white suits and the hair. There was a showman in Angus with, of course, all the mental equipment to back that up. It was fantastic and there were verbal jokes all the time. He wore that fame and success wonderfully and just savoured every moment. But the last two books he wrote, *Setting the World On Fire* and *As If By Magic*, were not very well received. The other side of the coin of Angus, and his showmanship and his wonderful verbal skills, was a man who was quite prone to depression, and had been all his life. I think that depression came back upon him in a terrible way when these two books were not well received. There was a famous critique of *As If By Magic* by Martin Amis, who was then a young up and coming writer and critic. He fascinated Angus and I know that that weighed on him really for the rest of his life, which is an awful thing to think about.

Bigsby: He also surely made a mistake in leaving Suffolk, where he used to live, and going to France?

Tremain: He was already ill by then, though. I remember seeing him just before he left and it struck me that actually his mind was somewhere else. It seemed to me very precarious that he should be leaving the country at that point. As to his reputation, all one can say is that you just don't know when you die, as a writer, whether your reputation is going to last. If he hadn't been ill perhaps he could have salvaged everything with one last wonderful book. I remember thinking that is what will happen. We are all allowed a dud book every now and again. He had two which were not greatly liked, but he could have salvaged everything, I think, if he had been able to come back with something that was as strong as his early work.

Bigsby: When you left university you did some school teaching and worked as a publisher and did actually publish two books, though they were extraordinarily unlikely books for you to have published. Did you derive anything from those two books that was going to be subsequently useful to you, or did the mere fact of writing help you?

Tremain: Let me tell you what they are before I die of embarrassment. One was a book about Stalin and the other was a book about women's suffrage. I was working at the time as a very lowly sub editor for a historical magazine. In the nineteen seventies, which is when I am talking about, there was this mania for collecting magazines into great binders. They were called part works. There were cookery part works and there were historical part works and I was working on a part work that was very partial about the First World War, which in the office we irreverently, because it had given us our jobs, called Wonderful World War One. All I was doing was writing captions and tiny little introductions to things, but the editor came by one day and he said, 'They are very good these things you are writing. They are very concise and precise. Would you like to write a book for me?' So this wonderful word commission suddenly fell into my lap. If you are a freelance writer this is the word that you long to hear all the time, commission. I had written an article – because occasionally he would invite me to write articles for Wonderful World War One – about the Suffragette campaign, which had been going strong since 1911 but which came to a grinding halt. The suffragettes gave up for the duration of the war and only resumed after the war. So he wanted me to write something about that. I had done quite a lot of research for this article and he said he thought we should have a book about women's suffrage and Emily Pankhurst in the

Ballantine series, and would you like to write it, thirty-five thousand words, highly illustrated. Of course I said yes.

This has a sad story attached to it actually. I had no agent in those early days and this little book, which became part of the Ballantine *Illustrated History of the Twentieth Century*, sold something like a million copies because it sold on railway stations all over the world, but I had no royalties. I had accepted a thousand pounds, which seemed to me like just amazing riches in 1976, or whenever it was, but there were no royalties.

Bigsby: You also wrote a book about Stalin, but I won't go into that. Let me turn back to your creative work. You were writing short stories during your twenties and they were bouncing back.

Tremain: Oh, they were bouncing back, yes. Young writers often begin with short stories. They think that because they are short they are not difficult to do, but of course they are immensely difficult to do. I think that the short story has to have a kind of poetic coherence, which took me certainly years to understand. Some writers, like Ian McEwan, seem to come to it absolutely fully formed understanding how the short story works, that there must be nothing superfluous in it and that it needs a poetic precision to it. I think it took me years to understand that and possibly years to find subjects that were really original enough. Anyway, it took me ages to put it all together. I didn't publish a short story, I think, until 1981 by which time I had published two books. So I came to it the wrong way round.

Bigsby: Did your first novel find a publisher straight away or did that do the rounds as well?

Tremain: Yes, that did the rounds, which was depressing, but after about the sixth or seventh publisher it landed on the desk of somebody called Penelope Hoare, who has been my editor ever since. She has changed publishing houses and I have managed to follow her. She is just the best editor in London and she understands my jokes and makes them funnier.

Bigsby: That first novel, although we weren't to know it at the time, was almost staking out your attitude towards writing because we know what conventionally first novels tended to be…

Tremain: My life till then.

Bigsby: Yes, exactly, whereas this is at the other extreme from that. It features an older person, much older than you, and a man. Throughout your work there has been this tendency to create characters who are remote from your own experience, and that is surely quite deliberate.

Tremain: It certainly is now. *Sadler's Birthday* is a story of an old man who has been a servant in a big house, then the owners of the house die without any children and leave him the house so the social situation is turned on its head. He becomes the master of the place where he has once been the servant. I think when that idea came to me it was vaguely connected to my grandparents who lived in a rather grand way. We were in the socialist nineteen sixties, early seventies, when this idea came. I wanted to turn everything around so there was a tiny bit of autobiography in that. I don't think there is any character who is like me but I think that in the colonel and his wife there are some elements a little bit like my grandparents.

Bigsby: I suppose in many writer's lives there comes the moment when they write a work which turns out to be a breakthrough novel, that is to say it finds a much wider audience.

Tremain: And that may never happen.

Bigsby: With you it was going to happen with *Restoration*. You wrote that in Thatcher's Britain and there is surely a sense in which you were looking for another period as a way of addressing that. Did you ever think of addressing that directly? Were you ever tempted to write a contemporary novel about that world of the eighties?

Tremain: Yes, I was more than tempted. I thought that was what I was going to do. My mind threw up various ideas for books and it seemed to me what happened then – and of course can still happen again when you are working with the contemporary – is that life catches up with the book before you have even had time to write it. I remember that Ian McEwan was writing about Berlin at the time the wall came down and he had to change his whole ending because history had overtaken what was meant to be a very contemporary book. It was no longer contemporary, so he had to completely reconfigure it, and this is a perennial danger if you are writing in your own time.

The process of writing a novel is very slow and the process of publishing is slow so you are counting on maybe two or three years from actually first having an idea to it becoming a book that anybody can read, and three years in our own lives at this time is a huge time span. What seems to feel contemporaneous to us now today will not feel that way in three years time because the novelist risks always being in some kind of a time lag. I felt that Thatcher's Britain was moving so fast that I couldn't capture it and more and more time was going by with nothing written. So I started to look around for a period in history which had some kind of mirror to the time and it seemed to me that the Restoration was rather a good one because this is a story of a man who trades honour for material possessions, which was really the core thing of Thatcher's Britain. If I was quizzed on how well sustained are the parallels between what was going on in Thatcher's Britain – both with our obsession with money and show and the beginnings of our obsession with fame and conspicuous consumption – I think you will agree with me that in the sixties it wasn't like that. We had some wild behaviours but we didn't spend money on things. I am talking for myself, perhaps you did, but it wasn't how I thought society was going to go when I was very young and then it did go like that and I thought, well I really want to explore that, the kind of ethos in which we live in this country, well, globally in fact.

It seemed to me that all kinds of things were going on at the time of the Restoration, which followed on the very monochromatic period of the Interregnum, some of which is startlingly wonderful. The theatres opened again, the life of the river became very colourful and buoyant and music was heard. People felt liberated in a way, but there was also this new materialism, this obsession not just with money, but with power from which money flowed, which of course meant Whitehall. Somebody in this novel says at one point, 'Whitehall casts a shadow over the whole country and there are only very, very few places where the shadow does not fall.' It seems to me that that was true of the Thatcher era. There was a sea change. People behaved differently, thought differently, had different aspirations, so it was all born out of that. I think if you read it now you don't necessarily find the Thatcher era in it any more.

Bigsby: Did you find the voice immediately or did you have to feel your way towards it?

Tremain: I think I found it immediately because it is a first-person narration from the point of view of this man who you can't really call a hero, because he behaved so badly. Anti-hero might be better. I think I found the voice and then thought, 'Oh, no. This is too dangerous to write in the voice of this first-person retrograde man' so I started telling it in a much more normal way, in a third-person voice. I wrote about fifty pages like that and it just seemed to me tremendously dull, and in a way like the worst kind of historical novel. I thought, 'Who is this person telling me about this other person? Is anything true?'

There is a terrible pitfall of historical fiction, which is to do with dealing with real characters and I tend to skirt around them. They are there in the background, in the same way that in Tom Stoppard's play, *Rosencrantz and Guildenstern Are Dead*, Hamlet is there in the background, almost like a passing show, but it does seem to me tremendously dangerous if readers suddenly stop and think, 'Is this real or is it not real?' They have what I call a biographical unease about it. It seemed to me very important to make up as much as I possibly could and make things feel immediate and indeed funny. This is one of the aspirations of this book, that is it has always made people laugh, which is why it succeeded.

Bigsby: Penelope Lively has said that she did a degree in history and though that did not make her a novelist it determined the kind of novelist she was. She has written novels which are set in the past but rejects a description of herself as a historical novelist. You would echo that, wouldn't you? Although you have set a number of your books in the past there is something about that title, historical novelist, which seems vaguely pejorative in this culture.

Tremain: Who does it suggest, I don't know, Philippa Gregory, Mary Renault, possibly at the best. I think it suggests novels that aren't about very much, that they just tell romping good stories. I am all in favour of the romping good story. I love story telling. I think as novelists we undervalue story telling at our peril, and to tell a good story isn't as easy as you might think. I really believe that, but I think a novel that has a serious intention has to be about far more than just its story. There have to be ideas in it. There doesn't seem to be a term other than historical novel that can encapsulate the book with serious intent that happens to be set in the past. If anybody could come up with such a term I would be very grateful to them. I haven't in twenty years.

Bigsby: Your most recent novel, *Trespass*, reflects that interest in France that we were talking about earlier.

Tremain: *Trespass* is a novel set in the Cevennes in France, which is a region I now know very well. It is very beautiful, a national park in France, wooded and wild and almost impenetrable. There are very few roads in, and what roads in and out there are are dangerous cornice roads, so it is a place where I think the person who doesn't know it feels very vulnerable. For me it has a beauty and a sense of terror, and that combination of beauty and terror is I think very fertile ground for a story. It has always seemed to me that the Cevennes, which I have known for twenty years or so, is the kind of unknowable place where something really terrible might happen. So this was the genesis of this book. I wanted to write a novel set there in which the unthinkable thing happened.

I have never really written about a crime before, again to do with what you were asking me earlier. I think one of the reasons my novels go in different directions is that I am trying to set myself this new boundary each time. I really am interested in what happens to us when we pass the age of sixty, and I am now past that age. I think something round about that time does happen to us. We start to see the shape of everything that has gone before, and we start to measure ourselves against our contemporaries, our siblings. Have we done the thing we set out to do? Was the thing we set out to do the right thing? Have we loved the right people? We start to ask all these questions when we are in our early sixties. So I wanted to write a novel in which all the protagonists are at this moment of crisis in their lives and have to find a way forward. The question I am asking in this book is, how do you find meaning in a life at this point when maybe two thirds or more of your life is behind you? Michael Frayn has said that happiness is absolutely impossible because, if we are thinking about past happiness, we feel sad because it is no longer with us. If we are in a happy moment we are not really in it because we are worried about it slipping away and that future happiness might never come. So happiness is impossible. That's the question that this novel asks. What is happiness and does it exist?

Bigsby: In *Trespass* you take someone from one society and put him in another, and this is a narrative strategy you have used more than once. In *The Colour* you send your characters to New Zealand. In *The Road Home* you have an eastern European immigrant to this country. They all go on literal journeys but they also go on other journeys, moral journeys. Is that a kind of structure that you feel drawn to?

Tremain: Yes, and I think when people say that all my books are very different, somebody like you, who knows me very well, could probably say in a flash of an eye that actually they are all exactly the same because they are all about journeys of one kind or another, and it has to be said that the journey is a wonderful metaphor. Indeed the act of writing a novel is like a journey, particularly for me who doesn't know everything in advance. It is a journey into the unknown in some sense. It is precarious. I think that is what keeps me going. I am often asked who is your ideal reader, who are you writing the books for? I think the most truthful answer I can give to that is really that I am writing them for me. I am writing them to expand my understanding of the world, which may or may not involve research periods that will take me to different places, either actually, geographically, or in terms of the reading that I have to do. The whole process of getting an idea, then reading, takes ages.

At the heart of *Trespass* is a crime that paradoxically, awful though it is, sets everybody free, and I love paradoxes, so this act of putting it altogether and then eventually making something reasonably coherent out of it seems to me one of the most passionate things one could do with a life.

Bigsby: In *The Road Home* you seem to me to have been trying to stage both the dilemma of an individual trying to make something coherent of his life and a society trying to make sense of a change which some found disturbing.

Tremain: I think I was inspired by something that Malcolm Bradbury used to say. He used to say something along the lines of fiction, i.e. the imaginative world, is the best pathway through troubled times. What I understand now by that is that fiction, by examining in very intimate detail the life of individuals, can have an impact on the way people see a group. I think immigration, in this country, has become an issue that provokes greater anxiety than it did before I wrote *The Road Home*. It came out three years ago. When I was writing the book I was anxious to show the other side, to imagine what it is like to be somebody coming, with very little of the language and no money, from an east-European country where things were going badly, and all the things that have been precious to him, including his wife, have been taken away from him. He is one of my characters who start with nothing and have to remake their lives, or try to. It is very interesting to me that I think that Malcolm was absolutely right about that in that I do still get letters from people about that book saying that when they see great crowds of eastern European immigrants in the tube or working on their houses, whereas they used to feel that there were too many of them, to feel hostile to them, they now don't think that. Having seen the inside, the absolute interior, of these characters, they are able to think in a much more empathetic way, and we are very short on empathy, it seems to me, this far into the twenty-first century. Maybe in any kind of serious political debate it is always very difficult for the writer of fictions to hold her own. Is the work we do important or is it just diversion? What is its significance in the culture? This is one defence that I would make for it, that it does bring alive something that perhaps we have never thought carefully enough about.

Bigsby: You are now beginning to plan your next novel and for the first time you are going to return to an earlier work.

Tremain: It is always said that writing sequels is the worst thing you could possibly ever dream of doing but *Restoration* is an old favourite of mine. This voice has stayed with me for twenty years now and it seems to be the right time to take it up again and that is what I am going to do next. Twenty years have gone by. I am twenty years older. He is twenty years older, and we arrive, very neatly, in the terrible winter of 1683, which is two years before King Charles dies. So everything is going bad, everybody is getting old and they are poor. It is the credit crunch *Restoration*, so it leads us neatly on to a new exploration of this world.

I have been resisting this and everybody has said to me you can't possibly do that. It will never be as good as the first one, which probably it will turn out not to be, but there you are. I am going to do it.

In Conversation With
Jane Urquhart

- 14th November 2005 -

Jane Urquhart, poet and novelist, was born in Thunder Bay, Ontario, in 1949, graduating from the University of Guelph in 1971. Her first novel, *The Whirlpool* (1986) won the French Prix du Meilleur Livre Étranger. She followed this with *Storm Glass* (1987) and *Changing Heaven* (1990). *Away* (1993) won the Trillium Book Award while *The Underpainter* (1997) won the Governor General's Award for Fiction. She subsequently published *The Stone Carvers* (2001), *A Map of Glass* (2005) and *Sanctuary Line* (2010). She is also the author of four volumes of poetry, her 2000 collection being entitled *Some Other Garden*. In 2005 she was named an Officer of the Order of Canada.

Bigsby: We first met when I was sent to Canada by the BBC to do two programmes on the Arts in Toronto and the sharp-eyed producer of the programme had spotted a first novel by a young Canadian woman. It was called *The Whirlpool* and it was set at the bottom of Niagara Falls. Your new novel, *A Map of Glass*, is your sixth.

Urquhart: Looking at the cover of *A Map of Glass* it occurs to me that that could have been the cover for the very first one and even today, when I was looking at it, I thought, is there something alarming about the fact that I can pick a cover for my sixth novel that would have worked perfectly well for my first novel, and probably my second novel, and third novel, and fourth novel, and fifth novel. I suppose the thing that makes it work for all of those novels is the water, and the traditional Canadian pine trees. A woman on the front of *A Map of Glass* is fishing in the water, and then there is the traditional Canadian canoe, nosing its way for those who want to see it. It is like an Irish image, in a sense, because you can only see it if you want to see it. It is like McGee Island in Ireland which can only be seen by the McGee family. So, only Canadians can see this Canadian canoe moving off from the rocks.

I took risks with this book, which is a good thing on some levels, but it makes it almost impossible to give anyone a clear indication of what the progression of the narrative would be since I am not sure there is a progression to the narrative. But one hopes that there is enough that a reader would want to read it from the beginning to the end. And the only way that I can continue to hope that a reader will want to read it from the beginning to the end was that I wanted to write it from the beginning to the end, and since I am a lazy person I don't usually do that unless I want to find out what is going to happen.

What happens in this book happens both in the present and the past. I am often involved in arguments, with academics in particular, who say to me, 'Why don't you write about the present?' and I say, 'Because you can't. By the time you have finished it is the past.' But this takes place partly, allegedly, in the present and also partly in the nineteenth century. It takes place in Prince Edward county, which is the county in Ontario on the edge of Lake Ontario, not on the edge of the Niagara river but downstream. It also takes place a little bit in Ireland and partly in the city of Toronto. That is the present.

What I found interesting when I was dealing with the alleged present was that somehow it needed to be in an urban setting. The main character, whose name is Sylvia, is a woman who has never in her life gone to the city on her own. She lives in a small town in Prince Edward county. She lives in the same house that her father lived in, and her grandfather. She is surrounded by ancestral furniture and ancestral things and as a result she has developed a kind of terror of change, and at the same time a very heightened awareness of the details of the world around her. I suppose it has something to do with intimacy.

I think about this quite a bit actually, about what has happened to all of us, or those of us who are authors anyway, and are constantly on the road. I think we start to lose the ability to become intimate, not perhaps with each other, but with the details of life, the things one uses every day, the knives and forks and the grouse in the back yard and the tree in the back yard, and all of that. It starts to become fuzzy. This is a woman who has precisely the opposite problem. She can't let go of the details of her immediate life until she is forced to do so by circumstances, and those circumstances make up at least a good part of this book.

In the present Sylvia approaches a young man called Jerome as a result of the fact that he has discovered the body of someone that Sylvia was very close to. He lives in a studio in Toronto. He is an artist and he lives with his young lady friend. The nineteenth century part of the book refers to the ancestors of a man called Andrew who was Sylvia's lover and the person Jerome found beside the river. This takes place in Canada, in about the 1840s, on an island that does exist. For those of you who know Ontario, it is in the harbour almost off Kingston. It may be a mile offshore and the name of the Island is not Timber Island, as I call it in the book. It is Garden Island, and Garden Island really was inhabited by a family who made their living and did rather well for a certain period of time harvesting timber, from the lower great lakes, to begin with, then, gradually, as the wood ran out, from the upper great lakes.

Bigsby: Canada is a settler country, an immigrant country. I presume your family came from Ireland?

Urquhart: Half my family came from Ireland. My mother's side of the family came from Ireland. My father's side of the family came from Coventry. My father's family would have come much earlier, probably late eighteenth century, early nineteenth century, and they came to Prince Edward County, the very county in which a lot of this book takes place, so I hasten to add that Kingston, Ontario, was not in Prince Edward county. It is in another county. Then my mother's side of the family came from Ireland during the famine in the 1840's.

Bigsby: How much in this novel comes from your family history and how much have you just imagined yourself back into that world?

Urquhart: I utterly imagined myself back into that world but, interestingly, I was doing something in that novel which had been going on in my family forever, and that was imagining ourselves back into Ireland because my mother's side of the family dominated completely and were very, very suspicious of my father's side of the family. You can imagine Irish Catholic, English Protestant, big suspicion. Anyway, in the Quinn family, the Irish Catholic side of my family, the side I was permitted access to a certain extent, there was an old saying: "You could marry into it but you couldn't marry out of it." So once you were in you couldn't even go back and visit your own relatives. It was that fierce. Those same relatives spent all their time imagining themselves back on the other side of the water in this imaginary place called Ireland which had been idealised well beyond anything that resembled reality. They would weep and cry, sing sad Irish songs, and they would get ferocious about political events in Ireland, all that having never laid eyes on it.

Bigsby: That is the story of immigrant countries, isn't it? You brought with you the stories and myths of another country, the other place.

Urquhart: And the other place, I think, has a tendency to grow in importance as the generations happen because obviously the first generation immigrant knows precisely how bad it was, and therefore hasn't really started to idealise things yet. But there is that cultural connection that causes the first generation immigrant to want to pass on to the children various aspects of the culture, and that goes on I think. In Canada it goes on right now, of course, because people from all over the world have come to Canada recently.

Bigsby: And there was no mythicising of England on the other side?

Urquhart: I suspect there was, but I was never permitted to have access to that due to the fact that I was a good Irish person. I had to pay no attention to things like the Orange Parade and all of that.

Bigsby: Do you have a house in Ireland now?

Urquhart: I do. Well, house is an exaggeration. I have a place.

Bigsby: So the myth has some power over you?

Urquhart: Oh, a huge amount of power. It is still alive and well and functioning in my imagination, even as we speak.

Bigsby: You were raised in a small town?

Urquhart: I was born in Little Longlac, northern Ontario, about a thousand miles north of Toronto. My father was a prospector and a mining engineer, though he preferred the prospector side. Romanticism was a disease on both sides of my family and mining engineer, up until very recently, seemed to me to be much more prosaic than prospector, until I realised that mining engineers were engineers of the underground which I love.

Bigsby: So you started life in a small town wilderness?

Urquhart: Yes, I was born there but the mine closed and then we moved to Toronto, but my father spent all his time up there anyway. That was probably his way of getting us into the city so he could run back to "the bush".

Bigsby: What did education mean to you when you went to school? Was it Canadian history, Canadian literature, or was it British?

Urquhart: I think you know the answer to that question – absolutely no Canadian history, no Canadian literature. As a matter of fact I think most of my teachers believed that there was no such as either Canadian history or Canadian literature. That is not entirely true. There was a man called Stephen Leacock who wrote a book called *Sunshine Sketches of a Little Town* and I quickly read one story from that collection, which was a humorous story and quite light, quite delightful, actually. But apart from that, no.

Bigsby: Not children's literature, then?

Urquhart: No. Children's literature again took place somewhere else completely.

Bigsby: So where did the idea of becoming a Canadian writer come from?

Urquhart: I am not entirely sure. I think I knew that I could be a Canadian poet, because that wouldn't take up too much space, and you could put together say a book that was sixty pages and slip it through somehow without anyone noticing, especially your mother. So I did that for a while.

Bigsby: How old were you when you wanted to be a poet?

Urquhart: In my twenties. That seemed to be okay. What I could not imagine being was a Canadian novelist. I couldn't imagine writing a great big book so that when I was writing the first big book, which wasn't that big at all, *The Whirlpool,* I just convinced myself. I called it "The thing," and I thought I was writing a very long, long, long, prose poem, and it just kept growing. Had I told myself I was writing a novel there is no chance I could have written it.

Bigsby: I am interested you say prose poem because the prose actually carries many of the qualities of the poetry?

Urquhart: Yes, I think it does. I find that I become uninterested quickly if there isn't a kind of cadence in the language that I use. I just lose interest. I can read with great pleasure spare prose, or fiction that is beautifully crafted and is not dependent on imagery, but I can't write it.

Bigsby: It seems to me you have an enormous advantage, however, in writing about a country that doesn't have that depth of literary tradition. In this country, where you can't be more than seventy-eight miles from the sea, there is not a patch of land that hasn't been turned into fiction, whereas Canada was not quite a blank sheet, but getting on that way.

Urquhart: That is why England seems so magical to us because we are walking around in this world that until the minute we get here we believe is entirely fictional, because someone made it up. We have read those stories. We entered those landscapes through our imagination and therefore even now I can hardly believe where I am half the time because of the fiction I read in school and in university and on my own. Also because of the pictures that I look at, the Constables and Turners. I think I am in magic land. I can't quite explain it. It is probably something that you would never experience.

Bigsby: The title of your novel is *A Map of Glass*, but in a way mapping is what you have always been doing. You have been mapping Canada, your Canada, almost from the beginning, precisely because there wasn't a map there already.

Urquhart: That is very true. I think that there are a number of us who as Canadian writers are doing that, and again we get back to this whole thing of whether we set things in the present or the past. But what you say about the mapping is also very true in that because we weren't given an official history, and because we weren't given an official canon of literature, we were also not handed a set of rules and the restrictions didn't apply either. History could be anything we wanted it to be. It could be a personal history or it could be a local history, for example. I find I am very drawn to the local history sections of our public libraries because in 1967, which was our centenary, people were encouraged to write down anything they could remember about the past of whatever village or town they lived in and to publish these things in small booklets which have ended up filling a vast local history. But we are not restricted by the whole notion of what history is. We are able to explore various points of view, which of course one should be able to do.

Bigsby: You talked about the absence of Canadian literature in your upbringing but when you started writing Alice Munro was writing, as were Mordecai Richler and Margaret Atwood. Were they not part of your consciousness when you first started writing?

Urquhart: Oh, they were absolutely part of my consciousness, yes, for sure, but I didn't think I could ever grow up to be like them, so what could I do? They were only ten years older than me, or fifteen years, but they seemed so much more grown up than me.

Bigsby: I mentioned the idea of mapping but you are also interested in the past, or perhaps traces of the past. It is powerful in this new novel. There are traces in the landscape that take you back to people who used to live there. There are traces in people's lives and the way they impact on other people. So isn't that also part of your interest in mapping, the desire to reach back to a discarded past or a past that can be so easily discarded, ignored.

Urquhart: Yes, there is a certain amount of retrieval, I think, in the process. I was really, really gratified, after I had published *Away*, my third novel, the one that dealt with Ireland, that a professor at the University of Toronto who came from Belfast asked me if I happened to be a historical geographer. I had never even heard of historical geography at that point and I immediately started to try and find out what it was so that I could answer in some sort of sane and sensible way. Now I have come to the point where the character who disappears in my book is a historical geographer. I love that idea of reading the landscape, which is what historical geographers do. I am not certain that they do it in Canada yet, but that did not prevent me from creating a character. This is the great thing about fiction. You can pretty much do what you want.

Bigsby: Perhaps you can explain the title, *A Map of Glass*.

Urquhart: *A Map of Glass* is a stolen title, although not entirely stolen you will be happy to know. It was the title of a work of art by a visual artist called Robert Smithson. He was one of the original "birth artists." Those of you who know something about visual art may remember that he made a large spiral jetty in Utah in the middle of the salt lake. He died tragically while trying to film this spiral jetty in a spiral way in an airplane. It didn't work and the plane crashed. But he also did a lot of installation work and he did things that he called mirror displacements. One of his mirror displacements was called *A Map of Broken Glass*. I didn't like the broken part, I just wanted the map of glass. Robert Smithson is the hero of my young artist, Jerome, in the book.

Bigsby: He is not the only real person to crop up in your novels. People make appearances who were a part of that past, and not just a fictive part of it.

Urquhart: Yes, they enter the novel in some way or another because I convince myself, when I begin, that the book is really going to be about that particular person. They draw me into the novel, the real people, but somehow they become minor characters en route. An American artist from the 1930s interested me enormously and I really believed I was going to write a novel about him but he became a minor character in a novel of mine called *The Underpainter* while the main character was entirely made up. So I seem to need to do both of those things.

Bigsby: Your invoking of *The Underpainter* it is a reminder that artists are for ever popping up in your work. A central character in *The Stone Carvers* is an artist. *The Underpainter* features an artist, as does *A Map of Glass*. Why?

Urquhart: Well, I have been marrying them. I have been married to two artists, visual artists, and now I have a stepson who is a visual artist as is my daughter's boyfriend. I am just surrounded by them. I try to keep them out but it is not working. That is my last novel about visual artists.

Bigsby: *The Underpainter* offers a term which describes this business of the layering of past and present: pentimento, a painting underneath a painting. That strikes me as partly the process by which you work when you have these two timescales. One is layered over another and the other is never quite invisible. It remains as a shadow.

Urquhart: Yes, I think that is true to a certain extent. I think it is also very true of the world in which I live in Canada. It is obviously true here, but it is true in a clearer way in Canada I suppose because of that uncluttered canvas you were talking about that is the Canadian landscape, but also the Canadian mindscape. With the exception of our native people, of course, we are all immigrants, as you have said. The longer ago our families came the more likely we are to be "settler" class, and it is very interesting to live in a country where everything was set up in the nineteenth century, or at least in Ontario certainly. It is not necessarily true of the west because the way that the migration took place was that it went westward. Therefore parts of the west are not settled by western culture, or weren't until the twentieth century. Even the grid work, the whole physical basis of our lives, was established in one century and in a very short period of time. The concession roads and the way they are laid out, the way the farming lots are laid out, the fence lines are laid out, the way the streets of the towns and cities are laid out, all that was all invented in the nineteenth century. So we have a particular past, a particular present, rather than a long, long, long past and a particular present. It is quite fascinating from that point of view, plus the kind of archival material available in Canada. It is fascinating and almost untouched, and that is a very different experience from even the United States.

Bigsby: Because of this interest in the past there is also an interest in memory and indeed we enter *A Map of Glass* through somebody who has lost his memory as a result of Alzheimer's?

Urquhart: Yes, I have become very interested in memory, I suppose partly because of the fact that here I am, in my fifties, and, who knows, it could happen to me any day. But I think it is because by the time you have been alive on the planet for fifty years so much has disappeared out of your life and so much is held only by memory. That includes people and landscapes. The whole notion of going back to something is always terrifying because you know that it is really not ever going to be there again, whether that is the human being you remember, or your childhood home, whether it is a street or a country lane. Anything is likely to have undergone massive change in fifty years. Maybe it was always like this, I don't know, but it feels as if it is a condition of our particular present. So memory seems to me to be terribly important all of a sudden in a way that perhaps it wasn't twenty-five years ago. It is something that is fragile and should be held on to as the only access to certain things that I have loved and cared about. That is likely why I was so obsessed by it at this stage.

Bigsby: And yet there is a tension because it is also necessary to forget. It is necessary to accept change, and in this novel there are those who fail precisely because they can't accept change.

Urquhart: That's right. I think that certainly the main character, Sylvia, is frozen into the past. She is so obsessed by the past that she can't get out without a kind of trauma.

Bigsby: She is almost autistic.

Urquhart: Yes, it is interesting because her family wants to diagnose her, her husband wants to diagnose her, and I decided, okay, if her family and her husband want to diagnose her, I am not going to diagnose her. There is a condition that is made reference to in the book, but the condition is never accurately identified. I would say that she is really closer to

Asperger's than autism, and even that is debatable. She is in a sense just an exaggerated facet of myself, though I don't identify with her in any real way. I think the impulse that drove me to write the book, that business of wanting to hold on to the past even while I was watching it disintegrate around me, may have been in a very exaggerated way part of the make up of her character.

Bigsby: When it comes to change in the novel, you refer to logging which effectively destroyed the landscape. There is no more logging, but they can't adjust to that. There are people who plant barley for the booze for the Americans but they only plant barley and destroy the soil. The sand takes over and slowly begins to bury the landscape. In fact there is a real place, isn't there, that gets buried by sand, a hotel?

Urquhart: Yes, it does, and that is a true story. It is part of the local history of Prince Edward County in Ontario, but also a story that my father often told, coming from Prince Edward County. It was about the hotel that is apparently still there, if anybody wants to go digging underneath the sandbanks, in a place called Sandbanks Provincial Park. What happened, of course, was that there was a great demand for barley from the American market. The farmers were making just a ton of money and they did not rotate their crops and eventually they destroyed the soil. At the same time the Americans slapped a huge tariff on Canadian barley just to add insult to injury and the sand bar that goes down the middle of Lake Ontario moved inland and kept on moving. So not only did it bury this hotel, it also destroyed several farms. Even the barley couldn't grow any more and people would have to abandon their farms. My father could see the third storey of that hotel when he was a child. By the time I was born it was gone.

Bigsby: There is a need to hold on and there is a need to let go simultaneously?

Urquhart: I think that is very true and the character of Sylvia is interesting to me in that she really does start to let some of it go by the end of the book, partly because she connects with a couple of young people. One of these young people, of course, is a new immigrant to Canada and seemed to be very, very alive and very present in her own life and therefore able to identify and adapt to almost anything, which was lovely and energetic and delightful for that reason.

In Conversation With Peter Ustinov

- 7th November 1998 -

Peter Ustinov, novelist, short story writer, playwright, actor, director, raconteur, winner of two Academy Awards, three Emmys, a Golden Globe, a BAFTA and a Grammy, was born in London in 1921 and died in 2004. He was fluent in six languages. He made his stage debut as an actor in 1938 and film debut in 1940, writing and directing his first film four years later. He appeared in more than one hundred film and television productions. He is probably best remembered for his appearances in *Spartacus* (1960), *Topkapi* (1964), *Death on the Nile* (1978) and *Lorenzo's Oil* (1992). Among his many plays were *The Love of Four Colonels* (1951) and *Romanoff and Juliet* (1956). His novels included and *Krumnagel: A Novel* (1976) and *Monsieur René* (1998). He is the author of several autobiographical works.

Bigsby: Your name might lead people to believe that you are not British but in fact you were born in London, in Swiss Cottage. But if we were to trace it any further back than that the story begins to get extremely complicated?

Ustinov: Yes, that's right. It is very interesting because I have discovered recently that my great, great, great, great grand uncle was the first Donatello in *Don Giovanni* creating the role with Mozart in Prague.

Bigsby: Don't I remember that your grandmother conspired to murder your grandfather?

Ustinov: Yes, she did but she didn't succeed. My grandfather left Russia. He was exiled because he became a Protestant, which was forbidden in the army. One thinks that many of these ludicrous things are Soviet but they existed a long time before that and the Soviets failed to eradicate them. In the Russian army at that time regular officers had to take an oath of allegiance every year to the Czar and to the Orthodox Church. My grandfather had fallen off his horse during manoeuvres – which is something I might have done too so I feel very close to him in a way – and had to lie on a board for two years. In those days there was no radio and no television and to read *War and Peace* in that position must have been very awkward. He fell in love with this girl from the so-called German Volga republic, which is the other side of the Volga. He married her and they were exiled together but as soon as they were out of Russia she ran away with an Australian sea captain. These things happened in that generation. She returned after a year with a child which was not his so he was forced to divorce despite his new Protestant convictions and went eventually, as an amateur archaeologist, to Palestine, which was then Turkish of course, and married my grandmother who was part Ethiopian and part Swiss. That was another story of the same kind because the Swiss went out to Ethiopia as a clergyman to convert them to the true faith and was converted himself.

Bigsby: That is only some of the bits and pieces.

Ustinov. That is only some of the bits. My mother's family is much more interesting because she was a painter and her uncle worked on all sorts of ballets for Diaghilev. Their father, my grandfather, was an architect who built the Russian chapel in Homburg, near Frankfurt, for the Prince of Hesse in 1902, I think. When she was eight, my mother remembers asking him, when he came back tired to St. Petersburg, 'How is it going with the Prince?' and him telling her, 'Not well. He is deaf in one ear and doesn't understand with the other'. So their father was an architect, too, and my grandfather's grandfather was the architect of the Kirov Theatre, the Mariinsky Theatre in St. Petersburg, and also rebuilt the Bolshoi after the big fire. There were many big fires, don't ask me which one it was, but they were always careless with plugs and cigarettes and so on. His father was a composer who was the last Italian director of the Russian opera. After that, they were all Russians. His father was a dancer and his mother was at the time a celebrated soprano, one of four sisters, all of whom were sopranos.

Bigsby: I would like to ask you one more thing about these national identities. You would think that with so many different national roots you would resist the idea of there being any substance to national stereotypes, but is there? Surely there is something in the stereotypes we have of Germans and Italians and so on, isn't there?

Ustinov. Yes, but they are very often out of date and that is what I don't like about them. There is no country which has changed more than Germany. It has really reverted to what it was before Napoleon walked across them and drove them into a unity. He is responsible for a great deal, Napoleon. They keep on blaming Hitler although they probably wouldn't in the future because if Pinochet gets off so would Hitler if he suddenly reappeared.

Bigsby: On the other hand, in your forthcoming book, *Planet Ustinov*, you quote a remark to the effect that in Switzerland whatever is not forbidden is compulsory.

Ustinov: That was a Swiss ambassador who said that. He was a Swiss ambassador in Washington and he asked if I liked it in Switzerland and I said I did but he said he preferred it in America. Then he told me that story. So everybody has a sense of humour. The German's sense of humour now is extremely lively and very elegant. I remember on my seventy-fifth birthday, when I was giving a performance in Berlin, seeing Roman Hertzog, President of Germany, in the front row and he was laughing a great deal. Afterwards I said, 'Thank you for laughing so much because it helped me a great deal.' He said, 'I enjoy laughing, but of course it is much easier if there is a pretext.' I saw him two weeks ago when he gave me a medal, which was very charming, and while it was going on and people were applauding he shook me by the hand and said, 'There is nothing in the world you need less than this, but it is your own fault that you are here. You deserve it.'

Bigsby: When you were young you went to a wonderfully named preparatory school, which sounds Dickensian – Mr. Gibb's Preparatory School for Boys. Was it there that you began to develop your talents as a performer? Was it a defensive gesture in school?

Ustinov: Yes, I was stout as a boy and I couldn't do things very quickly. I was very slow in learning how to tie a football boot lace. I always had to have help and so I developed a sense of making people laugh as a defence mechanism. I am sure it was that but it probably came naturally because nature understands that if you are stout you need to develop that very quickly. I know that I was the goalkeeper in the school football team because they thought I occupied more of the goal than other boys and therefore risked stopping a ball. I was very bad at maths and we won quite a few cricket matches because they made me the scorer. I will draw a veil over that sort of thing. I don't think this should be transparent.

Bigsby: And did your skills at mimicry begin then?

Ustinov: Yes, they began then.

Bigsby: You went on from that preparatory school to public school, Westminster, where presumably you had to wear strange clothing?

Ustinov. England, I think, is the only country I know where occasionally elderly men dress up as small boys to play some game or other. There is a tremendous nostalgia for school here. I keep on being invited back to a place from which I escaped with pleasure. I have been back and it has changed entirely because now it is coeducational and they dress in ordinary clothes. I had to dress up, at the age of thirteen, with a stiff collar, top hat, tail coat, striped trousers and a furled umbrella. I never unfurled the umbrella. I walked through a hailstorm because I could never furl it again and I knew that so it really became a walking stick in disguise. I must say it was not much fun in those days because we were also selected, because we came from that particular school, to stand and look solemn at George V's funeral and then at George VI's coronation. We had to be tremendously excited and happy and I hate doing that to order.

Bigsby: And you rubbed shoulders with some rather I was going to say strange people, but the sons of some strange people, the son of Ribbentrop?

Ustinov. Yes, and my father was having trouble at the German embassy at the time. I had a choice between British and German nationality, though as you said I was born in London. I sat next to him – he is still alive, a rather charming fellow now, covered with freckles and rather overgrown. The silly ambassador, his father, wanted him to go to Eton because he had heard that all sorts of battles had been won on the playing fields of Eton and he wanted the son to find out how it had been done. You go there. You keep your eyes open. But Eton refused to have him though he had already bought the top hat. The government twisted Westminster's arm to have him and there he was with the top hat in Little Dean's Yard, the virtual headquarters of the Anglican church, full of bishops walking around staring at nothing and gaining inspiration from trees. Into this place, where the Bishops' baby Austins and Morris Minors were parked, came this enormous Mercedes every morning, gasping with external exhaust pipes and moving in fits and starts in order not to hit the Morris Minors. Then Ribbentrop got out with his tail coat and his Nazi party youth badge, a sort of swastika with a red diamond, and one heard him through Little Dean's Yard, with choir practice going on in the distance, talking to the chauffeur before going into the abbey to pray for our defeat.

Bigsby: I would have thought that some of the sons of the aristocracy in this country were probably doing that along with him?

Ustinov: Yes, I don't know whether I can tell an absolutely scabrous story here but I am sure I can. I had a hideous tendency to giggle. I have never lost it. I don't do it quite as often but then it was awful and I was taken by my parents – he was still employed by the German embassy, and I was still German – to a visitor who had obviously impressed the Cliveden Set and was with the head of Reuters who thought it was wonderful what they were doing with the new Germany. This man was a leading civilian Nazi. He didn't speak English very well but was very loud. I promised that, if I was taken along, I would not laugh if anything untoward happened. We were all at lunch and he was extolling the new Germany and saying how efficient it was and how we were all inspired by Hitler in those days and all the guests were listening terribly interestedly: 'Yes, really? How interesting.' All that was going on and suddenly he said, 'I will give you an example of how efficient the new Germany is. If anything happens in my office which makes me feel something untoward I have on my desk a bottom.' He got the word wrong. 'I have on my desk a bottom and I only have to press my bottom,' he said, 'before policemen will come out.' I had to be steered out into the garden and it was raining.

Bigsby: We established earlier on where the genetic connection to theatre came from but you had your debut at an unfortunate time, the end of August 1939?

Ustinov: Yes, but my father always wanted me to be a lawyer because he himself failed to be one as a result of the outbreak of the 1914 war. I never wanted to be a lawyer but I had a premonition and said to him, 'Look, I will be an actor, which is the same profession but much less dangerous to my fellow men'. He didn't really care for that but once I started he brought friends to see me and then went out before the end in order not to be seen, but it was always too late. I had always seen him.

Bigsby: You had your debut in the London theatre immediately on the edge of the war and indeed you then entered the army but that didn't actually stop your theatrical career.

Ustinov: Well, no, my role in the army was the longest run I ever had. I was playing a private to which I was not really suited as a part. I would have preferred something not further up, further down if necessary. I knew that I would survive somehow.

Bigsby: Here you were, a product of Westminster, officer material, but you remained a private throughout the entire war. How did you do that?

Ustinov: They actually made me a civilian for a time out of embarrassment when I wrote a film called *The Way Ahead* but I wouldn't have missed it for anything because I knew that though at the time I loathed it, loathed every minute of it, and have never wasted more of my own or anybody else's time than there, in retrospect I would find it invaluably funny and could then talk about it with authority because some of the NCOs then seemed to have come straight from the Crimean war with only a coffee break in between. They were unbelievably awful and ignorant and silly.

Bigsby: I shouldn't disparage your war service because you did actually capture a town, didn't you?

Ustinov: I captured Maidstone, because I broke away from my parent unit. They were trying to test the Home Guard to see how efficient they were. I suspect *Dad's Army* is a very, very good requiem for the whole thing because it was exactly like that. I knew we were going to have trouble because they dug a trench across Britain in case the Germans came. A trench! And the trench went across the grounds of Dover castle. That is where it started. But, yes, I captured Maidstone by going across the traffic not down streets. I went and knocked on front doors and men in pyjamas came out and I said, 'This is a military operation.' 'Oh, yes,' they said, 'Well, come in then.' And then I was taken to the back door and went into the garden, over the hedge, to the next garden and knocked on the back door where another man in pyjamas said, 'Yes?' and I said, 'Military, military,' 'Right, come in.' I got into the centre of Maidstone by showing myself as little as possible in the street and going through houses. There was the General in charge of it and we had no ammunition obviously so I said, 'Bang,' and a young officer called Mr. Biddle, I remember that very well, who was a referee and who unfortunately had a stutter, said to the general, 'I am sorry sir you are dead,' and the General said, 'Oh, no I am not' and refused to acknowledge that he was dead.

He went away, alive, to direct some other operations and was furious with me and I was told I was dead. I said, 'No, you can't have it both ways. I shot him first.' And then they asked me all sorts of questions and I said, 'Well, listen. Either I'm dead or I'm not. I can't answer questions if I am dead.' They said, 'Don't you be impertinent.' That is the way the whole Home Guard seemed to operate and they locked me in the Guard Room, which was a silly thing to do because it was full of machine guns and things. I seized one of them and ran out and before I was overpowered I spilt ink over all their maps and they were absolutely beyond fury and said, 'Now you answer this question. Are you a member …?' So I spoke to them only in German. I gave them my number and eventually they called my colonel, who was a man who looked rather like a tortoise but had buck teeth. He came out of the front of his uniform, so much so that you could see the name of the maker and he said, 'Now what is all this?' I said, 'Well, I am sorry sir, I presume that the exercise is there so that people can assess what it would be like to have German-speaking people among them who can't speak any English'. I told him that I had been dead. I had had every type of adventure. I had shot the General, then I had been killed myself, and now I was a prisoner. He began to find that vaguely amusing and said, 'Did you have to speak German?' I said, 'They are not going to get the luxury of people coming in here speaking perfect English. What are they going to do when they get the real thing?' 'Yes, I suppose so,' he said, 'I think you are right of course. Just follow me out, stay close to me and there won't be any trouble.' That is the story of how I captured Maidstone. Did I get an award for it? No, I did not.

Bigsby: And all of this time your theatrical career was going on. How did the army respond to the fact that you had this other life, this successful theatrical life?

Ustinov: Towards the end, with great embarrassment. I had a colonel, when I was suddenly attached to a theatrical unit, who had previously been an agent, and towards the end of my four years he asked me into his office and then locked the door, which I didn't like very much. Then he said, 'Well, Ustinov, funny old thing, life, isn't it? We are all human beings. You don't take any notice. What difference does it make?' I began to worry about his sanity and then he said, 'I will be going back to civvy street. I don't know what awaits me there. Anything is possible. I will try and pick up the old strands. Will I be able to do it? Your guess is as good as mine. Ah, it's a funny old thing isn't it?' Then he said, 'You have got a play on in London. It seems to be running well.' I said, 'Yes,' and he said, 'You interested in a Rolex?' and I said, 'No, I have a watch already sir.' 'Rolex is it?' he replied. I said, 'No, but there are other makes.' I didn't know how to get out of that at all. He was obviously very keen to sell it. It is an odd colonel/private relationship.

Bigsby: You acted with many of the major actors of Britain including a favourite of mine, Sir Ralph Richardson. I think he was a favourite because I suspected he was as eccentric off stage as he sometimes appeared to be on stage. Was he?

Ustinov. Absolutely. You would see him and he would greet you ecstatically and then ten minutes later he would greet you again as though he hadn't seen you the first time, but with tremendous ebullience. He was always very surprised to see you at all and he was of course delightful. I had to direct him in the first film I directed and that was quite an experience because I wasn't used to this kind of extraordinary eccentricity. He liked to drive motorbikes. There was a wonderful moment I remember when suddenly he came in in the morning and said, 'Hello, it's a wonderful day, ouch,' and every time he talked he whistled. I made a sign to my assistant to come and listen to him. He understood immediately what was wrong and went back to telephone Ralph Richardson's house because Ralph, on that day, was athletically eager to get on with it: 'Come on. Can we start shooting (whistle)?' and didn't notice the whistle. And I said, 'Something is wrong' so they phoned his home and he had a very complicated system with bridgework because he had crashed so many cars and motor bicycles and even aeroplanes. There was a rumour he had been invalided out because he cost the British government too much money in aircraft which went into hedges and I could well believe it because he had this kind of lunar approach to everything, 'Come on let's go. Bang!' And this bridgework would have been left at home. They said they had found it so a Rolls Royce came out. Meanwhile the assistant came and said, 'You are wanted on the phone.' 'I don't want to talk on the phone. I want to start acting (whistle).' I said, 'You have plenty of time to go.' 'I don't want to go. I will sit in my room and sulk (whistle),' and it was impossible to get rid of him. Then suddenly he went to the phone because I said something may have happened at home. He said, 'Why do you put ideas like that into my head (whistle)?' I said, 'I am terribly sorry but I can't imagine why they are phoning you.' He took it and came back and said, 'I'm terribly sorry. I am suffering from a slight migraine. It will go. It is something I acquired during the war (whistle). Can I go and lie down for a moment? They are bringing my medicine from home.' So we allowed him to go and rest and God was that a relief. Twenty minutes later the Rolls Royce arrived and the chauffeur brought this small box, which was taken to his room, supposedly containing his medicine. Suddenly he came out and said, 'Ha! It is a miracle drug. I feel very much better.' and we started work.

Bigsby: I remember in one of your novels you say that there was an actor who was better on a horse than he was off it. How are you acting on horses?

Ustinov: I am very nervous about horses. My great uncle was the commanding general of the Cossacks Savage Division. None of those genes has come my way. I don't know how it is done because, on a horse, first of all you are very far from the ground, and you don't see the face of the horse, which worries me. All you can judge it by is the ears and they go all over the place. There come moments of extreme crisis when one imagines that the ears are consulting each other and so I am not really one for a horse.

Bigsby: Among the people you have acted with was Laurence Olivier, who you appeared with in *Spartacus*. How did you get on with him?

Ustinov: Very well, but he and Charles Lawton were absolutely the antithesis, of course. Larry Olivier once told me, in his cups I must say, that his ambition was to be the first theatrical peer. He said that when he wasn't yet a knight and I thought that was a very strange ambition to have, but Lawton had made his compromise with everything. His favourite phrase was that acting is merely whoring and he loved that idea. When they were together in Hollywood there was Laurence Olivier, with Roger Furse, his designer, signing laundry bills and discussing whether it wasn't too much and could they perhaps not send one pair of underwear this week because everything was accountable to the British. They were there as a kind of paid holiday really. They got paid, of course, but Lawton didn't care. He had already made his compromise. He had acted in some of the worst films ever made as well as some of the best and he had got his Renoirs and his pre-Columbian collection and his swimming pool. I remember him in his swimming pool because he floated very much like an iceberg, well, the opposite of an iceberg, because ninety per cent of him was visible. I don't want to say anything about Olivier which could be construed as critical, because he was a great actor, but he acted very much what he had rehearsed meticulously and he got it right and he wanted to be exactly what that was. But Lawton had a quality, which I prefer, which was that he never forgot to give the impression that it was actually happening and that he had never been rehearsed, which is something I understand personally very much better than the other system which I think is antithetic to film because film is a thing that actually happens at the moment. Even if you want to give a sense of history, Romans didn't behave so very differently from the way we live. Not really. They didn't have to be heroic the whole time. They relaxed too, and when critics said it was ridiculous that Robert Taylor should have said to Deborah Kerr, 'Bring the kids over for the weekend to Capri,' this is exactly what the Romans would have done. They would have said the equivalent of that.

I remember on *Quo Vadis* I was very worried by Mr. Mervyn LeRoy, the film's director. I had never met him before. We met on a huge set in Rome and he looked at me and said, 'How are you darling?' 'I'm alright, thank you very much,' I said. 'Have you any pointers for the part of Nero? 'Nero? Son of a bitch.' I said, 'Yes, yes, there is that of course, but don't you think we could perhaps between us make it a little subtler, a bit more shaded.' That worried him and he suddenly did a tap dance. I thought that was part of his concept. I watched. I was very naïve. I hadn't been a student too long before that. Then he stopped tap dancing and said, 'I used to be a hooker.' That was good to know but it didn't lead me any closer to Nero. So eventually I said, 'Okay' and thought, my God, several months of this is going to be absolute hell. But as I was going out he didn't want to leave the wrong impression so he called after me and said, 'The way I see Nero, this is the kind of guy who plays with himself nights.' I didn't immediately understand how I was going to give this impression and I thought it was pretty silly but now I begin to believe it is probably the profoundest thing ever said about Nero, which leads me to believe that the Americans are the only people who can be really faithful to ancient Rome because they are so similar.

In Conversation With Shirley Williams

- 23rd November 2009 -

Shirley Williams, daughter of Vera Brittain, was born in 1930 and educated at Somerville College, Oxford. She unsuccessfully ran for parliament in 1954 and 1955 but was elected in 1964. From 1971 to 1974 she served as Shadow Home Secretary. In subsequent Labour administrations she served as Secretary of State for Prices and Consumer Protection, Secretary of State for Education and Paymaster General. In 1981 she resigned from the Labour Party to form the SDP. In 1988 she supported a merger with the Liberal Party to form the Liberal Democrats. In 1993 she was elevated to the House of Lords. Among her books are *Politics Is for People* (1981), *Ambition and Beyond: Career Paths of American Politicians* (1993) and *God and Caesar: Personal Reflections on Politics and Religion* (2003). Her autobiography, *Climbing the Bookshelves*, was published in 2009.

Bigsby: Doris Lessing has said that people today forget the scars that people carry from the First World War. It was a wound that never quite healed. Was there an extent to which that was true of your mother?

Williams: Oh, yes, I think certainly. One of the things that my mother, Vera Brittain, tried to do in *Testament of Youth,* which was her most famous book, was to try to get across the characters of the young men she had lost, to immortalise them. I think as a very young child I understood that. Obviously the First World War meant nothing to me in any direct way, but I did feel that that is what she was trying to do and that was why she put her writing as the highest priority in her life, higher certainly than her children, higher than any other part of her life. I could see why, and as she worked her way through explaining and describing and bringing these young men alive, so I think some of the wounds of the First World War began to heal, never completely, but to the extent to which she could become a functioning human being again. So I understood that. After all, she had been a nurse throughout the whole of the First World War, dealing with people with gangrene and with the effects of being gassed, and so forth. It was a pretty rough kind of nursing, closer to butchering in some ways than to nursing. So I think she had to make up for what she had gone through.

Bigsby: She lost her fiancé and her own brother.

Williams: Yes, and her best friends.

Bigsby: In fact, when she died she was buried in Italy with her brother.

Williams: Her ashes were scattered on her brother's grave.

Bigsby: That was something you were involved in facilitating?

Williams: Yes, I went with her literary biographer, but also her very close friend Paul Berry, to Asiago, which is where my uncle, who I of course didn't know at all, had been buried. It was a charming scene because the war cemetery in Asiago is a place that Italians love to have picnics on. You saw these families sitting all around the cemetery with their picnics and bottles of wine and bread and I thought that was wonderful. I didn't find it in any way irreverent.

Bigsby: You said something interesting just now about your mother's priorities because although, in *Climbing the Bookshelves,* you do talk about her loving you and you loving her, what is quite clear is that earlier on that love didn't seem to exist. In the pecking order the work took primacy.

Williams: Yes, but don't forget we are talking about a period in which many, many parents who were professionals had very little to do with their children. They would have a nanny until they were about five. They would then go off to prep school until they were thirteen and then go off to boarding school until they were eighteen. The only time many of these children of well-off parents ever saw them was in the holidays, and not much even then. So we are not talking about now, when I think parents spend a lot of time with their children, and, if anything, get cross with them if also devoted to them. It was a very different and much more formal world.

Bigsby: You speak rather more warmly of your father, at least as someone who believed you should be able to do whatever you wanted to do.

Williams: Don't let me give you any false impressions. I didn't see a great deal of my mother in this period when she was driven by the need to finish *Testament of Youth*, which she finished when I was very young, in 1933, and then went on to *Testament of Experience*, and so on. But I did come to love her very much when I was an older teenager, and when I came back from the United States having been evacuated there for three years. In a way I rediscovered my mother, but by this time I was thirteen. I was old enough to read, to think, much more clearly than when I was nine, and I think that meant that from then on we had a very close relationship. She was a wonderful person to go walking with. She knew the sounds of birds and the names of plants, rather like an Edwardian lady's diary. It was the kind of thing you learned as a young Edwardian woman, which is what she had been. So she gave me a good sense of comradeship because of the long discussions we had on the walks we took.

My father impinged on me much younger because he had lost his mother when he was quite young. His mother had been a suffragist. In the course of that she had established quite a strained relationship with her husband, who was a Church of England vicar at a time when the Church of England was totally opposed to women's suffrage. You couldn't make a living in the Anglican church at that time – we are talking about the period before the First World War – if you or your wife were thought to be supporters of women's suffrage. It was considered to be completely outrageous. So he never could get a living and eventually they parted. She went and worked in a mission in the East End of London so as not to stand in the way of his career, because she didn't feel she could give up her belief in women's suffrage. My father was only sixteen or seventeen when she died and he always had a huge affection for her. So I was in a sense something he saw as being a fruit of her own commitment to women's suffrage. I think I picked that up very early on.

Bigsby: Your family was reasonably well off but when it came time to go to school you chose to go to a local elementary school, and this was in some way your introduction to people who existed on a different level, who came from a different class, a different background.

Williams: It was my immediate introduction to that, but I had already established an extremely close and affectionate relationship with my mother's young housekeeper, who was only eighteen when I was born and so wasn't hugely elderly from my point of view. I was very fond of her. She was a very affectionate woman and when she married she married a wonderfully warm man. I was very close to them. In fact I suppose in some ways they were my alternative parents. My mother also had a number of people she knew well from the First World War who came and saw her and they were by no means all from some protected upper middle class. They were, in some cases, people who had been badly mutilated in the war. So we had a very steady procession of people from different class groups. We also had people from many different countries.

Bigsby: But don't I remember that at school you pretended you were from below stairs?

Williams: I pretended I was my mother's housekeeper's daughter, sure. I didn't want my head bashed on the tarmac too much and that was the only way to do it.

Bigsby: And you became this Cockney kid?

Williams: Yes, and it was a huge revelation at that time because very few people crossed those terrible class barriers in those years, very few.

Bigsby: You were born in 1930 and were therefore nine when the war broke out. Your parents decided to evacuate you to the United States thinking that was the way to keep you safe. Actually putting young children on ships across the Atlantic at that time wasn't necessarily a way to keep them safe.

Williams: But you have got to add the other bit in, which is that my parents had reason to believe that they were likely to be wiped out as soon as there was a German invasion.

Bigsby: Yes. Which side of the family was it that was on the Gestapo list?

Williams: They were both on it. Uniquely, I think they were the only ones who were on the list as a couple.

Bigsby: Your father had been in Spain during the Spanish Civil War.

Williams: He was a war correspondent for the Loyalists and my mother had written *Testament of Youth*, which was anathema to the Nazis because they hated pacifists and anything to do with that. So they were both on the Gestapo black list. My mother in particular was sent to Coventry by quite a lot of other authors. They stopped talking to her. She was quite a prominent figure in the PEN Club so I think some of them were dying to get back at her and they did literally stop talking to her. A lot of people ceased to be her friends because she continued to be a pacifist. She was tipped off by a friend in the Foreign Office about the danger she faced.

They had not seen the Gestapo black list but she was tipped off that she shouldn't take risks.

Her problem, and my father's, was whether they should keep us and possibly risk us being orphaned and left on the streets, or send us away with all the dangers you have described. They both resolved that they couldn't go themselves. They were both very high-minded people. My mother thought that if she went to America as a pacifist she would be denounced as a coward and do a lot of damage to the pacifist movement, though my father was engaged in some very active work to try and bring the United States into the war.

Bigsby: When you got to America, to Minneapolis, you seem to have felt a sense of release and adventure, not homesickness. You revelled in this new world.

Williams: Absolutely true. It was absolutely wonderful, and it was not New York. It wasn't a sort of semi-sophisticated coastal town in the United States. It was genuinely deep America. The school was tremendously informal. We were asked to call our teachers by their first names, Alison and Pam and things like that. Back in England it would have been a near caning offence to call your teachers by their first names. Meanwhile, the academic mountain was a really low one. Very few people were studying algebra and trigonometry and all the stuff I had studied in England, so it was pretty simple to keep up with, and they were much more interested in social relations than they were in academic achievement. I remember when I was about twelve being invited to what was called the first formal, which was just like Jane Austen really. You went to the first formal, which was a dance, and you looked around to see who might be a suitable young man for the future. Then eventually you married somebody else when you were about eighteen. Everyone was married by twenty or twenty-one. So I remember being invited to the first formal and being frightfully annoyed about it because I had never learned to dance and didn't want to dance. I didn't want to spend the whole evening with a boring boy, so I refused.

The invitation was from the captain of the football team at the boys school and there was no invitation more to be prized than this one. My girlfriends simply couldn't understand how I could possibly bring myself to refuse. But I did, and I was then referred to the social councillor for being maladjusted. I should add a postscript to this because, when I got back to England a year later, when I was thirteen, the very first thing I was told by the headmistress of St. Paul's – by this time I was at a well-known English girls school – was that girls could not speak to boys on their way to or from school without risk of being very strictly disciplined. So it was two cultures thousands of miles apart.

Bigsby: You were back in England because your family brought you back. Now it was 1945. Yours was a very politicised family. Politics was the language you spoke even as a teenager. How much did that 1945 government, with all its social welfare legislation, encourage you to think that politics was indeed the direction you wanted to go?

Williams: I think almost completely. I share with Peter Hennessy the view that that was the great government, leaving out the wartime government which was obviously a very special case. Among post-war governments I think the Attlee government was the most remarkable, in terms both of leadership and courage. It's worth remembering that while we now have an economic crunch, which means that we seem to have completely lost any ability to think bravely, in 1948, when the National Health Service was founded for the first time ever, we had a vast debt to the United States. We were up to our neck in borrowing. The United States had just cut off all lending and told us we had to pay it back, but in the face of all this the Labour government of that year started the Health Service and went on to increase pensions and bring in benefits, and so on. It was an amazing achievement by any standard and it was an achievement largely of political courage and political will. It was quite staggering, I thought, and it totally fired me with a feeling that one could actually build a better society, which is what politicians are supposed to want and most do, actually.

Bigsby: At the age of eighteen you went to Oxford, with everything it had to offer, though one thing I forgot to mention earlier is that while you were in America you very nearly became a movie star. The film was *National Velvet*, but you lost out to Elizabeth Taylor. Had you got the part you would have had to marry Richard Burton.

Williams: I know, and seven others. I would rather not.

Bigsby: The only reason I invoke that now is because one of the things you did when you were at Oxford was to act. You played Cordelia in *King Lear*, a production which toured internationally. Were you ever tempted to think that you might like to continue with that after you left?

Williams: Briefly, yes. I think what I really wanted to be was an opera singer but my voice isn't quite right for it. I actually sang in Trafalgar Square. I sang *We Shall Overcome* outside the South African embassy at the time of apartheid.

Bigsby: At Oxford you were a contemporary of Robin Day and Tony Benn and used to go running with Roger Bannister, though not as fast as him. At that time you couldn't really go into the Oxford Union?

Williams: No, we locked ourselves to the railings as a way of protesting, but the Oxford Union and the Cambridge Union both persistently decided not to have women speakers, and that went on until only about, I guess, twenty years ago.

Bigsby: But you did become involved with the Labour Club and once you had left Oxford you ran for parliament at what, even today, seems a very young age.

Williams: Let me break in because the first woman chairman of the Oxford University Labour Club before me was Iris Murdoch. A little known fact.

Bigsby: You ran for parliament in 1954.

Williams: I was described in the press as the school-girl candidate. There were endless pictures of me in scarves and thick white socks. The Conservative candidate was a very elegant glass manufacturer and he managed to make me look like a hopeless tramp. I got fairly close. I didn't get anywhere near beating him but I did manage to maintain the Labour vote, and I should say one thing about that. It was a very deeply feudal constituency, and the only way I could get people in the cottages to talk to me – and a lot of cottages were tied to a farmer – was by canvassing them between the bean poles in their back garden, because they were terrified of being seen talking to me. We used to attempt to say quietly, behind the bean poles, 'Have you thought of voting Labour?' They would shrink behind the bean poles and, if they saw any signs of the farmer coming by, they would ask me to leave. It was quite interesting. It was a real introduction to what English life was like then.

Bigsby: How did you get adopted, because here you are, a young woman apart from anything else?

Williams: Because the chairman liked me, and the constituency was quite small. I had another crack in 1955 when the General Election followed in the same constituency. Failed again. Then again in 1959. That is the story of women, anyway.

Bigsby: Then you stood again in 1964 and won. Now there was a Labour government. Harold Wilson had a majority of two and had to go to the country again two years later. At last you had your hands on some power and you got some posts quite rapidly.

Williams: If you think that being a parliamentary secretary is a feeling of power, think again. It is the first rather rickety rung on the ladder, that's true, but the ladder is quite tall.

Bigsby: In time, though, you were going to hold some significant posts.

Williams: I became that dreadful thing known as Secretary of State for Prices. That was a cabinet post.

Bigsby: This was at a time of prices and incomes policies, not a comfortable position to be in.

Williams: You swim and the water keeps coming up again, but it is a great way to avert criticism hitting the government too hard. So I was put in that position.

Bigsby: What was it like to be a woman in a House of Commons that wasn't terribly woman-friendly?

Williams: It still isn't. British politics is dominated by class and very often young men find their way to the top, get promoted, find constituencies they can run for within a club. The major Conservative club at that time, and until very recently, was the Carlton Club. It refused to have Mrs. Thatcher as a member. It was completely opposed to having any women members. But the funny thing was that the Labour Party wasn't much different because they had a couple of clubs. One was for intellectually posh people like Roy Jenkins, and I never got asked to join that even though I was a fellow member of the cabinet.

So there was a very strong tendency to reject women from these clubs, which were in fact, and still are to some extent, quite essential elements in how politicians influence others, push themselves forward. I could tell many stories but I will just tell one. I went into the smoking room at the House of Commons with a young male Labour MP and I was sitting with him having, of all things, a dry sherry, a nice respectable thing to have, when an elderly gentleman, one of my Conservative peers, leant over and said, 'Take her out. This is obscene'. A few months later, when I heard bells ringing for a private members bill to be voted upon, I ran in from an outside meeting and I rushed up to my peer, a sweet man, and said to him, 'The bells are ringing for a vote. What private members bill is it that we have reached?' He looked very embarrassed and said, 'I would really rather not say.' So I said, 'Come on, tell me. I have got to vote in six minutes,' because by this time the clock was running down. He said, 'No really, I would rather not.' So finally I said, 'For heaven's sake' And he patted me on the head and said, 'Don't you trouble your pretty little head about it.' The next day it turned out to be the homosexual law reform bill. So that was the way it was to be a woman in those old days.

Bigsby: You do the men an injustice, though, because they did set aside a room for you with an ironing board, didn't they?

Williams: It wasn't just for me. It was mostly for Mrs. Thatcher. There was a chintz settee, as well, on which one could have the vapours I suppose. I remember going to that room and Mrs. Thatcher was often ironing there. She was a great ironer and on this particular occasion I had been beaten up like mad in the House of Commons because I was Prices Minister and the Conservative backbenchers had been told to make it clear that the level of inflation, which was then seventeen per cent, was my personal responsibility. We had been in power for one week, I should say. Afterwards, I saw Mrs. Thatcher in the Members' Room. I noticed that she had been standing behind the Speaker's Chair listening to me answering questions. So she said, rather nicely, 'You did all right.' So I said, 'Thank you,' and then she said, 'After all, we have got to make sure they don't get the better of us.' The question is, who are they?

Bigsby: You write with some admiration about Harold Wilson, not least because he kept Britain out of the Vietnam War.

Williams: I think Harold Wilson is a badly underestimated Prime Minister. He wasn't popular with the press and he used to paddle around in long shorts with his dog. He wasn't at all glamorous but he was excellent in two ways. One was that he brilliantly kept us out of the Vietnam War. He would appear in America and make friendly noises but no commitment of troops, or anything like that, and then come home.

On one occasion, Lyndon Johnson was the President, a real bully. He simply didn't invite him to dinner so there was Harold Wilson, in the Blair House as it was oddly called, which was the place for strangers, waiting for a phone call that never came. So he got no dinner at all. He just had to stay there being humiliated. But he would still never give way.

The other thing that I thought very impressive about him was that he really was genuinely a man with absolutely no sense of discrimination at all, none about colour, none about race, none about religion, none about gender, the last of those being very rare. He just appointed people according to whether he thought they were able to do the job. He was determined to bring more women into government and he did for the first time appoint women to the Foreign Office, economic affairs, transport, overseas aid and so on. The only problem was that of the eight women he appointed, four were Barbara Castle and Barbara Castle once said to me, perfectly truthfully, 'I shall go down in history as the woman responsible for more ladies rooms in parliament than anybody before or anybody since.' Perfectly true.

Bigsby: You were out of power in 1970, back again in 1974, but only just, so that again you had to go to the country in 1976.

Williams: They always have to think twice before electing a Labour government, and then they do.

Bigsby: That was the period of the Lib-Lab pact, the Alliance. Now once again we face a coalition government. Is that really a workable system? Can it be anything other than a temporary arrangement?

Williams: No, it is temporary, but I want to make an important distinction. It was not a coalition. The Liberals took no seats in the government at all. What they did do was what Nick Clegg is suggesting. If there is a minority Conservative, or a minority Labour government, the party should say, 'Show us the Queen's speech. These are the laws we can vote for, because they are common with our own policies. These are the laws where we won't support you. It is entirely up to you to decide whether you bring them forward, but we will vote against them. You don't enter a coalition. That is my view now. I don't think that the Liberal Democrats should enter a coalition with either party. I think it is democratically proper to let the party that has the biggest number of votes, whether it is Conservative or Labour, come to government.

Bigsby: But that means you would continue to be doomed never to be in power because every time a government is returned with a considerable majority they forget about any promises they made about proportional representation.

Williams: That may be true, but I don't quite agree with you. I think that if you have a minority government, and you play absolutely fair and say these we will support, these we won't support, eventually they will need to try to persuade you to support them. Incidentally, one of the things I feel passionately about is that in the light of very deep public anger with members of parliament we need massive parliamentary reform, and part of that parliamentary reform has to be electoral reform, but not only that. It has to be parliament deciding on its own agenda. It has to be parliament standing up to the Whips. It has to be parliament electing its own chairmen of committees. It has to be chairmen of committees being given the power to bring things to the floor. We have to change the whole thing.

Bigsby: Without proportional representation how will you ever gain leverage on power? We have it in Scotland and we have it in Europe, but why would the two major parties ever have a vested interest in giving away power?

Williams: The point at which they would have done it in the past was 1983. We had two per cent less of the public vote than Labour. We elected twenty-six MPs. Labour had two per cent more, twenty-four per cent against twenty-two per cent, and for that they got more than two hundred and fifty MPs. There must be a point at which even the long-suffering, and if I may say so, extraordinarily placid British public must think it a bit odd that one party should get ten times as many MPs as the other when it has got two per cent more of the vote.

There is another factor, too, which is important to mention. No British government since Macmillan, I think I am right in saying, has actually had a majority of public support behind it. All our governments now are governments who have got more people who voted against them than voted for them and there comes a point at which democracy is made such an ass that, one likes to think, even reformers who are not Liberal Democrats will see that we really can't go on with a system as twisted and distorted as that.

Bigsby: That Labour government, edging towards 1979, was faced with the Winter of Discontent, with its series of strikes. So you were booted out of power. Then comes the critical moment as Labour has to decide how it is going to go forward. There were those who argued that you had lost because you were insufficiently on the left. Michael Foot was leader of the party. Tony Benn ran a significant faction. There was a battle within the party which you manifestly lost. Was there ever a chance that that battle was winnable?

Williams: I don't think so, and I have got any number of articles, meetings etc. to show that this is true. I did start that battle in 1972. I was one of the leading figures in what was called the Campaign for Democratic Socialism and what happened was, along certainly with David Owen, Bill Rogers and various other people, we fought for about nine years. We went to all the conferences and put down resolutions, and so on. I was on the National Executive Committee of the Labour Party, elected onto it by the Unions as it happens. I think that we lost virtually every single vote. We had vote after vote after vote. We were losing, but what we were losing was policies that we thought were absolutely essential, everything from being a member of NATO – don't forget the Cold War was still going – to leaving the European Union. We were all very strong supporters of Europe. These were official Labour policies, by the by. They were policies that we stood on platforms for. We also said that editors of newspapers should not be obliged to follow a closed shop because we thought that was a serious invasion of the freedom of the press. So there was a range of things, from civil liberties through to foreign affairs.

I decided that the one thing I could not do was stand on a platform in 1983 and say the reverse of everything I believed to be true. I could not have stayed but I don't believe that at that point we could have won. God knows, we tried hard enough and the only reason in the end that the more moderate aspects came out was partly because Labour lost the '83 election and the '87 election and began to see that the thesis that a very left party would do better wasn't true. When Neil Kinnock became leader he began by going along with this line and then realised that it was running itself straight into the sand and finally fell back on what was happening in Liverpool, where, you remember, there was a taxi which was taking dismissal notices around to Council workers. Neil Kinnock had the guts to stand up and denounce that.

Bigsby: The SDP was founded in 1981. Roy Hattersley was the kind of person who could have joined, but didn't.

Williams: He is a very old friend of mine and I know why he didn't because in a way Roy is tribalist about the Labour Party. I am not saying it in a blameworthy way. My grandchildren are tribalist about Arsenal. But Roy thinks like that. As you know, he has fallen out with Blair and certainly with Brown because his picture of the Labour Party is, in a sense, his parents'. It is his family. It is something he feels very strongly about. It is not the Labour Party that exists now, and it wasn't the Labour Party that existed then. It is a virtual Labour Party which he loved so much, but it is not the real one.

Bigsby: There is an argument that the SDP was a kind of John the Baptist for the arrival of Tony Blair, although that is not a role I think you will probably accept.

Williams: Doubting Thomas is closer to it.

Bigsby: Roy Hattersley has argued that had you, and all of the so-called Gang of Four, stayed, that process of occupying the middle ground would have occurred much earlier.

Williams: I doubt it. We were there for a very long time. We had very little affect on the decisions that were made by the Labour National Executive. To put it quite straightforwardly though he was an absolutely lovely man, personally, I think many, many people felt that Michael Foot was not the person who could turn the party round, and at that time nor did he see that he needed to do so. What one also saw was a growing influence of the trade unions of the far left. I felt then, just as I feel now, that the CBI and the bankers shouldn't tell the Conservative government what to do. I think that the trade unions, and I am a trade unionist, should not tell Labour governments what to do. I think one doesn't want these huge corporate forces effectively guiding the paths of political parties.

Bigsby: Today Tony Benn has the image of a kindly grandfather who everybody loves. You were vitriolic about him at that time. You thought he was a pernicious influence.

Williams: Not quite true. I remember very well what I said. I said he was one of the sweetest people in politics.

Bigsby: You can hear the 'but' coming.

Williams: You can hear a 'but' coming, but you left out the other part of the 'but,' and I am going to make it balance because it is all true. Tony is a very attractive personality but what I said was, and I believe it to be true, he is to some extent the victim of his own eloquence. He hears himself talking, and many people do this, Tony Blair was another one, and he becomes more and more persuaded of what he is hearing through his own ears. He gets carried away. Let me give you an example, because it is in the papers today. You have got someone like Tony who made the most brilliant speeches on the subject of the need for regime change in Iraq but we now know that all the time he had already committed himself to a war. How did that happen? I don't think because he was a total liar. I think it was because he was persuaded by his own eloquence, without stopping to think whether that eloquence was very closely related to reality.

Bigsby: Yes, and something we will touch on in a minute if we have time, is faith. I am very struck by the fact that Tony Blair's answer to questions is often, 'I understand why you are saying that. I understand entirely. But I believe that ...' not, 'I think.'

Williams: I think that is something he had in common with Tony Benn, I really do. I think Tony would be quite capable of saying I believe that, and he would believe it, but I don't think in some cases he would have thought it through.

Bigsby: The two parties, the Liberal Party and SDP, came together again seven years later. Is there any truth in the *Spitting Image* version of that, with David Steele being the little figure in the pocket of David Owen.

Williams: Almost a total lie. David Steele is a brilliantly astute politician. He is also a very patient politician. He put up with quite a lot of scorn from David Owen, who is much taller for a start, and instead of taking offence or marching out or saying, 'I'll have no more to do with you,' David Steele just went on with what he wanted, which was in the end a combination of these two parties, finally getting there, managing to keep good relations with David Owen, to some extent at least. I think he must have been furious because in my view it was seven lost years, none of which made any sense at all because, as you rightly said, in our electoral system you cannot have two parties at the centre-left fighting one another. It just won't work, and naturally enough David Owen's continuing SDP went on to destruction. I think many of us saw that it would but David was a very determined person. Now he would admit it was a mistake, but it was a pretty desperate mistake and it lost us many years of working together. It undoubtedly did the merged party a great deal of damage at the time.

Bigsby: I'm interested in your fascination with other countries. You have taught at Harvard and have been a member of various organisations in the United States, but you were also involved in advising the Russians on their Constitution.

Williams: That was a fairly daft episode, but I did, that is true, along with a very distinguished Canadian professor called Charles Taylor, who is a brilliant philosophical writer, and a colleague at Harvard called Michael Sandel who is now the professor of government there. The three of us went through the gates of the Kremlin at the invitation of Mikhail Gorbachev to try to work out a Constitution. I remember that as we got there a very young, rather lazy, Russian official said, 'Too many cooks spoil the broth,' pointing to the door out, but we stayed. We stayed for a week and we worked on it all and found the greatest difficulty we had was with that great Russian belief that if you put something in a Constitution it will happen. So they were constantly coming to us and saying, 'We want a right to shelter. We want a right to a job.' We had every sympathy with them but we knew that the words would not make any difference. But it was very exciting. It was quite astonishing. And then, of course, very quickly Russia fell into what I can only describe as the grip of jungle capitalism. Although I may have sounded a bit moderately right-wing just now, I strongly believe that capitalism if self-regulated is desperately dangerous and I saw that with my own eyes in Russia and Eastern Europe, where one saw the most savage kind of capitalism, with a complete gangster system to go along with it.

Bigsby: I get the impression, though, that you are an admirer of aspects of America. You are married to an American. But isn't there something very odd at the moment as America seeks to spread its ideas of democracy at the very moment its own version is so flawed. The 2000 election was effectively corrupt. Chicago politics has a history of corruption, as does Illinois politics. Is it the Enlightenment values that you respond to in America?

Williams: I was Professor of Elective Politics at Harvard. One of the things I spent most time on was arguing that America absolutely had to clean up the amount of money in politics. When you consider that Bloomberg, the Mayor of New York City, spent one hundred million dollars on getting re-elected, something like ten dollars for every single citizen in New York, it is simply appalling. We now have Lord Ashcroft here, which isn't very good news either, but it is on a different scale. So, yes, I am strongly against the corruption of American politics. It is very serious, right down to the level of state legislators. I am very critical indeed of the way in which the United States has exported so-called democracy. It hasn't really been democracy at all in any sense that we would know, the attempt to impose on Iraq a presidential system. It was ludicrous. Now, in Afghanistan, it is even worse. No, I love America for its enterprise, its innovation, its imagination. It is a country full of possibilities. It is not a country whose politics I particularly admire. I never have, and have never lectured as if I did. I guess if you wanted to ask whose politics I have most admired it would be Scandinavia, not America.

Bigsby: You said that over the last thirty years there are three Prime Minister you admire. They are Margaret Thatcher, Tony Blair and the present Prime Minister, for whom you have become an adviser in a particular area.

Williams: I admire Mrs. Thatcher, but not for her policies. I made it quite clear I was strongly against them. I thought they went much too far in destroying small businesses and chucking people out of work and indeed creating vast inequality, so let me put that on the table quite clearly. What I admired her for was getting from Grantham, a rather remote little town in Lincolnshire, all the way to Prime Minister and I think you would have to admire anybody who did that for their sheer determination. So I want to say that quite clearly. I didn't say I admired Mr. Blair. I thought he was outstanding, but I didn't admire him. I thought he was willing to mislead the country seriously over Iraq. Damn it, I spent three years arguing about this in the House of Lords every single day, where my party was the only large party opposed to Iraq, with people like Charles Kennedy and Ming Campbell. We just went on and on and on about Iraq, asking question after question, and I think people recognised that.

But I am currently an advisor to Gordon Brown. The reason is quite straightforward. When I was still at Harvard I got invited by Senator Lugar and Senator Nunn, who are the two Senators who have been most prominent in worrying about nuclear proliferation, to join their committee called Nuclear Initiative. They invited me to join because they wanted some people from other countries there and they invited me on because I knew them both somewhat in my role as critic of American politics. I then served on that committee, and I am still on it, now, for ten years. It is now called The Nuclear Threat Initiative and it gave me a tremendous amount of access to information and knowledge because what they were primarily involved in was making secure the literally thousands of nuclear weapons that were scattered all over the former Soviet Union.

When Gorbachev fell and, as you know, power effectively fell into the hands of Yeltsin who was drunk some of the time, huge efforts were made by this committee to secure all those nuclear weapons, and it actually happened. Nuclear weapons in Ukraine and Kazakhstan all went back to Russia and were either destroyed or put under safe guard. In other words they really avoided what might have been a major war. So I had been on that thing and then I was invited by Gordon to be his adviser because of that knowledge. Then, nothing to do with Gordon Brown, I got invited by the Australian and the Japanese governments to serve on the international commission on nuclear proliferation and nuclear disarmament, and I have just completed a vast global trip to everywhere on that issue, Egypt, India, Pakistan and Japan.

Bigsby: If there is one aspect of your career that still raises the temperature of some people it is comprehensive education. Looking back, do you think it has been a triumph or do you have your doubts?

Williams: No doubts. It would have been a triumph. What actually happened was that we had no majority to push through an education bill. It was entirely permissive. If you go to Kent today you will find the 11+ is safe and sound and still lives. There is a completely old fashioned 11+ system. Kent is not an outstanding education authority. As the Black Paper writers would have it, it should be now streaks ahead of any other county. It is not streaks ahead of every other county and some of the most effective counties are places like Cambridgeshire, North Lancashire and Hertfordshire, and so on, which have got comprehensive systems.

Now why did that happen? Because some authorities refused. Norfolk is a very good example. They wouldn't do anything at all. They never replied. They didn't go ahead with comprehensive education for years on end, where Kent didn't go ahead at all. So there has been a lot of patchiness. What happened was that the Black Paper writers [a group of people opposed to progressive education and the introduction of comprehensives] tried to damn everything to do with comprehensive schools. I will be quite blunt. Literally thousands upon thousands of young men and women are in university who, if they had gone to a secondary modern school, though many of them were well taught, would never have been able to take an A or O level. I think it was absolutely dotty, as a country, that we thought we could chuck away something like three quarters of our children with no opportunity of getting a professional or higher education. It just takes my breath away that England – not Scotland or Wales – is a still sufficiently a class-bound country to think that must be the right answer. It cannot be the right answer.

Bigsby: Have you found a way of getting politicians to react more quickly to the unintended consequences of their actions and their legislation?

Williams: Yes, and I will give you one very good example. When I was working for Tony Crossland, as his Minister of State in the Education Department, he told me that as a minister he put in enough money to be able to look at an experiment five years after it had been introduced to see if it had worked. His particular example was polytechnics. He put by money to look at whether polytechnics had actually had the outcomes that he hoped, which included doing research into local and regional issues, making sure that vocational qualifications were regarded as seriously as academic ones. I think it was a tragedy that the polytechnics were brought to an end and replaced by universities because the great weakness in England, and especially in its economy, is the absolute absence of a proper respect for skill. As a country we suffer horribly from that compared to, say, Germany or Scandinavia where proper skills are highly admired and respected. British people feel they have to apologise because their son is an electrician. For God's sake, we need electricians, frankly more than we need media studies experts, and we don't seem to understand that. Anyway, the answer is you need to have what they call post-legislative scrutiny. What that means is that every single bill of any significance ought to be reviewed in five years or ten years time and then the lessons from it should be drawn.

In this country we have had something like twenty-three criminal justice acts since 1997. We have created over three thousand more criminal offences since 1997. We never follow up to see what the effects of our laws are. We just pass more of them. We don't repeal the old ones. We just go on and on loading law upon law upon law, and it is disastrous because increasingly people don't even know what the law is, let alone obey it. So the straight answer to your question is that either we ought to write into every single law that we pass a sunset clause, which means that it dies out after five or ten years, or there must be a system of going back to it, scrutinising its effects, looking to see whether it achieved what it set out to achieve in all those lovely florid speeches at the beginning of second readings. I think we would be much better off if we did. We have got as far as pre-legislative scrutiny. We do now look at laws in draft, and not only when they are being debated on the floor, but we don't have post-legislative scrutiny. In the House of Commons they don't have either. It is a great shame.

Bigsby: Should we be allowed a referendum on the new European Constitution?

Williams: On the Lisbon treaty, absolutely not. What we should be allowed a referendum on is if we want to stay in or go out. To have a referendum on what are essentially relatively limited constitutional changes, as distinct from major constitutional issues, would simply tie up the whole of parliament in referendum after referendum. I completely agree with the Scottish referendum. It was right on devolution. I agree completely with the referendum on the EU, when the occasion warrants, but to have a referendum on all these relatively minor changes, and they really are minor changes, would simply make a mess. Go and look at California.

Bigsby: In your opinion how can MPs and peers regain the respect of the people.

Williams: Both parties have consistently been totally cowardly about MPs salaries. They have rejected time and again the advice of the so-called Top Salaries Review Board. They have always said to MPs, 'It would be very unpopular for us to increase salaries so we will increase expenses.' They actually advised people to get more expenses rather than raising salaries. Today the salary of an MP is sixty per cent of that of a general practitioner and sixty per cent of that of a headmistress or headmaster of a large secondary school. With great respect, I don't think anybody who knows the responsibility of an MP can really pretend that it is much less than that of a GP, or a secondary headmaster or headmistress. So we have had a kind of cheating, as much by governments being cowardly as by MPs using expenses having been told they can. I think it is appalling, and I myself believe that the more major frauds, like for example claiming interest on a mortgage which is already paid, or switching houses in order to get a capital gain, should be punished before an ordinary civil or criminal court as the case may be. That would be proper. There should be no special protection for MPs. But that means that the parties should face up to the fact that they should follow independent assumptions about what an MP should be paid.

But I believe that the expenses issue is only a very small part of the problem we now confront, which is a massive loss of trust and faith in MPs, much of it because we are much more transparent than we used to be. I knew lots of corrupt MPs in the past but nobody ever asked them questions because it wasn't thought to be polite to do so. So what we have to do is make a major reform of parliament, with smaller numbers of MPs, much more transparency and a decent electoral reform.

Lightning Source UK Ltd.
Milton Keynes UK
UKOW050840010312

188119UK00001B/26/P